The Spiritual Transformation
of Jews Who Become Orthodox

The Spiritual Transformation of Jews Who Become Orthodox

ROBERTA G. SANDS

Published by State University of New York Press, Albany

For information, contact State University of New York Press, Albany, NY
www.sunypress.edu

Library of Congress Cataloging-in-Publication Data

Names: Sands, Roberta G., author.
Title: The spiritual transformation of Jews who become Orthodox / Roberta G.
  Sands.
Description: Albany, New York : State University of New York, [2019] |
  Includes bibliographical references and index.
Identifiers: LCCN 2018027991 | ISBN 9781438474298 (hardcover : alk. paper) |
  ISBN 9781438474281 (pbk. : alk. paper) | ISBN 9781438474304 (ebook)
Subjects: LCSH: Jews—Return to Orthodox Judaism. | Spiritual life—Judaism.
Classification: LCC BM565 .S26 2019 | DDC 296.7/15—dc23
LC record available at https://lccn.loc.gov/2018027991

10 9 8 7 6 5 4 3 2 1

There's a whole big tradition out there, and there's a whole Jewish tradition that's so beautiful. It was locked away; you didn't even know about it. At first, you didn't even know about it; then you knew about it, but it didn't seem very accessible; then it starts to become accessible . . . it's very cool. I love that process. So now that things are becoming more accessible, it's good, it's good, it's a good place to be. But it's still exciting.

—"Ben," Orthodox for ten years

Contents

List of Tables

Acknowledgments

The research described in this book was developed together with Rivka Ausubel Danzig, who died tragically in 2006 following a courageous struggle with illness. She was my partner in the conceptualization, implementation, and initial analysis of the study. I feel privileged to have had the opportunity to work with Rivka, whose penetrating intellect, creativity, perceptiveness, and spiritual depth were awe-inspiring. I am grateful for her contributions to this study and deeply regret that she did not live long enough to participate in the writing of this book.

Rivka and I collaborated on the study "*Baalei teshuvah's* Spiritual Transformational 'Soul Work.'" I appreciate the funding and support we received from The Spiritual Transformation Scientific Research Program, sponsored by the Metanexus Institute on Religion and Science, with the generous support of the John M. Templeton Foundation. I am particularly appreciative of the support provided by Solomon H. Katz, founding president of the Metanexus Institute and director of its Spiritual Transformation Scientific Research Program. Others affiliated with this program, especially Joan D. Koss-Chioino and Hava Tirosh-Samuelson, as well as other grant recipients, offered encouragement to further our work.

This research was made possible by individuals who cannot be named because they were promised anonymity. I am grateful to the *baalei* and *baalot teshuvah* who shared their experiences and challenges in their individual interviews and in focus groups. They are remarkable individuals whose determination and perseverance are documented in this book. I also appreciate the participation of key informants, also promised anonymity. I wish I could name this distinguished group of rabbis, rebbetzins, and community leaders.

A number of individuals helped with the implementation of this research. I am especially grateful to Robyn Rapoport Spero, our proficient research coordinator, who participated in all phases of the research, including screening potential participants, interviewing, coding, and data analysis. I also thank the following individuals for their assistance in various capacities: Gail Feinstein, Susan Frager, Jennie Goldenberg, Tirzah Goldenberg, Miriam Hirsch, Chanie Holzer, Nicole Ives, Rebecca Stern Lamm, Charna Shapiro, Rashi Shapiro, and Victoria Stanhope.

Thanks also go to former dean Richard Gelles and support staff of the University of Pennsylvania School of Social Policy and Practice, and to the Social Work Mental Health Research Center (especially Phyllis Solomon, Steven Marcus, and Craig Abbs) that existed at the time of this study. My immersion in the field of social work as a social work educator at the University of Pennsylvania and elsewhere, as well as my social work practice experience, influenced the theoretical perspective taken in this book.

Two chapters of this book include versions of previous publications. I thank John Wiley & Sons for allowing me to use a modified version of my article "The social integration of *baalei teshuvah*," *Journal for the Scientific Study of Religion*, 48(1), 86–102, ©2009 by the Society for the Scientific Study of Religion. I also thank Taylor & Francis for permission to use a modified version of an article I co-wrote with Rivka Danzig, "A model of spiritual transformation of *baalei teshuvah*," *Journal of Religion and Spirituality in Social Work: Social Thought*, 26(2), 23–48. DOI: 10.1300/J377v26n02_02; https://www.tandfonline.com.

I have benefited from the work of scholars who preceded me in studying Jews who become Orthodox. These include Janet Aviad, Sarah Bunin Benor, M. Herbert Danzger, Lynn Davidman, and Debra Kaufman. Thanks also go to Cynthia Darling-Fisher and Nancy Kline Leidy for allowing us to use the Modified Erikson Psychosocial Stage Inventory (MEPSI) in this research. I also appreciate the valuable reader reports on my manuscript obtained by State University of New York Press. Thanks also go to Rafael Chaiken for guiding me throughout this process and Eric Schramm for valuable suggestions.

Many friends and family members have been here for me as I worked on this project. I thank my daughter, Bonnie (Blima) Moskoff, who, after she became Orthodox, sparked my interest in *baalei teshuvah* as a research topic. I appreciate her reviewing chapter 5 and the questions she and her husband, David, answered during the writing of this manuscript. I thank Dorit Roer-Strier of the Paul Baerwald School of Social Work and Social Welfare of the Hebrew University of Jerusalem, with whom I have conducted research on the impact of a daughter's *teshuvah* on family relations in Israel, the United States, Argentina, and South Africa; and the research team in Israel, coordinated by Minny Mock, that enriched my understanding of the process of becoming Orthodox. I also thank my son Philip Wilhelm for being there for me. Finally, and significantly, I thank my beloved husband, Samuel Klausner, for his advice, encouragement, perspectives, insights, and support throughout this undertaking. I appreciate his prodigious knowledge and wisdom, as well as his tolerance of the time and energy it took in writing and completing the manuscript.

Philadelphia, PA
May 6, 2018

Introduction

The Context of Spiritual Transformation

Seated beside a partition separating the women's section from the men's, the women wedding guests chatted excitedly among themselves. After the musicians returned from their break and introduced a lively tune, a few friends of the bride beckoned the women to form a circle on the dance floor together with Shani, the bride. All of a sudden, several other friends of the bride placed red and green pointed paper hats on their heads and joined the circle. Holding hands, the women with the hats moved into the center of the circle and danced with Shani while the others clapped. Then women in the outer circle joined the center circle, dancing with Shani and her friends.

The next round was similar to the first except that this time friends of the bride took out long, shimmering white lights that they waved in circular motions. As the music became louder, the dancing became more spirited. The mother of the bride joined her daughter, the two of them dancing together in the center while others danced around them. One by one, Shani's friends joined the mother-daughter pair in the center circle. Round three was similar except that this time the bride's friends brought out hula-hoops, wrapped them around their hips, and put on a demonstration.

When the music became softer, the program for the bride changed. Shani's friend Malka took out a large shopping bag and announced, "Shani's transformation!" Explaining that she raided Shani's closet, Malka got into a pair of Shani's blue jeans and put on her friend's sweatshirt and Nike sneakers, modeling the outfit while the group stood around her in a circle and clapped. Malka and Shani danced together, laughing. Next, Malka put on a jeans skirt and took off the blue jeans, keeping the sweatshirt and sneakers on. A few friends danced with Shani and Malka while others joined hands and danced around them. After that, Malka

1

replaced the sweatshirt with a long-sleeved blouse, cast off the Nikes, and put on flats and knee-length socks. Finally, she replaced the jean skirt with a long dark blue skirt.

Shani (formerly Sandra) is a baalat teshuvah, a formerly non-observant Jewish woman who embraced Orthodox Judaism. She became observant around the same time my daughter, Blima (formerly Bonnie), did, while both were studying at a seminary in Israel. After Shani returned to the United States, she became part of a group of other women who had become observant, and who were also among the wedding guests. Shani worked a few years as a nurse at a New York hospital where, through a patient, she met the groom. Having become acquainted with Shani through my daughter, I was invited to attend her wedding as well.

This book is about the transformation of Jewish men and women in the United States who were raised in relatively secular Jewish homes and later became Orthodox. In doing so, they made changes that went far beyond alterations in their attire and the adoption of Hebrew or Yiddish names; they changed their worldviews, their priorities, the ways in which they identified as men or women, and the manner in which they patterned their daily lives. They went through a reeducation process in which they acquired a new set of guidelines about what they could and could not eat, how they were to relate to men and women, how to observe the Sabbath and holidays, and, more generally, how to establish holiness in their lives. In the process, they joined a new community and made changes in their identities.

I am using the term "spiritual transformation" to describe the lengthy process of religious, spiritual, and lifestyle changes of *baalei teshuvah* (Hebrew, "masters of return," lit., masc. pl.) and *baalot teshuvah* (fem. pl.).[1] In this book, I describe their starting points and examine their initial processes of searching, exploration, learning, and decision making, and then their later processes of additional learning, socialization, adaptation, and social and psychological integration. In this introduction, I present the concepts that are used in this book; set out the theoretical perspectives; portray the Jewish historical context of Jewish spiritual transformation; describe my research methods; and explain the social context of the study.

The thesis of this book is that the spiritual-religious transformation of Jews who become Orthodox is an all-embracing, protracted, open-ended process that gives rise to a radical revision of one's internal being and external environment. While the initial exploration and search process that leads to a commitment is exhilarating, the process that follows is arduous, as it makes demands on one's time, relationships, work life, and self-confidence. It requires reeducation and resocialization and involves spiritual struggles, leading to a profound change in one's worldview, identity, and community. Although these efforts lead to an enriched life and provide a framework for living a meaningful life, they do not necessarily result in psychological integration and social inclusion.

Several books have been written about the *baalei teshuvah*'s "return to Judaism" in the United States and Israel (Aviad, 1983; Danzger, 1989; David- man, 1991; Kaufman, 1991). These sociological studies describe and analyze the experiences of the cohort of Jewish youth that became Orthodox in the wake of the hippie, anti-war, and countercultural movements in the United States, and disillusionment with Zionism in Israel. Aviad and Danzger give special attention to educational institutions (yeshivas for men and midrashas (referred to as seminaries for women) in Israel where the youths were studying. Most of these books focus on people in the early stages of religious change, leaving aside questions about how they live out their commitment in later years (Aviad, 1983; Benor, 2012; Danzger, 1989; Davidman, 1991). Two of the early books are about women (Davidman, 1991; Kaufman, 1991), whose movement into Orthodox Judaism appeared to diverge from feminist ideology. A more recent volume offers an ethnographic, sociolinguistic perspective on the language and cultural learning acquired by newcomers to Orthodox Judaism (Benor, 2012). Other books describe the experiences of *baalot teshuvah* and their mothers in Holland (Mock-Degan, 2009) *and baalei* and *baalot teshuvah* in Brazil (Topel, 2008).

The present volume, written twenty to thirty years after most of these predecessors, is concerned with a later cohort that became Orthodox during the last three decades of the twentieth century and the first two years of the twenty-first century. It reflects a generation that is post-hippie and less politically oriented than the generation described by previous authors. Although other books describe educational socialization in learning institutions or programs (Aviad, 1983; Benor, 2012; Danzger, 1989; Davidman, 1991) and informal settings (Benor, 2012), the present volume looks at socialization toward ongoing community participation. Whereas previous studies were informed by sociological and sociolinguistic theory, this book incorporates psychosocial developmental theory to understand age/stage-related challenges that *baalei* and *baalot teshuvah* faced when they first became Orthodox and the challenges they had while trying to integrate into existing Orthodox communities.

This book is unique in its use of spirituality and spiritual transformation as a lens for viewing the process of becoming a *baal teshuvah* and living out one's commitment as an Orthodox Jewish adult in the community. It raises questions about inner experiences and external expectations that were not examined in previous studies. These include:

+ How do *baalei teshuvah* navigate the landscape of Orthodox Jewish communities as novices?

+ What internal and external obstacles do they face?

+ What supports their spiritual development?

+ How does their spiritual life change over time? Do they continue to grow or, instead, do they reach a plateau and stop?

+ To what extent do they become integrated psychologically and socially?

+ What are the psychological and social costs and benefits of their spiritual transformation?

I begin by clarifying the terms "spirituality" and "spiritual transformation" and what they mean in general, in Judaism, and in this book. Then I introduce other terms related to spiritual-religious change.

Terminology

Spirituality

Traditionally, the term spirituality has been connected with religion (Pargament, 1999). The opposite of materiality, it refers to the insubstantial or transcendent. Over time, however, spirituality has come to describe a personal religion, feelings about God or nature, an attitude of reverence for life, or aesthetic appreciation, which can be experienced within or outside a religious system. Nowadays some individuals describe themselves as spiritual but not religious (see, e.g., Fuller, 2001). This conceptual division may have been stimulated by the baby boom generation of the twentieth century whose spiritual searching was not necessarily associated with organized religion (Roof, 2003). This produced a "New Age" type of spirituality that influenced the popular perception of spirituality. Generally, however, religiousness is equated with the institutional (i.e., associated with a church, synagogue, or other organized entity) and spirituality with the emotional, experiential, and cognitive (Pargament, 1999).

Recognizing that the terms spirituality and religiousness are "fuzzy," some social scientists have attempted to define them more precisely (e.g., Hill et al., 2000; Zinnbauer et al., 1997). Hill et al. (2000) concluded that the two concepts overlap in that both include a sense of the sacred and a search process. In addition, religiousness can at times include a search for non-sacred goals (e.g., affiliation, social identity) so long as it facilitates the search for the sacred. Furthermore, religiousness (but not spirituality) encompasses means and methods that facilitate the search for the sacred that are supported and validated within a particular group of people (Hill et al., 2000). Empirical studies examining the relationship between spirituality and religiousness in Christian samples have found that, although there are differences, generally the two go hand in hand (Marler & Hadaway, 2002). A study of a national population of Jews in the United States found that the two concepts correlate modestly (Sands, Marcus, & Danzig, 2008).

There is little consensus about the nature of Jewish spirituality. In his introduction to a two-volume edited work on the subject, Green (1986) defines it as the "striving for life in the presence of God" (p. xv). As he explains, "The cultivation of a life in the ordinary world bearing the holiness once associated with sacred space and time . . . is perhaps as close as one can come to a definition of 'spirituality' that is native to the Jewish tradition and indeed faithful to its Semitic roots" (p. xiii). Berman (2002) suggests that the biblical concept of *kedushah*, holiness, comes closest to the biblical and rabbinic understanding of spirituality, which is "about the process of bringing God's values into the world" (p. 4). These values, which are based on God's attributes, include interdependence, tolerance, and striving for justice (Berman, 2002). Green's and Berman's definitions are consistent with Hill et al.'s (2000) focus on the sacred (holiness), but in Judaism one brings the sense of holiness and God's values into everyday life.

Paraphrasing a statement in the *Shulkhan Arukh*, the code of Jewish Law, Strassfeld[2] (2002/2006) writes:

> We are called to walk through life with a consciousness of the presence of the Holy One always. We are to do so as we walk, do business, and interact with people—in other words, when we are engaged in all the "mundane" activities of daily life. For the *Shulkhan Arukh*, awareness is the goal of life. The whole rest of this book is commentary on how to achieve that awareness. (p. xix)

In this book, spirituality is viewed as both a *subjective experience of closeness to God* and *the performance of actions related to living within the framework of the Torah*. Subjectively there is a feeling of connection to God that is experienced in tandem with performing religious obligations (*mitzvot*, commandments; sing. *mitzvah*). The framework of the Torah refers to teachings within the Hebrew Bible, writings of the prophets, the Talmud (rabbinic teachings), Jewish law (*halakhah*), and other sacred writings. As suggested in this definition, spirituality and religiousness are integrally interconnected.

Spiritual Transformation

Like spirituality and religiousness, the term spiritual transformation is fuzzy. Generally, it refers to the process and outcome of changing one's beliefs, values, attitudes, and behaviors related to a transcendent or higher power. Pargament (2006) defines it as "a fundamental change in the place of the sacred or the character of the sacred in the life of the individual" (p. 18). The research undergirding this book was on the spiritual transformation of *baalei teshuvah*. It was one of some twenty studies on spiritual transformation funded by the Metanexus Institute on Religion and Science, a project of the John M. Templeton Foundation. I developed this study together with my colleague, the late Dr. Rivka Ausubel Danzig. We focused on Jewish Americans who made changes in behavior, attitude, and beliefs in either of two contexts: (1) intensification within Judaism (e.g., from Reform to Orthodox) or (2) a shift from no religious commitment among those previously nominally Jewish to a devout religious life.

The quintessential spiritual transformational experience within Judaism is called "*teshuvah*," a Hebrew word for "return" that Steinsaltz (1987) described as a return to "the Divine source of all being" (p. 3). Broadly defined, *teshuvah* is a spiritual reawakening, a desire to strengthen the connection between oneself and the sacred (Steinsaltz, 1987). The term also means "repentance"—remorse over one's past errors, the desire to make amends, and actions that demonstrate a changed way of life. It is a gradual process enabling one to restore one's spiritual core, which has become damaged through sin, to "a state of integration, both with God and within oneself" (Englander, 1985, p. 212). The term *teshuvah* is relevant to all Jews who engage in a process of repentance and recommitment.

Traditionally, the term *baalei teshuvah* was applied to Jews who were formerly observant, drifted away, repented, and returned to traditional practice. In this volume, the focus is on Jews who were not raised Orthodox and thus are not "returning" to the Judaism that they abandoned but instead are returning to the tradition of their ancestors. The spiritual transformation of *baalei teshuvah* refers to both the processes and actions that bring them closer to God, and encompasses spiritual and religious changes that operate together.

The transformation occurs as *baalei teshuvah* expand their knowledge of Torah, experience holiness, and perform *mitzvot*. This requires major changes in their previously held beliefs, values, obligations, priorities, attitudes, and behaviors. Making such changes is demanding, requiring academic learning, socialization to religious community norms, commitment, and perseverance. Feelings such as awe, gratitude, and wonder that are commonly associated with spirituality may arise from the processes of bringing one's life in synchrony with the commandments.

The spiritual transformational processes of *baalei teshuvah* involve every facet of their lives (Steinsaltz, 1987). They must reorient themselves so that God, the Torah, and the observance of *mitzvot* are central to their beings and fully manifested in their daily activities. Such a reorientation necessitates that *baalei teshuvah* learn about and gradually accept religious laws and practices, study sacred literature (Danzger, 1989), and incorporate their learning into their everyday activities. Observance of *mitzvot* (traditionally, these are enumerated as 613 commandments), such as keeping kosher, reciting daily prayers, and observing the Sabbath, infuses their lives and is expressed in their marital relationship, interactions with extended family and friends, educational pursuits, occupational goals, parenting, recreational activities, and communal life. These changes can become visible to researchers in participants' narrative accounts of their spiritual journeys, in the language they use, and where they locate causality (cf. Snow & Machalek, 1984).

Accordingly, this book is about internal and external changes. *Baalei teshuvah* reconstruct their individual and social identities. They change their core beliefs, emotional lives, perception of self, and ideology, as well as the social community with which they identify. While taking on new religious behaviors, they relinquish those that are no longer appropriate. They dress modestly, eschew popular culture, and live according to norms of the religious community they join. Such changes in a person they knew intimately can create difficulties in relationships with parents, siblings, and other family members. In the process of changing, *baalei teshuvah* acquire new friends and lose some old ones. Their new reference group consists of other Orthodox individuals and their families, rabbis, and others who participate in the institutions and communities with which they associate. They alter their sense of time so that the Jewish clock and calendar—with times for daily prayer, the Sabbath, fast days, and holidays—are primary, and change their priorities from the material to the spiritual.

The sweeping changes that *baalei teshuvah* make may be considered a "paradigm shift," a term Kuhn (1970) used to describe a change in worldview, where a previously held perspective that is no longer considered valid is replaced by one that seems to answer questions that could not be answered by the old one. Kuhn considered the new paradigm incommensurable with the previous one, for the rules that guided the previous way of thinking no longer apply. Although Kuhn was describing scientific revolutions, the term does help explain the radical changes *baalei teshuvah* make and the problems facing the newly Orthodox in effecting inner changes and dealing with friends and family who think according to the paradigm that the *baalei teshuvah* held in the past. To illuminate the process of change, a number of terms will be explained.

Terms Related to Religious Change

Religious change is a common topic of study in the social sciences. Generally, this refers to an alteration in one's beliefs, practices, and affiliations in relation to a higher power. It includes conversion from one established religion to another, joining a new religious movement, switching from one denomination to another, religious intensification, disaffiliation, and abandoning religion altogether. The terms conversion, switching, and religious intensification are most germane to understanding the spiritual-religious transformation of *baalei teshuvah*.

Conversion generally refers to a change from one religious system to another, such as from Christianity to Islam, or a change from a non-believer to a believer. This can occur on the societal level, "mass conversion," such as when one religious group imposes its religion on a conquered people or when a subjected group realizes that the pathway to privileges is through conversion (Klausner, 1997); or it can occur on the individual level. On the individual level, the change can be sudden and dramatic, such as St. Paul's conversion on the road to Damascus, also referred to as "quantum change" (Miller & C'deBaca, 1994), or it may be gradual (James, 1902/1958). There is an abundance of literature on conversion on the individual level, which examines motivation and describes stages of change. Some research studies suggest that conversion is motivated by the desire to heal from emotional deprivation during childhood (e.g., Ullman, 1989), whereas others find personality changes as a result of conversion (Lawton & Bures, 2001; Paloutzian, Richardson, & Rambo, 1999).

Another term used by social scientists who study religion is *switching*. This refers to moving from one division to another within a given religious system, but it can also apply to switching to no religion (Roof & Hadaway, 1979). In Christianity, switching generally occurs between denominations such as from Methodist to Episcopalian. Switching among American Christians is common, with rates varying from 15 to 40 percent (Hoge, Johnson, & Luidens,

1995; Newport, 1979; Roof, 1989; Roof & Hadaway, 1977; Stark & Glock, 1968). Social scientists have observed a flow from lower-status, theologically conservative denominations to higher-status liberal ones (Stark & Glock, 1968), from mainline to "fringe" groups (Roof & Hadaway, 1979), and shifts out of religious affiliation altogether (Hout & Fischer, 2002). Switching has been associated with a variety of factors such as younger age (Demerath & Yang, 1998; Newport, 1979) and circumstances such as marriage and moving (Hoge et al., 1995; Musick & Wilson, 1995). In Judaism, switching applies to moving from one movement (e.g., Conservative) to another (e.g., Reform).

Religious intensification occurs when one remains in a previous religious tradition but strengthens and deepens one's commitment. Rambo (1993) defines intensification as a type of conversion, that is,

> the revitalized commitment to a faith with which the convert has had previous affiliation, formal or informal. It occurs when nominal members of a religious institution make their commitment a central focus of their lives, or when people deepen their involvement in a community of faith through profound religious experience and/or life transitions like marriage, childbirth, and approaching death. (p. 13)

Nominal Christians who become evangelicals are intensifiers, as are "born again" Muslims (Aslan, 2017, p. 224). In this volume, conversion, switching, and intensification are viewed as forms of religious change. The spiritual transformation of *baalei teshuvah* is a kind of religious change that is similar to these three terms. Because religious intensification is within the same religion that one had ties to in the past, this term seems to fit best with the situation of *baalei teshuvah*. There are some individuals interviewed for this study, however, whose trajectories resemble conversion from no religion to another because they grew up with little or no exposure Judaism and later became Orthodox. The term switching could also be applied to *baalei teshuvah*, but this term will not be used because it underestimates the magnitude of the change made by those who become Orthodox.

Besides the social science concepts that have been described, religious communities have terms that they use in their everyday speech. *Baalei teshuvah* are often referred to as "BTs" in contrast with "FFBs," those who are "*frum* from birth." The Yiddish term *frum* means religious, observant, pious, or Orthodox. Although neither of these acronyms accurately depicts the two groups,[3] I use them in this book because they are employed frequently in

Orthodox communities and were used by participants in the study. In this book, the terms religious, observant, *frum*, and Orthodox will be used interchangeably. Throughout this volume, BTs who are quoted use a number of Hebrew and Yiddish terms. As explained by Benor (2012), *baalei teshuvah*, not unlike FFBs, incorporate Hebrew and Yiddish loan words in their English speech and switch back and forth between languages. Where these terms are first used, they are defined.

Theoretical Underpinnings

This book is about spiritual transformation, which, like other types of religious change, is complex, multifaceted, and dynamic (Rambo, 2010; Smith & Stewart, 2011). I examine this change from two perspectives—the individual (psychosocial) and the group (sociological). *Baalei teshuvah* make internal changes as they move into adulthood and experience life as adults. Psychosocial developmental theories focus on changes in the biological, psychological, and social arenas that occur at different stages of the life cycle. In chapter 2 of this book, in which I describe the processes of *baalei teshuvah* leading to commitment, I use the term "state" instead of stage, because states are fluid and tend to unfold in a nonlinear pattern. Here I refer to developmental theorists who use the term stage.

Psychosocial Perspective

Psychosocial developmental theories provide a structure through which to understand what is occurring within individuals and their environments at different periods of life. They offer a perspective on internal and external stimuli that encourage life changes such as becoming Orthodox. The prominent developmental theorist Erik Erikson is known for his conceptualization of eight stages of human development. Articulated in several books (e.g., Erikson, 1950; 1959/1980; 1968), Erikson's psycho*social* theory departs from Freud's psycho*sexual* theory in encompassing biological, psychological, social, and cultural factors that influence growth over the entire life cycle. Erikson's eight stages are sequential, expressed as polarities, and hierarchical, with each built on its predecessor. Each stage is characterized by a developmental crisis or challenge with which the individual must grapple. During infancy, the period of the first stage, one encounters the crisis of *basic trust vs. basic mistrust*, which is concerned with feeling that one can count on others and have confidence in oneself. This crisis is particularly relevant to this volume because the seeds of faith are rooted in this period. As Erikson (1959/1980) said, "Whosoever says he has religion must derive a faith from it which is transmitted to infants in the form of basic trust" (p. 67). The other crises associated with childhood are *autonomy vs. shame and doubt, initiative vs. guilt,* and *industry vs. inferiority.* These have to do with the development of self-control, taking action on one's own, and competence, respectively.

Erikson's (1959/1980) stage of *identity vs. identity diffusion,* which is associated with adolescence, is characterized by the exploration of ideologies, beliefs, values, and occupational possibilities and the forming of an identity. At this stage, one might explore different religions as a means of finding oneself. The process is not complete during adolescence; it continues to develop as new roles and opportunities become available. In this study, I was interested in spirituality as an aspect of identity, that is, "spiritual identity" (Hoare, 2009; Kiesling & Sorell, 2009; Kiesling, Sorell, Montgomery, & Colwell, 2008), and how one's spiritual identity may change in adulthood. Erikson (1959/1980) viewed identity (or ego identity) as encompassing an inner perception of "self-sameness" (p. 94) and continuity that is matched by a similar perception by others, suggesting that others play a part in defining individual identity. I was also interested in how Erikson's adult stages of *intimacy vs. isolation, generativity vs. stagnation,* and *integrity vs. despair,* which are concerned respectively with forming close personal relationships, nurturing others, and achieving wholeness, intersect with the experiences of BTs.[4] Typically, intimacy is associated with young adulthood, generativity with middle adulthood, and integrity with older adulthood, but in Erikson's conceptualization, all the stages exist in some form throughout the life cycle The formation of ego identity is "a lifelong process spanning all eight of his postulated psychosocial stages" (Côté & Levine, 1987, p. 276). In her review of Erikson's published and unpublished writings, Hoare (2009) concluded that "the spiritual element and corresponding values, practices, and principled behavior are integral to Erikson's mature adult identity" and "that faith is essential to human wholeness and ego vitality" (p. 184).

Since Erikson, a number of developmental theorists have been examining changes that occur during adulthood. Among them, Jeffrey Arnett (2000, 2004) has concentrated on "emerging adulthood" (the period from the late teens through the twenties). Arnett characterizes emerging adulthood as a time of "profound change and importance" (Arnett, 2000, p. 469) in which people engage in identity exploration in relation to work, love, and worldviews. They begin this process by seeking exposure to a range of life experiences prior to making a commitment. As they move along during this period, they become more purposeful. They explore potential careers and relationships, examine the worldviews of their parents and others, and arrive at their own beliefs (Arnett & Jensen, 2002). The adults in this study who became observant in their late teens and twenties engaged in such exploratory processes.

Daniel Levinson and his colleagues (Levinson with Darrow, Klein, Levinson, & McKee, 1978; Levinson with Levinson, 1996) focused primarily on middle adulthood, but in describing early, middle, and later adulthood, they introduced the concept of the *life structure*, "the basic pattern or design of a person's life at a given time" (Levinson, 1978, p. 41). Levinson is concerned with the individual's sociocultural world, the aspects of the self that are lived out and those that are neglected, and participation in the external world. The components of the life structure that Levinson examines at each "era" in his 1978 book about men are based on choices, primarily those relating to work, love relationships, friendships, involvement in religious life, community involvement, leisure, and goals. In a parallel book on women's development, the author states, "The primary components of a life structure are the person's relationships with various others in the external world" (Levinson, 1996, p. 22). At a given period, certain components are central, some are peripheral, and some are unfulfilled (Levinson, 1996). In this book, I found that components of the life structure—work, family, religious community, and friends—became reconfigured along a spiritual-religious axis. As individuals moved along in the process, they altered their priorities and worldviews. These changes in their life structure are akin to a paradigm shift.

Sociological Perspective

The sociological perspective taken in this volume is that the spiritual-religious transformation of *baalei teshuvah* entails a change of group affiliation where the new group's norms are different from those with which the BTs had been familiar. The change involves a movement from one's primary socializing group to another one. The primary group is usually one's family of origin, which orients the younger generation in accordance with its values, beliefs, religion, and culture, but the extended family, schools, peers, and religious institutions and communities also contribute to early socialization. Primary socialization is crucial to children's psychosocial development as it enables the younger generation to function in a way that is attuned to cultural norms and demands.

Socialization is not, however, restricted to childhood. It occurs throughout the life cycle through diverse socializing agents, including educational institutions, the internet, the media, and cultural institutions (Grusec & Hastings,

2007). It is brought about by a variety of means, such as modeling, performance of rituals, and the correction of missteps (Grusec & Hastings, 2007). A process of "secondary socialization" or "resocialization" (Berry, 2007) takes place as one takes on new roles. For example, becoming a professional necessitates academic and social learning at universities, during internships, on the job, and through mentors and role models. During professional socialization, one acquires knowledge, skills, values, and attitudes that are relevant to the new profession. Likewise, when one moves from one job to another within a professional field, one is socialized toward the norms of the professional culture in the new setting.

In the case of *baalei teshuvah*, resocialization entails movement away from the relatively secular norms in which they were raised toward those of a religious tradition that requires considerable learning. Because their parents socialized them to regard Judaism secondary to the primary goal of integrating into the larger secular culture, BTs lack the cultural tools (Swidler, 1986) they need to function adequately in the religious culture they join. They need to become reeducated and resocialized to the new culture. This book highlights the struggles they have in attaining competence in their new environment and how they work toward advancing their knowledge and skills (see especially chapter 4). Their experiences are similar to those of new immigrants, who become resocialized to a new society. Whereas immigrants assimilate, to varying degrees, to their new environments, *baalei teshuvah* de-assimilate to free themselves of secular influences that are incongruent with norms of their new communities and then assimilate to their adopted Orthodox communities. In order to understand these processes, we turn next to a discussion of immigration and assimilation, which have been part of the American experience since its founding and are integral to the Jewish experience in the United States.

Immigration, Assimilation, and Religious Intensification

The United States is a nation of immigrants. Compared with other countries, it has achieved a high level of success in integrating people from diverse religions and ethnicities into a common whole. One of the consequences of successful integration, however, is that the various ethnic, religious, and cultural groups that are amalgamated lose their respective legacies as successive generations become increasingly assimilated into American society. This book is about a sector of Jewish adults who became aware of their lost legacy and tried to recover it through a spiritual migration (cf. Cowan, 1996).

Jewish immigration to what is now the United States of America dates back to the colonial period and has continued intermittently since then. The earliest group of immigrants consisted of Sephardic Jews from Brazil whose roots were in Spain and Portugal. Jews born in England, France, Germany, Holland, and Poland also immigrated in the late colonial/early national period, while Sephardic Jews remained predominant (Sarna, 2004). From the mid-1820s to the mid-1870s, most of the Jewish immigrants were from Central Europe (Sarna, 2004). During the last two decades of the nineteenth century and the first two decades of the twentieth century, large waves of emigrants from Eastern Europe arrived. It is generally understood that their departures were prompted by pogroms (organized massacres), discrimination, poverty, the fear of being inducted into the army, and the desire for a better life. Other waves of immigrants consisted of those leaving Europe before and after the Holocaust; and refugees from the former Soviet Union and the Middle East. *Baalei teshuvah* interviewed for the study described in this book are the descendants of immigrants from Europe who were religiously traditional or embraced a secular Yiddish Jewish culture and/or a socialist ideology.

The immigrants who came to the United States during the late nineteenth and early twentieth centuries found themselves in difficult circumstances. Their principal challenge was economic survival, but they also were confronted with a society in which the dominant language, social norms, and religion were different from theirs. They arrived with few resources and gravitated to low-income, urban, Jewish neighborhoods where they lived in crowded tenements and worked as peddlers and garment workers, among other occupations.

Motivated to rise from poverty and enhance opportunities for their children, some started their own businesses. As a concomitant to the desire to "make it" economically, the immigrants sought to become "Americanized." For the most part, they sent their children to public schools where the children acquired language and other skills needed to navigate in American society. When they could, the families moved out of tenement neighborhoods into more prosperous areas. In their struggles to succeed, some striving business owners kept their stores open on the Sabbath, violating religious law, and committed other religious infractions, such as eating non-kosher food. With increased interaction with ubiquitous Christians, subsequent generations accommodated further. Their adaptations in dress, speech, and religious behavior may have brought about their acceptance, but these changes also moved Jews away from Judaism. Some put up Christmas trees and exchanged Christmas presents as they assimilated into American society.

Jewish assimilation into the dominant white Protestant culture has been unremitting. Successive National Jewish Population Surveys (NJPS) (1970, 1990, 2000–2001) have found decreasing numbers and percentages of Jews and an increasing proportion of interfaith marriages (NJPS, 2000–2001). The Pew Research Center (2013) study on American Jews came up with similar findings. At the same time, Jews exceed other Americans in their level of higher education, occupational standing, and income (Burstein, 2007). In comparison with African Americans, whose visibility as a minority has impeded their integration, Jews have been able to move into the white Protestant culture more easily (Brodkin, 1998). This is not to say that there were no obstacles. Jews in the United States have faced antisemitism, exemplified in quotas limiting the number of Jews admitted to certain colleges and medical schools; employment discrimination; restrictive covenants on living in particular neighborhoods; and exclusion from certain private clubs. Today Jews are presidents of universities and large corporations, serve as congressmen, congresswomen, and senators, and have held cabinet-level and advisory posts in presidential administrations.

Jews in the United States express their Jewishness in religious, cultural, and secular ways. One way is through affiliation with synagogues associated with Jewish religious movements, also referred to as branches and denominations. The major Jewish movements are Orthodox, Conservative, and Reform. Orthodox Judaism adheres most strictly to the stipulations of Jewish law (*halakhah*) as articulated in the Hebrew Bible (the Torah) and interpreted by the rabbis of the Talmud (known as the "oral law"), and later codified and expounded upon. Within Orthodox Judaism, there are numerous streams including, but not limited to, Modern Orthodox (observant of religious law while open to the secular world), Haredim (scrupulously observant, closed to the secular world), and Hasidim (very pious and with a tradition of mysticism). The term Haredim also is used to encompass Hasidim (Heilman, 2006) as well as those described as "Yeshivish," who identify with Jewish learning academies (yeshivas) in their focus on Torah learning and their language and cultural style (Benor, 2012). Haredim are sometimes referred to as "Ultra-Orthodox," "Black Hat," and "Torah Jews." In contrast, the Reform movement accepts the Torah as a "living document" that makes it possible for adherents to adapt to social changes and incorporate innovations that may conflict with rabbinic law (Central Conference of American Rabbis, 2004); the Conservative movement lies in between these two groups with its acceptance of Jewish law in principle but allowing for elasticity in interpretation (Raphael, 1984). In addition to these major religious sub-groups, there are smaller movements such as

Reconstructionism and the Jewish Renewal Movement. Other Jews identify as Jews but not with any specific religious movement, calling themselves secular, post-denominational, culturally Jewish, secular humanists, or "just Jewish." Regardless of their identification or nonidentification with a religious movement, some affiliate with Jewish community organizations. These include, but are not limited to, the American Jewish Committee, the Anti-Defamation League, HIAS, B'nai B'rith, Hadassah, the National Council of Jewish Women, the American Israel Public Affairs Committee (AIPAC), and J Street, as well as other organizations that espouse Jewish values or support Jewish educational, philanthropic, and cultural programs or causes in the United States, Israel, and elsewhere. Others express their Jewishness by reading biographies, novels, and nonfiction works about or written by Jews; subscribing to Jewish periodicals; listening to Jewish music; visiting Jewish sites during travels; following news about and visiting Israel; or through their political choices.

The participants in the study described in this book were raised in homes that identified primarily with the Reform and Conservative movements, with a minority raised with little or no religious orientation. Overall, religious observance was light or negligible, while for the most part Jewish identity was affirmed. At the time they were interviewed for this study, 35 percent self-identified as Modern Orthodox, with the rest describing themselves as right of Modern, Centrist (also right of Modern), Yeshivish, Hasidic, some combination or in-between category, or an invented group such as "BT Orthodox."

According to an analysis of data in the National Jewish Population Survey of 2000–2001 on switching between Jewish religious movements (Orthodox, Conservative, Reform, and non-specific), 62 percent stayed within the same group, 29 percent moved away from a traditional movement, and 9 percent moved to a more traditional denomination (Sands, Marcus, & Danzig, 2006). Thus, it is normative to continue to identify with the same movement in which one was raised and commonplace to become less observant than one was while growing up. Migrating to a more traditional movement is counter-cultural with respect to Jews and Judaism in the United States.

If Jews who intensify their observance of Judaism represent a minor-ity among Jews, why should one write about them? Moreover, why focus on *baalei teshuvah*, who intensify by becoming Orthodox, rather than those Jews who strengthen their commitment in other ways such as increasing synagogue attendance or lighting Sabbath candles? While the latter actions, too, are forms of religious intensification within Judaism, the changes of *baalei teshuvah* are more dramatic and far-reaching than simple behavioral changes. Their embrace of the strictest of the major Jewish denominations in the United States requires greater commitment, a higher level of participation, and more sacrifice than taking on discrete religious behaviors (cf. Iannaccone, 1994). A case study such as this is a "telling case" of religious intensification, one that can make theoretical relationships visible (Mitchell, 1984) and thus contribute to understanding those who engage in other kinds of intensification within Judaism and other religions. In the United Kingdom, the population of strictly Orthodox Jews is increasing at a higher rate than that of the non-strictly Orthodox Jews and is expected to continue to grow in the next few decades (Staetsky & Boyd, 2015). Religious intensification in which participants have embraced the most stringent alternative is a widespread phenomenon, occurring in Christianity, Islam, Hinduism, Buddhism, and other religions of the world (Antoun & Hegland, 1987; Marty & Appleby, 1991–1995; Zeidan, 2003).

The term "fundamentalism" is often used to describe religious groups that embrace strict alternatives, including Haredi Judaism (Heilman, 2005). These groups are generally viewed as conservative, anti-modernist, insular, and oppositional (Emerson & Hartman, 2006; Marty & Appleby, 1991). Marty and Appleby (1991) identify the common feature of the diverse fundamentalist movements discussed in their five-volume edited book as "a process of selective retrieval, embellishment, and construction of 'essentials' or 'fundamentals' of a religious tradition for the purposes of halting the erosion of traditional society and fighting back against the encroachments of secular modernity" (p. 6). Fundamentalist Orthodox Jews (i.e., Haredim) are scrupulous in their observance of religious rituals, live in separate religious enclaves, and guard against the intrusion of secular culture (Heilman, 2005). They idealize men who devote themselves to the study of Torah and valorize women's domestic role. The men grow beards and wear distinctive black suits and hats, while the women dress modestly in long skirts, long-sleeve blouses, and, if married, various types of head coverings (e.g., hats, scarves, wigs). By appearance and practice, they can be identified as different from other Jews and Christians. Although only some of the *baalei teshuvah* interviewed for this study can be described as fundamentalist, most have been influenced by the Haredim because Orthodox Judaism in the United States has moved to the right (Heilman, 2005, 2006; Soloveitchik, 1994) and organizations that recruit potential *baalei teshuvah* and educate them tend to be dominated by the Ultra-Orthodox (Shapiro, 2005).

In embracing a strict version of Judaism, *baalei teshuvah* resist the paths followed by most American Jews today whether they affiliate with less strict religious movements or define themselves as "culturally Jewish," secular, or "just Jewish." The BTs object to the diluted form of Judaism they experienced or observed in liberal Jewish movements, preferring the authenticity they find in

Orthodox Judaism (Danzger, 1989). They oppose the moderate, mainstream, or cultural Judaism in which most of them grew up and are affirmative about their identity as observant Jews. Their aim is to recover the religious tradition of their more distant forebears as they envision it and express it in their everyday lives. They are supported in this endeavor by a social movement that promotes and supports their transformation, but they are viewed skeptically by some outsiders.

The *Baal Teshuvah* Movement: Reactionary, Cult, or Revivalist?

The *baal teshuvah* movement consists of individuals, institutions, and organizations that encourage Jews to explore Judaism and help them participate in Orthodox Jewish life. Although Jews proselytized gentiles during the early centuries of the Common Era, they later came into conflict with Christians over this activity (Laytner, 1996), creating a practice among Jews of refraining from proselytizing gentiles. This did not, however, preclude fostering religious observance among other Jews. The late Rabbi (Rebbe) Menachem Mendel Schneerson (1902–1994), charismatic leader of the Lubavitcher Hasidic sect (also referred to as Chabad), promoted reaching out to non-observant Jews and encouraging their gradual adoption of religious practices. In the United States, and eventually throughout the world, Chabad established local affiliates, Chabad houses, with that purpose, notably around university campuses and other underserved communities. At campus Chabad houses, students gather for Sabbath (Shabbat or Shabbos) dinners, holiday observances, and educational programs, and may seek answers to their spiritual questions from Chabad rabbis. Chabad has established similar missionizing programs around the world (see chabad.org).

Some organizations associated with the *baal teshuvah* movement focus on education. Several yeshivas and seminaries in Israel and the United States prepare BTs for fuller religious participation. Described in the early literature on *baalei teshuvah* (e.g., Aviad, 1983; Danzger, 1989), they instruct students in Jewish law, religious practices, Jewish philosophy, and sacred texts. Many of the institutions in Israel have dormitories, enabling a process of immersion in an intensely religious environment. In addition to these efforts, some organizations hold weekend and weeklong programs, such as the Discovery seminar, in which magnetic speakers lecture about theological issues. The Lincoln Square Synagogue in New York has made participation in Orthodox religious services accessible through its Beginners' *Minyan* (Davidman, 1991), a model adopted by other synagogues and outreach organizations. In addition, organizations such as Aish HaTorah, Etz Chaim, Project Seed, and Hineni have been providing guidance and education to individuals who are exploring Judaism or wish to deepen their knowledge and understanding. Moreover, information is available to potential *baalei teshuvah* and others through websites, audio recordings, and linear translations of Hebrew religious texts and prayer books.

Although valued by those who become Orthodox, the *baal teshuvah* movement is often perceived negatively by others. Considering that *baalei teshuvah* represent a divergence from mainstream Judaism, which is accommodationist, and instead embrace tradition, there are those who characterize the *baal teshuvah* movement as reactionary. Interviewed for studies by Sands and Roer-Strier (2004), mothers of women who became Orthodox expressed displeasure that their daughters were reverting to a religious way of life that they saw as outdated and restrictive. The mothers were also troubled by the patriarchal character of Orthodox Judaism (Roer-Strier & Sands, 2004) and commented that they could not understand how their formerly feminist daughters became Orthodox (Sands & Roer-Strier, 2004).

Another common perception held by the mothers was that their daughters were participating in a cult. The term "cult" has a technical sociological meaning, but because it has been popularly used as a pejorative term and is subject to various interpretations, it is no longer a meaningful concept (Richardson, 1993). Popularly, cults are separatist, authoritarian, religious, or quasi-religious groups that lure middle-class youth and "brainwash" potential recruits (Ellwood, 1986; Richardson, 1993). The term "cult" has been applied to groups like the Moonies, Jews for Jesus, and, in the *baal teshuvah* literature, an Orthodox outreach organization (Tapper, 2002). When groups like these appeared to be growing, some writers expressed concern that Jewish youth would be susceptible to them (Schwartz & Isser, 1987). Because "cult" has negative connotations and is often misapplied, a more neutral term, new religious movement (NRM), is now preferred (Bromley & Shupe, 1995). The updated term, however, does not fit the *baal teshuvah*, because this is not a new development, having had a place in Judaism for centuries. On the other hand, the turn toward Orthodox Judaism by Jews who were raised with little religious observance can be regarded as a revitalization movement.

In a seminal article on this subject, Wallace (1956) defined a revitalization movement "as a deliberate, organized, conscious effort by members of a society to construct a more satisfying culture" (p. 265). Individuals in a given society as well as the society as a whole maintain a mental image or model of a society or culture—what Wallace calls a "mazeway"—as a means to promote stability and reduce stress. Under heightened feelings of dissatisfaction or stress, when individuals and/or the society or culture finds that their existing mazeway does not work, they are open to change. Wallace describes a sequence of stages in which a society moves from a steady state through periods of individual stress and cultural distortion to a period of revitalization and a new steady state. During the period of revitalization, the mazeway is reformulated and changes are made in the organization of the society and communication patterns to enable cultural transformation. Once the changes are accepted and incorporated into daily routines, they become the "new normal."

Wallace's (1956) model has been applied to revitalization movements among Native American societies (Champagne, 1983), Black Muslims (Laue, 1964), and Catholic Charismatics (Daniel, 2010; Lane, 1978), as well as to feminist theology (Porterfield, 1987). More contemporary literature, however, gives greater attention to power relations, viewing revitalization movements as resistance to the dominant political establishment (Yokes, 2007). Similarly, the *baal teshuvah* phenomenon can be viewed as a revitalization movement that resists the dominant mainstream cultural Judaism.

Among the types of revitalization movements that Wallace (1956) describes are "revivalist movements," which give emphasis to cultural practices, principles, and values that were part of the mazeway of previous generations but are not currently present. In the case of the *baal teshuvah* movement, traditions that were part of the mazeway of previous generations but have been lost to contemporary, secular Jews are revived. The *baal teshuvah* movement has the added feature of the presence in their communities of Jews who have maintained traditional practices.

The individuals, institutions, and organizations that constitute the *baal teshuvah* movement make it possible for partakers to acquire the social and academic learning they need to become part of preexisting Orthodox communities. As this book shows, the journey from mainstream, moderate, or cultural Judaism to Orthodoxy is arduous. Most of those who pursue this path have significant gaps in their religious education and are unfamiliar with the norms of the group they aspire to join. With the help of individual Orthodox Jews and outreach organizations, they engage in an extensive reeducational and resocialization process. This process can be intellectually stimulating, exhilarating, and elevating, but it also generates a great deal of anxiety and insecurity. Those who persist with the process benefit from becoming anchored in the Jewish religion, where they find purpose and meaning, and from feeling connected to a religious community. Furthermore, their learning and the resources of their religious communities equip them to be parents who impart a meaningful framework for living to their children. In later chapters, the resocialization process is be more fully explicated. I turn next to the research study that is the basis for this book, and the research methods that were used to learn about the process of spiritual-religious transformation.

The Research Study

This study was conducted from 2003 to 2006, with data analysis continuing for years after the official termination of the research. Using a constructivist grounded theory research approach, the study was designed to inquire qualitatively about how men and women who were raised in relatively secular Jewish homes became Orthodox and were able to incorporate Orthodox Judaism into their daily lives. Grounded theory is a research strategy introduced by Glaser and Strauss (1967) in their landmark book *The Discovery of Grounded Theory*. The authors explained how one could systematically study a phenomenon and build theory inductively from data. This study was influenced by the work of Charmaz (2006, 2009, 2014), a second-generation grounded theory scholar, who has articulated a more contemporary, flexible version of grounded theory. With constructivist grounded theory, the goal is to generate concepts, develop analytic categories, and/or build theory from data, but it is assumed that the knowledge produced is not "discovered" but co-created by research participants and the researcher, and that the research process and product are influenced by preexisting categories of knowledge, structural conditions, and emergent situations (Charmaz, 2014). Constructivist researchers try to enter participants' worlds to learn how they see reality, but the researchers also reflect on their own reality and how their social locations influence what they see and how they construct what they see (Charmaz, 2014).

Our core research team consisted of Rivka Danzig, Robyn Rapoport Spero (research coordinator and interviewer), and me. We met regularly during the course of the study to discuss our data and the next steps. In addition, we had interviewers who lived in or near the three Orthodox communities where the interviewees were located, whose work was supervised by Rivka Danzig. All these team members were Orthodox except the present author, who identifies with Conservative Judaism. Two interviewers were *baalot teshuvah*. Overall, the composition of the research team provided us with the advantages of an insider status that are discussed in the qualitative research literature (e.g., Merriam et al., 2001; Shah, 2004). Insider status gave us access to a sample[5] and enabled us to understand *baalei teshuvah*'s language, ask meaningful questions of the data, and attain an authentic cultural understanding. I was a partial insider-partial outsider because of both my familiarity with *baalei teshuvah* through my daughter and previous studies and my non-Orthodox religious orientation. My partial outsider perspective enabled me to raise questions about ideas and practices that seemed new or unusual. My social location was also as an academic in the field of social work who had practiced as a clinical social worker. As a clinician, I was trained to be aware of and reflect on my own feelings and to make strenuous efforts to prevent personal reactions from spilling over into my work with others. I also benefited from the perspectives of others on the team whose ideas enriched my understanding.

The data for this study came from individual interviews, focus group meetings, and key informant interviews—with no overlap in participants in each of these activities. Each of these three methods provided a different lens with which to look at the spiritual transformation of *baalei teshuvah*. The individual interviews had the advantage of eliciting in-depth information about the spiritual journeys of those who engaged in the process. Focus groups had the benefit of responses stimulated by group interaction that did not emerge in individual interviews (Morgan, 1997). The key informant interviews elicited reflections from persons who had firsthand, on-the-ground knowledge of *baalei teshuvah*'s process of change. The individual interviews were the principal method of data collection. The two other methods were used to supplement, complement, and crosscheck findings from the interview data, a process known as triangulation (Denzin, 1989; Taylor & Bogdan, 1998).

The individual interviews with *baalei teshuvah* took place in three different East Coast metropolitan areas. Interviewers living in these same general areas interviewed forty-eight individuals, half men and half women, half religiously observant two to twelve years, and half religiously observant thirteen or more years[6]. The stratification by years observant and by gender produced a more gender-balanced, older, and more experienced sample than those in the earlier studies of Aviad (1983), Davidman (1991), and Kaufman (1991). This also made it possible to learn about the transformation from newcomers and those who were long-time BTs. Each of the interviewees was asked to construct and discuss a timeline depicting his or her spiritual development over time.[7] In our study, we asked interviewees to divide their spiritual-religious lives into time periods and to give them titles. (The interview questions can be found in Appendix A.) After each interview, the participants completed the Modified Erikson Psychosocial Stage Inventory (MEPSI; Darling-Fisher & Leidy, 1988), a quantitative instrument consisting of eighty questions. This instrument was incorporated into the study in order to obtain an external quantitative measure of where the participants were in terms of Erikson's developmental stages. The results of this inventory are presented and discussed in chapter 3.

The sociodemographic characteristics of the 48 interviewees are listed in Table I.1. Interview participants[8] worked in a variety of occupations (not listed in the table). Eleven were in human service or therapeutic professions, such as psychology, social work, nursing, and physical therapy. Nine worked in business or finance and were either self-employed or worked for others. Other participants were doctors, lawyers, teachers, guidance counselors, college professors, scientists, administrators, and other specialized occupations. A separate analysis comparing men and women found that they had similar levels of education and occupations. Forty participants worked, two were retired, and six were students or homemakers.

Table I.1. Characteristics of Interviewees (N = 48)

Age	
Range	31–58
Mean	45.4
S.D.	7.5
Gender	
Male	24
Female	24
Number of Years Observant	
Range	2–38
Mean	14.4
S.D.	9.0
Marital Status	
Married	44
Separated	1
Single	3
Spouse Status	
Baal or *Baalat Teshuvah*	35
Raised Orthodox	4
Raised, lapsed, returned	3
Convert	2
Not applicable (unmarried or separated)	4
Number of children*	
Range	0–6
Mean	3
S.D.	1.69

continued on next page

Table I.1. Continued.

Highest Level of Education	
High school	2
Some college	3
College graduate	17
Master's degree	12
Law degree	5
Ph.D.	6
M.D.	2
Unknown	1
Jewish Parents	
Both parents	47
Father only**	1
Religious Movement Identified with Growing Up	
Reform	10
Conservative	26
Reform & Conservative	3
Traditional/non-Orthodox	1
Reconstructionist	1
None	7
Age When Became Observant	
Range	15–55
Median	29.5
Mean	31
S.D.	8.9
Self-described Stream of Orthodoxy at Time of Interview	
Modern Orthodox (MO)	17
"Right of MO"	2
"Centrist"	1
Between MO/Centrist and other	3
Yeshivish	4
Hasidic	7
Haredi	1
Combination	3
Other	4
"Just Orthodox"	3
Can't answer	3

*Forty-five participants had children; three had none.
**The mother had a Reform conversion, which is not accepted within Orthodoxy.

Two Orthodox mental health professionals (a husband-and-wife team) conducted two focus group meetings, each with a different set of Jewish professionals who were *baalei* and *baalot teshuvah*. The meetings were conducted at two different professional conferences for Orthodox health and mental health workers in which we knew *baalei teshuvah* were well represented. The first focus group, which took place during the first year of the study, had eight participants, six men and two women, who were professionals in health (including mental health) and education. Their ages ranged from 31 to 61, and they had been observant from 11 to 35 years. The second, conducted ten months later, was with ten mental health professionals, eight women and two men who ranged from 28 to 57 years of age and had been Orthodox from 10 to 38 years. We used the focus groups to home in on questions about the psychosocial development of *baalei teshuvah*. As with the individual interviews, we asked these participants to create and discuss their spiritual developmental timelines. The interview guides for these focus groups can be found in Appendix B.

As for the key informant interviews, Rivka Danzig and I interviewed ten individuals who had direct expert knowledge about and professional experience working with *baalei teshuvah*. All these interviews except one were conducted by phone. The key informants consisted of eight men and two women who were rabbis, wives of rabbis (rebbetzins), therapists, educators, and *keruv* (outreach) workers from the same geographic areas as the interviewees. They spoke from the perspective of their work roles; for example, those whose work was with youth could provide insights into the experiences of young people, and those who worked on the community level could talk about how *baalei teshuvah* integrate. (The interview guide for the key informant interviews can be found in Appendix C.) The individuals who transcribed the individual and focus group interviews lived in different cities from the interviewees. Interviewers for the key informant interviews wrote narrative summaries describing the responses.

Consistent with a grounded theory approach (Charmaz, 2006; Glaser & Strauss, 1967), data analysis was concurrent with and followed data collection. The interviews were transcribed soon after they were conducted and thus were available for reading as the project proceeded. Two of us wrote analytic memos in which we summarized the interviews and identified theoretical issues and other aspects of the interview that were salient. The research team discussed about ten interviews together and from them began to identify what we called "an evolving model of spiritual transformation." We tested the model on subsequent interviews and made changes. The team developed an initial set of codes based on the individual interviews and revised the codes a few times thereafter to correspond more closely with the data. After training, two individuals coded the interviews. For this book, I reread the transcripts, developed additional codes, and applied them to the data.

With respect to the two focus group sessions, two of us debriefed with the facilitators after each session to obtain their impressions of the content and process of the meetings. Subsequently, each of the research team members listened to the tapes and/or read the transcripts. The research coordinator then organized and transcribed participant responses question by question, then identified themes that were related to responses to each question. Next, the team collectively discussed the transcripts and the analysis, adding additional interpretations that we recorded in minutes. The team engaged in a similar process with the narrative summaries of the key informant interviews.

Comparisons were made between the findings of the individual interviews and focus groups and key informant interviews as a means of triangulation. Discussions in the focus groups enriched findings from the interviews, prompting us to return to the interviews. Similarly, key informants sensitized us to issues we had not noticed previously but were present in the individual interview transcripts.

The Social Context of this Study

The period in which the participants in this study moved into adulthood (late 1960s to early 1990s) and became Orthodox was a time when traditional norms were becoming more relaxed and society was becoming more open. The country was developing increased acceptance of different religious, ethnic, and cultural groups, and the groups themselves were celebrating their differences. Evangelical Christianity became a conspicuous political force, making it customary for politicians to bring God into public discourse. Universities faced challenges about curricula that focused on knowledge about and created by white men, resulting in the addition of women's studies and revised multicultural curricula. This atmosphere made it possible for a Jewish man to run for vice president in 2000 and an African American man to be elected president in 2008 and reelected in 2012.

While the country was becoming more tolerant of cultural differences, similar developments were occurring within the Jewish community. The Reform, Conservative, and Reconstructionist movements were becoming increasingly open, ordaining women as rabbis and cantors; accepting lesbian, gay, and bisexual members; and, in the case of some Reform rabbis, conducting marriages of interfaith couples. Women in all three of these religious movements were able to wear religious garments traditionally worn by men, read from the Torah, and lead prayer services, and they were counted in the quorum, or *minyan*, required for religious services (traditionally ten men).

In the face of liberalizing trends in Jewish communities, sectors of Orthodox Judaism became wary. Traditional Jewish communities in Europe have a history of resisting reform movements (Wurzburger, 1997). Following the *Haskalah*, the Jewish Enlightenment, and the emancipation of Jews from European ghettoes in the eighteenth and nineteenth centuries, the opening of the secular world to Jews became problematic to religious Jews. Some Jews, such as those in the Reform movement, modified their religious practices as a way of accommodating to their host European societies. Other Jews tried to maintain their traditional religious practices while partaking of secular knowledge (*Torah im derekh erez*; Torah with secular education); still others had a separatist ideology (Wurzburger, 1997). Those traditional Jews who saw accommodation as a gateway to assimilation and assimilation as perilous opposed adapting to the secular culture (Heilman & Friedman, 1991). Today's Haredi communities continue to resist assimilation, accommodation, and secularization and convey this to potential *baalei teshuvah* when they are exploring Judaism in educational programs (Aviad, 1983; Shapiro, 2005).

The Question of Gender

Since the women's movement of the last few decades of the twentieth century, much discussion has been had about the unequal position of women within Orthodox Judaism. Among the concerns are the separate men's and women's roles, limits on women's participation in religious services, restrictions on women's singing in the presence of men (due to the doctrine of *kol ishah*), and the requirement that married women go to the ritual bath (*mikveh*) after several clean days following menstruation. Although some writers have tried to clarify the basis for discrete gender roles in Jewish law (Berman, 1973; Biale, 1984), feminist Jewish scholars view such distinctions as inequitable (Heschel, 1995; Plaskow, 1990). Two sociologists who studied *baalot teshuvah* have tried to understand women choosing a way of life that appears to run counter to feminist sensibilities (Davidman, 1991; Kaufman, 1991). Davidman (1991) conducted an ethnographic study of the newly observant in two communities, one Modern Orthodox, the other Lubavitch; and Kaufman (1991) interviewed *baalot teshuvah* living in a variety of Orthodox Jewish communities around the country. Davidman (1991) found differences between the Modern Orthodox and Lubavitch BTs, the latter younger and less educated in secular universities. Both authors observed that the *baalot teshuvah* were attracted to the family orientation of Orthodox Judaism. Other social scientists that made Hasidic women the focus of their research have highlighted the complexity of women's adaptations to feminism (Fader, 2009; Morris, 1998). Sands and Roer-Strier (2004; Roer-Strier & Sands, 2001, 2004; Sands, Roer-Strier, & Strier, 2013) conducted studies of *baalot teshuvah* and their mothers in Israel, South Africa, Argentina, and the United States; and Mock-Degan (2009) did a similar study in Holland. In all these, the mothers voiced a feminist perspective in response to their daughters.

Although this book is about the process of spiritual-religious transformation without specific focus on gender, the gender-balanced sample of interviewees made it possible to examine gender issues as they relate to changes the BTs made. Gender issues are discussed where evident in the interview data. The book draws attention to women's separate roles, the struggles of some women over feminist issues, and the adaptations of women and men as they moved into and became part of gendered communities.

Themes and Format of the Book

This book emphasizes the extensive life changes that are made *after* one makes a commitment to Orthodox Judaism. In reading this book, one will become aware of several prominent themes, some of which have been already touched on:

+ Spiritual transformation is a lifelong process.

+ Social connections draw *baalei teshuvah* into Orthodoxy and help them adapt to life in Orthodox communities.

+ One is most receptive to examining and moving into another spiritual-religious orientation during late adolescence and early adulthood, and during times of transition, such as new parenthood, marriage, divorce, and the death of a significant other.

+ Because of gaps in their Jewish religious education and the need to participate in religious life with others, *baalei teshuvah* engage in an extensive learning activities before and after they become Orthodox.

+ Spiritual struggles occur before one makes a commitment and continue while living an Orthodox Jewish life.

+ *Baalei teshuvah* make psychological and social changes that lead to (but do not necessarily ensure arriving at) psychological and social integration.

+ *Baalei teshuvah* gain a framework with which to view adverse events positively, to heal from past wounds, and to appreciate the nonmaterial aspects of life.

+ The transformation changes them thoroughly, changing their identity, family life, living situation, career, and daily life.

This book is organized around findings of the research study that pertain to the process of considering, deciding upon, and taking on the responsibilities of an Orthodox Jew. Chapter 1 portrays the backgrounds and early experiences of the men and women who later become Orthodox. It captures their constructions of their family lives, their early memories of thoughts about God, spirituality, and religion, and the experiences that were conducive to or impeded their spiritual development. Chapter 2 is about their search process and the journey toward commitment. It identifies and describes different phases of the process, including conflicts and ambivalence, leading toward a decision. In keeping with the developmental perspective used in this book, Chapter 3 examines differences among participants who became *frum* at different ages and life stages. It also looks at the developmental issues of participants who were at different ages or stages at the time of their interviews. This chapter should be of special interest to readers who are acquainted with the developmental literature, but it can be skipped if this is not a focal concern. Starting with chapter 4, the emphasis is on the open-ended socialization and reeducation process, which involves help from mentors and role models as well as personal efforts to learn. As novices, the BTs learn from teachers and others whom they view as knowledgeable about Orthodox Judaism and community norms. In chapter 5, the focus is on challenges related to marriage, the family of procreation, and relations with the family of origin, which also involves reeducation. In chapter 6, the struggles the BTs experience in maintaining belief in the light of untoward life events, gender role expectations, and other issues are addressed. Chapter 7 pertains to the psychological integration of the new identity as an Orthodox person and to social integration into an existing Orthodox community. The eighth chapter describes how *baalei teshuvah* attempt to live out their spiritual-religious orientation in their daily life. In the final chapter, I discuss and integrate these issues further and propose components of a theory on the process of spiritual-religious transformation in Judaism and potentially other religions.

Throughout this book, the reader will find quotations from participants in this study.[9] In all cases, pseudonyms are used. The pseudonyms selected reflect the range of names the participants used, which are Hebrew, Yiddish, and Anglo-American. The reader may also notice slight differences between the spelling of Hebrew and Yiddish words in quotations and in the text.[10] The analysis represents a composite of individual narratives, comprising what Richardson (1988) called a "collective story." Accordingly, the narratives of "similarly situated individuals who may or may not be aware of their life affinities" are amalgamated so that the experience of the group and the social, cultural, and historical contexts of their experiences can be recognized (Richardson, 1988, p. 201). Here the narratives represent *baalei teshuvah* as a community. In a few cases, details are presented about individual narratives, but for the most part the focus is on the collective narrative.

Summary

This book is about the spiritual-religious transformation of Jewish men and women living on the East Coast of the United States during the early years of the twenty-first century. It is based on a qualitative research study of the spiritual journeys of *baalei teshuvah* from diverse Jewish backgrounds. It explores participants' perceptions of the families in which they were raised and examines their accounts of the experiences that led them to radically change their beliefs, behaviors, and values so that these are consistent with the way of life of Orthodox Jews in the religious communities they joined. The findings of the study are based on in-depth interviews with *baalei* and *baalot teshuvah*, focus-group meetings with health and mental health professionals who are also *baalei teshuvah*, and interviews with Orthodox community leaders who work with this population. Theories of psychosocial development and socialization are used to interpret the findings.

The aims of this book are to examine the processes involved in spiritual-religious transformation; the relationship between spiritual changes and psychosocial development; the reeducation and resocialization that occurred along the way; the significance of spirituality and spiritual struggles; and the extent to which *baalei teshuvah* integrate these changes psychologically and socially and make changes in their identities.

Chapter 1

Beginnings

An appropriate starting point for this inquiry is to consider the recollections of the upbringing and early experiences of the forty-eight interviewees who became *baalei teshuvah*. In this chapter, I describe the participants' constructions of their family backgrounds and religious experiences; their earliest memories of thinking about God, spirituality, and religion; personal-familial challenges; and the people and experiences that inspired their spiritual development while growing up.

Most developmental theories acknowledge the importance of childhood experiences in shaping individuals' lives. As mentioned in the introduction, Erikson (1968) asserted that faith development is rooted in his first stage, *trust versus mistrust*, and expands in later stages. Likewise, the formation of identity is a lifetime project that begins in childhood, comes to the fore during adolescence, and undergoes modification in the process of development (Erikson, 1959/1980). Parents and other caretakers provide the primary influence on young children, but as children develop, other relatives (e.g., grandparents, aunts, and siblings), neighbors, peers, and teachers become increasingly important (Erikson, 1959/1980). The social-cultural, environmental context is of fundamental importance in Erikson's psychosocial theory, as well as theories of Levinson and his colleagues.

Parents are also the primary agents of religious socialization of children and adolescents, but extended family, religious leaders, and other community members play a role in this area, too. For Jewish children, religious socialization includes the ways in which they identify as a Jewish ethno-religious group as well as formal instruction, attendance at religious services, travel to Israel, home observances, and participation in Jewish camps and youth groups. Jewish

31

religious socialization takes place within the home, synagogue, and neighborhood. Children learn their parents' attitudes toward religion and the rituals they practice, and observe the consistency between what they profess and how they act. Children and adolescents also discern the attitudes of peers and others in their neighborhood and schools, and ways in which their parents' attitudes and practices are congruent or incongruent with those of other children's parents. Considering the developmental and socialization influences, I will start with a description of participants' background characteristics.

Research Participants' Family Backgrounds

In Table I.1, I described the socio-demographic characteristics of the forty-eight men and women who were interviewed for this research (referred to as participants, interviewees, *baalei teshuvah*, and BTs). Here I will provide more information about their families based on the accounts in their interviews.

The BTs were diverse with respect to their socioeconomic backgrounds and places in which they lived. Although it was required that research participants spend most of their formative years in the United States, one emigrated from Europe and another from Israel as young children. They grew up in many sections of the country—the South, Southwest, West, Northeast, and Midwest—before moving to the cities in the Northeast where we found them. Some grew up in large urban environments where there were many Jews, whereas others lived in communities in which they were part of a small Jewish minority. Several spoke of their families' economic difficulties during their childhoods whereas others portrayed growing up middle class or financially privileged. No specific social profile fit all.

Most of the forty-eight interviewees were raised in intact families, with eight having parents who were divorced.[1] A few from intact families spoke of dissension between their parents or between themselves and one parent whereas others reported that their families were close, warm, and loving. Four spoke of traumatic experiences growing up, such as abuse. One of the key informants, a rabbi/educator, talked about the importance of the BTs' relationships with their parents. In his opinion, having a poor relationship can block growth toward becoming *frum*. He said that some people have difficulty with the idea of a loving, compassionate God, but that emotionally balanced healthy people move ahead smoothly. He added that the more selfish a person is, the harder it is for the individual to do *mitzvot* (commanded obligations) which are, in essence, acts of selflessness. People with good *midot* (character traits), he said, do better in terms of changing and making the transition. The lack of such qualities pushes people away from the process.

The focus group discussions were primarily about adult experiences, but members' timelines pointed to significant childhood experiences. Timelines from Focus Group 1 noted bar mitzvahs, a serious surgery, parents' divorce, learning about the Holocaust, cultural affiliation, parental resistance to their wanting more Jewish involvement, and youth group membership as salient experiences. The timelines of the Focus Group 2 highlighted losses (e.g., death of a sibling, parental divorce), day school, Jewish camp, a youth group, Hebrew School, bat mitzvahs, and awareness of the Holocaust. The experiences identified in the timelines of the two focus groups echoed each other and the individual interviews.

Most of the 48 study participants spoke of having had close relationships with grandparents and other relatives. In contrast with the traditional Orthodox grandparents referred to in Danzger's (1989) study of *baalei teshuvah*, the grandparents were relatively secular. Still, the extended family got together for Jewish holidays and other occasions. There were traces of Orthodox Judaism in the grandparental, parental, and other relatives' homes.

Several BTs spoke of anti-Jewish attitudes on the part of a parent, extended family members, or peers that raised questions for them about their Jewish identities. A few mentioned that their families had Christmas trees or exchanged Christmas presents, indicating that the families were assimilating into the larger society. In contrast, others grew up in families that conveyed positive feelings about being Jewish and held traditional Friday night Sabbath meals, kept kosher, and attended synagogue as a family on the Sabbath and/or holidays. A few described their families as Zionist or spoke about attending Zionist camps, youth groups, or religious schools. Typically, the participants went to Reform or Conservative Hebrew or Sunday Schools, which they liked to varying degrees, and had a *bar* or *bat mitzvah*. More male than female participants recalled disliking Hebrew School, because, they said, it kept them away from sports and was disorderly. Six interviewees continued their religious studies during high school in post-bar/bat mitzvah or confirmation classes. Another six attended Jewish day schools. Ten said that they went to Jewish summer camps.

Based on the interview participants' descriptions, I was able to identify three types of Jewish religious orientations of the families of origin. The first of these are the *Minimalists* (n = 7). Participants in this category came from families that did not affiliate with a synagogue, send their children to a Jewish camp, or enroll them in Sunday or Hebrew School (except for short periods, or a minimum required for a *bar mitzvah*). The families of an additional three participants fit the criteria for Minimalist, but in these cases the BTs had some supplementary religious education. Influenced by relatives and others, two attended Jewish day schools and the third went to Hebrew School. I call these three families *Minimalists Plus*. For the most part, the BTs whose families were Minimalists or Minimalists Plus had some exposure to Judaism through Passover seders held at a relative's home or minimal celebrations of their *bar mitzvahs*.

Next were the *Mainstreamers* (n = 24). These came from families that attended synagogue a few times a year and enrolled their children in Sunday School or Hebrew School at some time. Generally, these families did not keep kosher. On the other hand, a mother may have been active in a Jewish women's organization or the parents may have participated in synagogue activities or Jewish charitable or Zionist organizations. One Mainstreamer family sent their child to a Jewish day school while several others enrolled their children in a Hebrew high school, a confirmation class, and/or Jewish camp but were otherwise modest participants in Jewish religious life.

The *Modern Traditionalists* (n = 14) took Judaism seriously within the parameters of Reform or Conservative Judaism. The families attended synagogue more frequently than the Mainstreamers, in some cases weekly or biweekly. They had some home observances such as a traditional Friday night family meal, lighting Sabbath candles, keeping kosher, and changing dishes for Passover. Three of these families sent their children to Jewish day schools and three enrolled them in Hebrew high school or post–bar or bat mitzvah seminars. One father reportedly attended religious services every morning.

These categories suggest that the BTs have different levels of family socialization and educational preparation for becoming Orthodox. Those from Modern Traditionalist families had a taste of religious observance but did not find these practices consistent. The seven from Minimalist families that provided little exposure to Judaism were disadvantaged. Those who attended day schools, went to Hebrew School, and participated in post–bar or bat mitzvah classes or seminars were better positioned to raise the level of their learning later.

Although there was variation in the extent to which Judaism was imparted, for the most part the families can be described as "culturally Jewish" in a number of senses. They saw themselves as Jewish regardless of the extent to which they were observant. They celebrated selected religious holidays (especially Rosh Hashanah, Yom Kippur, Chanukah, and Passover), at which times they enjoyed being together as a family and eating Jewish ethnic dishes.

Some marked the Sabbath by lighting candles and having a special meal or by attending services, but they did not abide by the restrictions of this day (e.g., not using electricity). They gave little attention to Jewish law. The BTs emerged from their various families identified as Jews. A common statement was "I knew I was Jewish."

To the extent that education, academic achievement, and community service are part of Jewish culture, the families seem to have embraced these values. Considering that the *baalei teshuvah* were well educated (see Table I.1) and many were professionals, families seem to have encouraged achievement and success in the secular world. A high level of education also suggests that they were socialized to think scientifically, that is, guided by observation, logic, and concrete evidence. Although this could be problematic to them when they were exploring Orthodox Judaism, their secular education led them to enjoy philosophical arguments, intellectual challenges, and novel interpretations. During the interviews, they used their intellectual skills as they reflected on the past.

Earliest Memories

As a means of starting the interviews without imposing our own perspectives on participants, we asked about their earliest memories of thinking about God, spirituality, and religion (see Appendix A). These questions helped prepare the participants for the rest of the interview while their responses showed where they were coming from before they became observant.

Earliest Memories of Thinking about God

Participants reported that they found it challenging to recall their earliest memories of thinking about God. Some reported that in their families there was no talk about God, whereas others spoke of being made conscious of God. Exemplifying the latter, Elliot said, "I just grew up with an awareness of God. My grandfather prayed, and my mother would talk about God." Others who reported growing up in families that spoke about God mentioned that their parents had their children recite prayers. Sherry's earliest memory was of her father's teaching her the *Shema*, a prayer affirming the oneness of God. She recalled, "He said that it was important for me to talk to God about how I was feeling and what I was doing." Allison recalled reciting the *Shema* with her sister at night "and of course when you do something like that just before you fall asleep, I think it triggers a whole presence of God." On the other hand, Paul was encouraged to recite the Christian prayer "Now I lay me down to sleep" before he went to bed. This prayer ended with, "And if I die before I wake I pray the Lord my soul to take." Fearing that he would die in his sleep, Paul added an additional line, "But don't let me die." Nora said that her mother modified the same prayer so that it included blessings for "all the people in my family and all the people that I loved." Rather than feeling frightened, Nora felt that God was protecting her.

Some BTs recalled thinking about God after the death of a grandparent, other relative, or friend. They wondered what happens to a person after death. Did he or she go somewhere, like heaven? What would happen if their parents died? Participants who grew up in Minimalist homes found talk about God puzzling. Maya, for example, was surprised when her mother told her that God did not want her to waste the bread that Maya had discarded. She said she was not accustomed to hearing discussions about God in her family.

A number of participants shared their earliest perceptions of God. Their varied responses included the following:

> It's generally been a God as a creator, as a giver, as the creator of all that is of the world . . . like this thing that was bigger than life that was outside of the world that created everything. The trees, the grass, you know, my family, life. (Batya)

> I definitely thought about God a lot as a child. I definitely believed that there was this sort of huge formless spirit that was looking after me and was taking care of me. (Erica)

> You know, I kind of think of this grandfatherly figure sitting on a big throne kind of thing. I guess somehow the image that I've also always had has not been of this loving father type figure, but more of the judge. (Annie)

> When I was a little girl and I used to go outside and sit on a lounge chair and look up in the sky, in the clouds, and think that God was there, was watching me, and I just wanted to be in the clouds. Like I just wanted to transport myself into the sky. (Nora)

> I knew that there was something that I couldn't explain that somehow things seemed to work out right. (Jerry)

It was a Santa Claus view of God—that God takes care of you and does good things for you, but you have no obligations. (Paul)

I always felt close to God. I grew up going to the beach very frequently, and going on my grandfather's boat on Sundays, and I always felt close to God. I love being outdoors, and I love looking at the moon and the trees and the plants, and listening to birds. And I always felt that *Hashem* was close. (Ellen)

These images suggest a powerful being that created the world, hovers above and within nature, and is protective but controls and judges. Other images, not quoted here, described a God that aroused their fear of punishment or guilt.

Two children of Holocaust survivors, both from Mainstream families, spoke of the presence of God in their lives. In one case, the family emphasized God but not religious practice. As Deborah said, "God was always important in our house, because it was God that saved her (my mother) and her family." The other child of a survivor who spoke of God's presence said:

I was bewildered. I didn't understand God. And I knew that God kind of saved our lives. I didn't know why He would allow the world to be operated this way, I guess. I was three years old, I don't know how complicated I could have felt about it. (Ezra)

Several interviewees recalled learning about or discussing God in Reform Sunday school, discussions that seemed to arouse skepticism. Karen recalled:

You know, somewhere between second and sixth grade, sitting in Sunday school with this teacher, I don't even remember who the teacher was. And I remember this boy. . . . We must have been talking about God, and I remember he said, he was like questioning her about the existence of God, and I remember he said something to her like, "If God exists, I'm gonna put this stapler down on the table, and why can't He lift it up or something." And I remember looking at him, thinking, and saying to him out loud, "Do you think if there is a God, He has time to like deal with your nonsense of lifting up the stapler? You know, like, come on." And, so I guess, that would be my earliest memory.

Others, who attended Conservative Hebrew Schools and religious services, regarded their upbringing as more culturally Jewish than God-centered. As Lauren explained, "God was mentioned in *davening* (reciting prayers) but we didn't think too much about God. We just thought, 'This is what Jewish people are supposed to do. And this is what we're going to do and this is the way it is.'"

Overall, the participants had some concept of God gleaned from family members, prayer, and religious school. Their recollections of their child's eye views reflect their young ages (mostly preschool or early school age). Although their ideas about God incorporated Christian and pantheistic elements, for the most part they were consistent with Jewish characterizations of God as powerful, just, compassionate, and awe-inspiring, and their age-related view of God as parental. God, however, was not the focus of the Jewishness with which they grew up.

Earliest Memories of Thinking about Spirituality

Interviewees reported that their early thoughts about spirituality occurred, for the most part, when they were older, that is, in their teenage years, during college, or after they did *teshuvah*. A few, however, spoke of nascent spiritual experiences that arose during childhood. Several BTs offered unsolicited definitions of the term spirituality, for example:

> spirituality for me would be feeling connected to God and feeling that there was a higher purpose than just living in the physical world. (Ezra)

> a connection between myself and God. (Sarah)

> I've always felt that you have to look beyond what is apparently in front of you. (Adam)

> And only recently have I . . . figured out that it means a relationship with God. (Allison)

The term *connection* seems to encapsulate participants' definitions of spirituality and the kinds of experiences they described. Interviewees provided numerous examples of early spiritual experiences in which they felt connected to God, *Hashem* (lit. the Name), or something vaguely meaningful:

I used to sleep with a prayer book in my bed. And I can remember that all the years, I needed some connection, even though I didn't know what it was at the time, I knew it was something. (Shifra)

I remember making a conscious decision in high school to light Chanukah candles because it was a connection to my ancestors. (Maya)

I would say probably the first time I really felt like I could have a connection to *Hashem* was that time that I prayed. That was really a big thing for me. It wasn't about community and it wasn't about heritage. It was about me talking with God. (Erica)

Probably my bar mitzvah. I mean, spirituality, the connection, a deep inner type of connection, or just a sense that, again, I always knew that there was Hashem. (Jerry)

Although they recalled discussing spiritual matters in Sunday School or Hebrew School, the spiritual experiences they described were in connection with the Sabbath, Passover, Chanukah, and attending religious services. They spoke about special feelings they associated with these occasions and the presence of immediate and extended family and friends. Ruth, whose family was Minimalist, recalled being exposed to her grandmother's Friday night dinners:

I have a lot of memories (of) my grandmother. Even though she wasn't observant, she always had Friday night dinner at her house with her whole extended family, which was, I think, this remnant of her religious life when she was younger. And so that felt, it felt like a spiritual feel to that in some way. It was like there was always *challah* (braided bread) and there was *matzah* ball soup, even though, again, it was not connected to ritual, but there was something spiritual about that experience for me. I think the family component and the Friday night ritual component was spiritual.

Although she described family visits rather than meals, Ellen spoke similarly about her grandmother, characterizing her as a good person who embodied spirituality.

Several interviewees mentioned the deaths of family members and friends as times of spiritual awakening and questioning. Arthur recalled learning about the death of his grandmother when he was four years old, at which time he thought about where she would be going. Another participant, Gabe, reflected about his grandmother's unveiling:

> I just began to think there was something very special about what was happening then; something other-worldly. For a six-year-old kid to think that . . . something out of the ordinary, spiritual, that there were spirits around that were (guiding her). I remember looking up in the trees nearby and seeing a bird fly and thinking to myself that bird must be Grandma. And that, that probably was my earliest introduction to thinking out of the box.

Gabe seems to have assimilated the concept of transmigration of souls or metempsychosis, whereby the soul of a deceased person takes the form of an animal or person. The concept is associated with Hinduism as well as other religions and cultures. In Judaism, the doctrine has been connected with adherents of Kabbalah, but it has been controversial (Kohler & Broydé, n.d.).

Some BTs described early memories of spiritual experiences that were secular or universalistic in character. They spoke of being moved by nature, music, or a baseball game and intrigued by study of Eastern mysticism. As Ben explained:

> Being spiritual, I think, mostly had to do with maybe going to a concert that I liked, or maybe going with my dad to a baseball game. Or something that just was a . . . there was some kind of a transcending experience that was more than just a game itself. We went there, so it was something really nice, we could go to the game. Or when I got old enough to go to concerts . . . I'd get some kind of a good feeling. But it wasn't attached to any kind of religion.

This participant described a pleasurable, elevating experience. Other BTs later transferred the spiritual feelings that they had in relation to secular music to the chanting of religious prayers.

Several interviewees could not come up with an early spiritual experience or were puzzled with the term. A couple of them expressed negative or indifferent attitudes toward spirituality. One man was particularly critical of the idea:

Depending on how you define the word, spirituality tends to rub me the wrong way—even now. That comes up in the category of things which are nutty and crunchy. [Chuckle] So . . . I'm not necessarily sure what you're defining under the general heading of spirituality. I mean that's—that can be a big heading. I tend to lump that under the sorts of things where, in college, people would make these flaky, inventive services to better express their inner need to, whatever they were expressing. I mean, that sort of thing I tend to run screaming from. (Joel)

Although participants struggled with the term spirituality and with recalling an early experience, few responded cynically like Joel. They did have a range of responses to the question about their memories of their earliest thoughts about spirituality. Across groups (Minimalist, etc.) participants spoke of experiences in which they felt connected to God, family, their ancestors, Judaism, nature, other-worldly phenomena, and, as mentioned, death. Sometimes the connection was through a symbol, like Shabbat candles. They did not describe early spiritual experiences as solitary; they associated them with being with loved ones on the Sabbath and Jewish holidays and going to synagogue with family and friends.

Earliest Memories of Thinking about Religion

When it came to describing earliest thoughts about religion, the core idea was *differentness*. Participants recalled knowing that they were Jewish and that being Jewish was different from being Christian. They felt different from neighborhood children who went to Catholic school or attended Protestant churches—but also different from Jews whose level of observance was less extensive than theirs. In addition to discussing their differentness in terms of religious identity, they also discussed their holiday celebrations, religious school attendance, synagogue life, and home observances.

Most of the participants attended public school, and even if they lived in predominantly Jewish neighborhoods, they had Christian neighbors and friends. Joshua said that he was cognizant of being different from his closest friend, especially around Christmas time, while Allison spoke about being attracted to her Catholic friend's Christmas tree:

and I loved that tree! I mean it was a classic American tale. And my mother, going out and getting as many Chanukah decorations as she could find. The apartment became solid Chanukah. And you know, it was incredible! And then every night was the gift, and each night the gift got bigger and bigger, and that kind of thing. And really trying to compensate and push that. . . . You know, because it wasn't a religious home but a very Jewish home.

Even though Chanukah is not a major Jewish holiday in the way Christmas is to Christians, Allison's mother tried to compensate for any deprivation her daughter might have felt through an embellished celebration of Chanukah. Mark, whose family had been celebrating both Christmas and Chanukah, recalled his discussions with his classmates about religion and his parents' similar response:

I think that when I was . . . in second grade, that some of my classmates and I were trying to figure out what religion was about. I presume from the discussion that they didn't have any more clues than I did. We celebrated both Chanukah and Christmas. That is to say, we got presents on both Chanukah and Christmas, I think. And I remember the discussion was . . . okay, there's three religions. There's Judaism, and there's Protestantism, and Catholicism. Well, what are the differences? And one of them suggested, well, I guess it's Jews celebrate Chanukah and Catholics celebrate Christmas and Protestants must celebrate both. So I said, "Oh, then that must be what we are." I told my parents that and I think that's when they enrolled me in Hebrew school. (Mark)

Batya spoke of celebrating Jewish holidays as a means of differentiating oneself from Christians:

Religion, I think, was celebrations . . . Religion was identity. Family. . . . Food, certain kinds of food, Jewish food, Jewish people, Jewish faith. It definitely had a sense of difference-ness, you know, like one of maybe my earliest remembrances is like Passover and not celebrating Easter, and Chanukah and not celebrating Christmas.

As suggested by Batya and sixteen other participants, celebrating Jewish holidays was a way of affirming one's Jewish identity. By partaking of some traditional aspects, like eating special food, families asserted their Jewish cultural identity in contrast with what they were *not*. It is notable that two of the most frequently celebrated Jewish holidays, Chanukah and Passover (National Jewish Population Survey, 2000–2001), occur around the same time as Christian holidays. Other ways of affirming their Jewish cultural identities that they described were participation in social action activities and demonstrating sensitivity to those who were discriminated against or suffering in some other way.

Despite a common perception that religion is equivalent to culture, many interviewees described their experiences within Jewish religious institutions and their home practices as meaningful in themselves. As mentioned in the introduction, the term religion is linked with institutions (Pargament, 1999). Among the Jewish institutions or organizations that the interviewees mentioned were synagogues and religious schools (Talmud Torah, afternoon supplementary or Hebrew schools, Sunday schools, and Jewish day schools), as well as Jewish youth groups and summer camps. Even though participants' synagogue attendance tended to be a few times a year, seventeen people referred to going to synagogue or *shul*. Lauren's parents were officers in their Conservative synagogue, which was "a very big part of our life," and Nora recalled loving her synagogue and Hebrew School:

> Well, I didn't think about religion per se, but . . . I went to Hebrew School from a very early age, and I loved being in the synagogue with my parents on the High Holidays and I loved the cantor, so I guess I loved religious practices, the feeling surrounding religion, and being in the synagogue from the time I was a young girl and going to Hebrew School, and, looking back, being in the synagogue with my parents and feeling safe and secure.

For Nora and others, the synagogue was a safe haven, a home away from home. Eli said that what he liked best about going to synagogue was the socializing. Dov spoke positively about learning about Torah in Hebrew School, studying for his bar mitzvah, and attending Hebrew High School afterward. Dov, who came from a Minimalist Plus family, had convinced his parents to send him to Hebrew School and have a bar mitzvah when he saw that his friends were participating in these activities.

The BTs also spoke of home religious observances. Several of their families had kosher homes and adhered to some eating restrictions during Passover. Shimon remembered that in his home, his mother kashered chicken that previously had not been soaked in salt water and the family had two sets of dishes. Batya said that when it was Passover, "We eat *matzah*, we have seders, we don't eat bread, we don't eat corn." Another BT, Seth, recalled his mother's cleaning the house before Passover and eating *matzah* during the holiday even though the family engaged in few other rituals. Others remembered their mothers' lighting Sabbath candles and their families' having a traditional meal. Cheryl said that she loved everything about being Jewish—"The more ritual, the more observance, the better"—and pushed her family to do more religiously. On the other hand, when Eliza was eleven, she started lighting Sabbath candles herself. As she explained, "My mother didn't light them, so I took that on. I also took on . . . doing (a) *yahrzeit* (memorial) candle for my aunt because nobody did that. And I've been doing it ever since."

BTs from Minimalist families had some awareness of Judaism as a religion and identified as Jews. As Marilyn recalled, "I've always known I was Jewish, I've always known that Jewish people do certain things, don't do certain things. But as for . . . I don't think there was ever a time when I didn't know that there was a religion there." Two BTs from Minimalist backgrounds recalled that their early feelings about Judaism were negative. Maya had thought it was "too organized," had "too many restrictions," and was "something for older people." Ruth thought it was too insular. Another BT from a Minimalist family, Howard, who said that he was aware of being Jewish as a label but was not exposed to Judaism in any form, recalled:

> I was brought up in a totally secular home. My parents identi-
> fied . . . themselves as Jews. There was no spirituality in the house.
> There was no religion in the house. You know, it was no particular
> practice other than they were Jewish. Certainly, (they) weren't
> Christian. So I'd say that my actual first thoughts of religion, like
> they were of God, was by watching the religion of my friends who
> were mostly Christians where I was brought up.

Nevertheless, Howard, like other male participants who were raised with little or no exposure to Judaism, had a *bar mitzvah* for which preparation consisted of memorizing from a recording the traditional reading.

In contrast, some participants had a relatively large amount of knowledge of Judaism as a religion. This included the six individuals who attended Jewish day schools. Nora, whose family fell into the Mainstream category, recalled that she benefited from learning Hebrew, hearing about Israel, and having a close friend whose parents observed the Sabbath. Nevertheless, Nora left the day school in ninth grade to follow friends who were switching to public school. Jacob, from a Modern Traditionalist family, expressed mixed feelings about being different from his Jewish peers:

having gone to a Jewish day school and growing up in a neighborhood that was Jewish but totally secular, the kids used to sort of
make fun of me, acted as though I was the rabbi, I was the local
Jewish kid. So I was very much aware that I was different and that
I had this Jewish religious training, and at times, you're ashamed
a bit and at times you're also awkward, but on the other hand
there was a certain pride in being a little bit more Jewish than
the next kid, and having a little Jewish background.

As mentioned at the beginning of this section, the core theme is *differentness*. The *baalei teshuvah* were cognizant that Judaism was different from
Christianity based on their celebrating different holidays, eating special foods,
affiliating with Jewish institutions, and having some home observances. The
feelings of those who were middle and high school age when they experienced
this differentness were probably heightened, and possibly negative, because of
sensitivity to peer group opinion during those ages. Awareness of Judaism as
a religion was greatest among those who attended synagogue, day schools,
and Hebrew School and had some home observances. Yet many responded
to the question about religion by affirming their Jewish identity, conflating
religion and ethnic identity. These responses are in keeping with Danzger's
(1989) observation that *baalei teshuvah* begin their journeys by identifying
with Jews as an ethnic group and later with Judaism as a religion. We turn
now to a discussion of the special challenges or obstacles some participants
faced while growing up.

Personal-Familial Challenges

In a previous publication, Danzig and Sands (2007) described early experiences that challenged *baalei teshuvah's* spiritual-religious development as a
"spiritual eclipse of the soul." As we defined it, the term refers to "the muting,
silencing, or blocking of spiritual needs as a consequence of adverse or non-
supportive experiences" (Danzig & Sands, 2007, p. 33). This occurs when a
person's interest in religion or spirituality is not recognized or is invalidated
by a parent or other significant early figure or by negative interactions in the
neighborhood, school, or community. The challenges I focus on here consist of
adverse events and conditions within the family and community that seemed
to impede not only their spiritual development but also their psychological
and social development.

A number of participants mentioned stressful life events that occurred when they were children. It was already mentioned that eight participants grew up in homes in which their parents divorced. At least three of them said that they were surprised and shaken by this experience and that conflict continued after their parents parted. One said that in the aftermath he began "acting out all over the place." Others spoke of changes in their living arrangements and difficulties with step-parents. A few spoke of abuse—emotional and physical—but were vague about what specifically had occurred. Two BTs spoke of the challenges they faced growing up with a parent with mental illness, and another talked about a sister with mental health problems. These painful situations can create a need for spiritual help, but none of these individuals spoke of turning to religion when they were children and these situations were affecting them.

Although a minority of study participants mentioned abuse or other difficulties while they were growing up, a member of one of the focus groups commented on the perception in the secular and Orthodox worlds that individuals who become Orthodox do so because they have emotional problems stemming from growing up in dysfunctional homes. As Edward said:

> there's a sense that I get, I could be wrong, my own projection is that there's something wrong with us, and that's why we've glommed onto *yiddishkeit* (Jewishness), and I would really hate for any of this study to focus on anything, well, the reason these people became this was because . . . they came from these homes, or these situations, and there must be something (deficient) about (us).

So far as I could tell from the interviews, the *baalei teshuvah* in this study did not become Orthodox as a way to cope with emotional problems or dysfunctional family histories. It is more likely that those who had such difficulties growing up were attracted to Orthodox Judaism as a positive framework for raising a family.

In their oral discussions of their timelines, many individuals described desires they had as children to increase their level of religious observance and their knowledge—aspirations that were thwarted by family members and mocked by peers in their neighborhoods. Annie is an example of a participant who felt inspired to keep kosher after learning about it in Hebrew School:

> I was coming home and telling my mother, "Oh, we learned you have to keep kosher. So now you have to keep kosher." And my

mother went to the principal and my Hebrew teacher and said,
"Look, whatever you want to teach her in school, that's fine. But
I'm not doing this in my house. So I don't want you to go and
tell her that this is what she should be telling me. I don't like it."
You know, my mother said to me, "Some day when you grow up
if you want to keep a kosher home (you can)," never dreaming in
a million years that that would ever be the case.

Eliza made a similar request of her mother and she, too, was rebuffed. Ellen
spoke of her parents' preventing her from going to Torah Camp and their
complaining about her involvement in a Jewish youth group. Similarly, Jacob's
mother complained to the rabbi at her son's day school about the school's
practice of checking whether the boys were wearing *tzitzit* (traditional under-
garment with tassels), which Jacob never wore. The message that these young
men and women received from their parents was that it was okay to be Jewish
but not too Jewish.

In their retrospective reconstructions of their engagement with Judaism during childhood, some participants, particularly those from Minimalist
families, expressed the sentiment that there was a Jewish void in their lives.
Brian described his religious upbringing this way:

> Well, basically, I was raised in a non-religiously affiliated family.
> Religion, spirituality, God, nothing of the sort was ever dis-
> cussed. . . . There was some very faint recognition of being Jewish
> at all. There was really no significant practice. . . . (I had) a very
> short stint at a Reform Sunday school, maybe a year or less as a
> child, I think five years old, six, seven, somewhere in that period.
> Didn't last; there was no pressure to continue. There was [sic] no
> Jewish names in our family given to my parents or the children.
> There was no celebration of holidays of any kind. No bar mitzvah
> or bas mitzvahs.

Others, who had more family exposure than Brian, were critical of their
parents' and relatives' religious behavior, such as attending synagogue only
a few days a year and celebrating Passover by having a family meal without
reading the story behind the holiday that is recorded in the *Haggadah*. The
BTs viewed these observances as superficial and lacking in meaning, and they
depicted their families as inconsistent. Maya, whose Minimalist family offered
her hardly any exposure to Judaism, lamented:

> I felt so cheated in a sense. That there was this whole part of who
> I was, or who I could be connected to, that was kept totally away
> from me. I mean, and it wasn't that my parents said, 'Keep this
> away from her,' it's just that my parents didn't know either, and they
> didn't participate in any of this, so it wasn't anything that . . . I
> was exposed to, and I felt very curious about all that. . . . Why is
> that something so alien to me, and people around me are going to
> synagogue on Rosh Hashanah and Yom Kippur, even if nothing
> else, and we didn't even do that.

Not only did Maya feel deprived of part of her identity; she and the others
from Minimalist backgrounds were unprepared to enter Orthodoxy.

A more blatant disturbance in the childhoods of some participants
was exposure to anti-Jewish attitudes in their peer group and within their
families. A number of BTs mentioned that they grew up in neighborhoods
and attended schools in which they were the minority religion. Jerry spoke
of being called names and being excluded from activities by his friends: "My
mother had our rabbi come and talk to me one day because I was really hurt."
Ariella said that her maternal grandmother was a "Jew hater" and that her
mother had internalized Jewish self-hatred.

In some families, anti-Jewish attitudes were applied to Orthodox people.
Parents conveyed the idea that Orthodox Jews were dirty, smelly, and ante-
diluvian, portraying them as old men with beards who observed strange and
outdated customs. Another participant from a Minimalist family, Paul, spoke
about the message his father expressed when he was a child:

> And he was very, very, negative on Orthodox things and things
> like that. I still remember that when I was little he would drive
> back from Manhattan sometimes, and he would sometimes drive
> through Williamsburg [an Orthodox section of Brooklyn] and
> he would point out the Hasidim on the street, and he would say,
> "Look how they live," with just disdain.

This statement is not surprising considering that Paul's parents and grandparents were in the process of assimilating to American society and wished
to avoid reminders of past generations that lived in poverty in *shtetls* (small
villages in Eastern Europe). The disdain produced a desire to distance themselves from people who looked like their European forebears and to assimilate
further. Allen recalled, "My mother's grandmother said it was better to marry

a Christian than an Orthodox Jew." Participants heard these negative attitudes from close family members and, for the most part lacking close contact with Orthodox Jews, did not have firsthand experience that would provide evidence to dispute them.

Seven participants were children of Holocaust survivors; the father of an additional interviewee took part in the liberation of one concentration camp where he experienced a traumatic shock. Most of these participants referred to their family member's history a few times during their interviews, reinforcing how important this was to them. Growing up in a home in which parents experience or repress traumatic memories is an especially trying situation that is likely to trouble the younger generation.

In her writings on *baalot teshuvah*, loss of a mother during childhood, and defectors from Orthodox Judaism, Davidman (1991, 2000, 2015) uses the term "biographical disruption." She describes this as a rupture that is so deep and profound that it marks a significant change in one's life course afterward (Davidman, 2015). The negative experiences described in this section can be considered biographical disruptions, but they were not experienced by all the *baalei* and *baalot teshuvah* and they do not account for the whole of participants' experiences. They had other experiences that drew them toward Judaism.

Inspiring Experiences

The other side of the challenges that thwarted the spiritual and psychosocial development of *baalei teshuvah* was the experiences that fostered their Jewish spiritual and religious development and promoted their psychosocial maturity. Danzig and Sands (2007) called these positive experiences "spiritual imprints" or impressions that may have left people with residues of spirituality. These included warm relationships with parents and grandparents, family religious observances, religious education and teachers, synagogue involvement, bar and bat mitzvahs, summer camp, and trips to Israel. Encounters with charismatic leaders and rabbis also were inspiring. Annie, whose family background was Mainstream, captured the meaning of spiritual imprints in her statement about a former Hebrew School teacher: "You plant this little seed and you don't think that it's bearing fruit but it's just in there and it just has to be nurtured."

Sherry, from a Modern Traditionalist family, described her early life as one in which she was given a positive foundation upon which she could build as she got older. She came from an intact, nurturing family that was active in the local Conservative synagogue and other Jewish organizations, kept a kosher home, traveled frequently to Israel, and sent the children to Hebrew School and Jewish summer camp. Following her parents' example, Sherry assumed leadership roles in a Jewish youth group. Her family attended services on the major Jewish holidays and got together with extended family for Passover. Sherry described her father as having a Jewish *neshamah* (soul) even though he was not religious. She said that her parents were accepting of Sherry's and Sherry's siblings move into Orthodoxy.

A number of BTs were raised in families that supported the Jewish community—locally, nationally, and internationally. Their parents were active in Jewish organizations such as B'nai B'rith, Hillel, and Hadassah and took their families to visit Israel, where some relatives lived. As Tamar explained, her family emphasized Jewish values, that is, being "active in Jewish organizations and Jewish youth groups. Certain mitzvahs were kind of just understood: being close with family, grandparents, visiting family." She was told it is important that Jews mingle with Jews, marry a Jew, and perform acts of loving-kindness (*chesed*). Eliza recalled that as a teenager she was sensitive to human rights. Arthur used the term *tikkun olam* (repairing the world)[2] to describe Jewish values. As he explained, "Judaism was doing things to right wrongs in society and look out for the people who didn't have anyone else to look out for them." The BTs whose families emphasized community service came from all three family categories.

In a survey on Jewish values among a national sample of Jews (Jones & Cox, 2012), some 84 percent of respondents stated that the value of social justice was somewhat or very important to them, and 80 percent said that caring for the widow and orphan was somewhat or very important. In addition, some 72 percent said that it was somewhat or very important to heal the world (*tikkun olam*) and to welcome the stranger. The *baalei teshuvah* interviewed for this study seemed to have assimilated these values along with feelings of solidarity with other Jews.

BTs whose families belonged to a synagogue reported that, for the most part, they attended services on the high holidays, Rosh Hashanah (1 or 2 days) and Yom Kippur (1 day). In contrast, Lauren said that her parents had a different perspective:

> Both my parents said, "You see, why only be in *shul* on Rosh Hashanah, Yom Kippur when it's not fun, when you can go on Purim and Simchas Torah when it is fun?" So they picked up on that and that probably kept us also involved. It wasn't just hours and hours. So that was really where the foundation was laid.

Participants who described inspiring aspects of their Jewish family life tended to be simultaneously critical. This is not surprising given that they were describing their backgrounds retrospectively as *baalei teshuvah*. Thus, when discussing their parents' keeping kosher, they explained that they were kosher in their homes but ate *treif* (non-kosher food) in restaurants. Similarly, they explained that after a traditional Friday night meal or Saturday morning services, the family would watch television, which is a violation of the Sabbath. They also mentioned driving to synagogue and having *bar mitzvah* parties in which lobster was served.[3] When discussing parents' celebrations of Jewish holidays, they spoke of the holidays their parents did *not* observe.

Consistent with Danzger (1989), many of the participants spoke of their grandparents as significant inspirations to their becoming Orthodox. The grandparents provided encouragement and monetary support toward the BTs' Jewish education, attendance at Jewish camps, and trips to Israel. Although most of the grandparents were relatively secular, one participant grew up observing her Orthodox grandfather:

> I grew up with my grandfather . . . going to *shul* twice a day, wearing *tzitzis*, *davening*, having black hat *rabbonim* (rabbis) around me, having their grandchildren come in their black pants and white shirts, so I wasn't devoid of Orthodox individuals around me. (Sarah)

In speaking of a grandfather who fell away from Judaism but retained some practices, Seth said that he felt connected to him because he was named after him. Other BTs talked about grandparents who kept kosher, attended synagogue regularly, had the family over for Friday night Sabbath dinners, or exuded qualities that seemed spiritual or religious. In the latter regard, Ruth said:

> My grandmother was sort of religious, in her own way [chuckle], you know, her husband was a communist, so she couldn't really do that much in the house. But in her own way, she had a very strong religious heart, and I think, spoke about God. I mean, I don't remember like specifically, but I felt like she had a very strong belief in God, and I was very close to her and I really loved her, and just thought the world of her, and I think that sort of had some effect. . . . There was something about the feeling of being with her and who she was that was just, you know, there was just something very, very spiritual about it.

Ruth grew up in a Minimalist family but her grandmother seemed to provide her with a gateway to spirituality. Similarly, Joshua said that his grandmother, who used to quote Jewish and secular scholars, conveyed "some kind of feeling" that stayed with him "and blossomed into something later in life."

Several BTs spoke of the deaths of grandparents and other relatives as eye-opening experiences. Seth, for example, learned about sitting *shiva* for seven days after his paternal grandmother died. He recalled relatives bringing a briefcase full of prayer books that were used during the prayer services. He was impressed that his uncle and a cousin who was ten years older than he both knew where to follow the service from these books and how to *daven*, which he had not learned to do.

Other *baalei teshuvah* highlighted particular experiences that they considered crucial to their spiritual-religious development. For example, Batya, who came from a Mainstream family, found her active involvement in a Jewish youth group fun and enlightening. She especially enjoyed the creative services that were held during a youth group retreat where she learned that God was accessible to her outside the synagogue:

> God was something that I could own. God was in a hotel at a youth group retreat. Do you know what I'm saying? Like, God was not just in this one place with the rabbi. God could be something I owned and understood and had a relationship with. So . . . those kinds of creative services really served me well because it taught me to talk to God and think about God and reflect about God in ways that I'd never done previously.

Other participants savored the opportunities for leadership and socializing in Jewish youth groups.

Jacob, whose background was Modern Traditionalist, spoke of attending Torah Leadership seminars that had aroused "spiritual stirrings" in him. These took place out of town over several days. There he met rabbis and song leaders who touched him deeply. In the suburban world in which he grew up, "cool" people were involved in sports. At the seminars, he found people who were able to integrate being "cool" with being Jewish. He was particularly moved by the *kumzits*, occasions when the group would sit together singing spiritually moving songs. David, like Jacob, connected with Judaism through music. When David was 16, he had the special experience of spending Yom Kippur at Shlomo Carlebach's synagogue. He recalled:

I started going away for *yom tov*. So I spent one Yom Kippur in the city (New York) at Shlomo Carlebach's *shul* . . . which was unbelievable. . . . I had heard him sing, I liked his music and stuff, but until you see him *davening* for the *amud* on *Kol Nidre* or *Neilah*[4] you don't know what's, I mean, it was like you saw the rays of light coming out of him. It was like really unbelievable! And seeing that! I had never seen anything like that. I was used to like the *chazzan* (congregational prayer leader, chanter) in my parents' synagogue was like being rushed through it and be done with it. There was no feeling in there, there was nothing to touch someone's soul. That was really the first spiritual thing that ever happened.

A number of BTs spoke of the significance to them of Jewish day schools and camps. There they increased their knowledge of Hebrew, Hebrew texts, songs, prayers, and Israel, which gave them some preparation for the life they later chose. Cheryl, who had been unhappy in public school, where she felt that she did not fit in, found her life "transformed" when she switched to a Conservative day school. Liora, the child of a low-income single Minimalist mother, attended an Orthodox Jewish day school on a scholarship. During a Sabbath visit with her grandmother, who engaged in some traditional practices but was not strictly observant, a *rebbetzin* (rabbi's wife) who was connected to the day school suggested this possibility. With her mother's consent, Liora attended this school for several years. There she learned some Hebrew and was exposed to a traditional Sabbath at the home of a friend. Today Liora is grateful to have had this experience. Others found that attending a Jewish camp facilitated their entry into Orthodox Judaism. Allison learned how to *bentch* (recite prayers following a meal) and got a feel for the Sabbath at her Zionist Jewish camp. Reflecting on his experience at Camp Ramah, which is affiliated with the Conservative movement, David said that it provided a stepping-stone to his moving into Orthodox Judaism:

I did not realize until later on in life, till I started to become religious, that that was an influence. That while they may not have intended it to happen, with some people it's just a natural progression from that to becoming religious.

A follow-up study of alumni of Camp Ramah found that they exhibited high rates of engagement in Jewish life as adults and that 17 percent affiliated with

Orthodox synagogues (Cohen, 2017). In addition to the extra learning that camp provided, it was spiritually moving. As Cheryl said of Camp Ramah:

> Shabbat at Ramah was a very, very, spiritual thing. The whole camp would dress up white and beautiful for Friday night together. And the whole camp would be shouting Friday afternoon. And there were so many traditions. Everyone would *daven* together. We would sing these beautiful melodies. Oftentimes we'd *daven* by the lake or something. That was really, really beautiful.

As indicated, participants who attended day schools and/or religious camps or were active in youth groups had some exposure to Shabbat and traditional Jewish practices that enhanced their spiritual-religious lives. The seven BTs from Minimalist backgrounds who lacked these experiences, as well as some of those from Mainstream Jewish families, missed such early socialization experiences. Their socialization would come later. Remarkably, very few participants spoke of having close friends or family members who were Orthodox. Encounters with Orthodox people would come later, too.

Summary

This chapter has described the formative perceptions and experiences of the participants in this study. Their experiences were diverse—no profile fits all—with some having a rich exposure to Judaism through family observances, day school, and summer camp while others, in retrospect, experienced a Jewish void. Early educational experiences in Hebrew Schools, Sunday Schools, day schools, and camp gave some of the BTs access to the Hebrew language, which is used in prayers and religious texts, and a Jewish peer group with whom they could identify. Those from Minimalist families who had little religious education during childhood were aware that they were Jewish and that this was important to who they were but they felt that something was missing. Those who grew up in neighborhoods in which they were a religious minority were acutely aware of their differentness.

For the most part, participants' early socialization as Jews was ethnic or cultural. They learned about Jewishness through holiday celebrations with family, eating ethnic food, having their own or attending others' bar and bat mitzvahs, and hearing about Jewish values such as social justice and family solidarity. They attended Hebrew or Sunday schools, where some of them learned how to read Hebrew script, and they went to synagogue a few times a year. Their early exposure, which varied in quantity and intensity, constituted a starting point that helped them form a Jewish identity and acquire knowledge.

In this chapter, I have presented interviewees' memories of their early perceptions of God, spirituality, and religion and depicted the positive and negative expressions of Judaism in their homes and elsewhere. Their recollections of their early experiences reflect their developmental levels (viewed God as parental) and relatively secular upbringing (spirituality is connected to nature; religion is connected to family connectedness). Their memories of negative experiences reflect adverse experiences and anti-Jewish socialization in their families and communities. The inspiring experiences that they described seem to have aroused embryonic feelings of spirituality while the negative experiences seem to have generated frustration, shame, and alienation. Judaism played a part in the early lives of most of the *baalei teshuvah*, but not a central part. A small number were coping with other problems in the family, such as parental divorce and abuse.

The BTs' recollections of their early thoughts when they were children are influenced by the family contexts in which they experienced them. As children, they were dependent on parents' decisions about their Jewish upbringing and thus they did not have much choice. During adolescence, they were on a path to becoming more individuated and moving toward finding their own direction in life. Participants in this study gave importance to parents, grandparents, family celebrations, school, and peers, who are significant figures during formative years (Erikson, 1959/1980). The recollections of the men and women did not appear different except that more men than women said that they disliked Hebrew School, and almost all the boys spoke of their bar mitzvahs while only some of the girls spoke about their bat mitzvahs. Based on the interviewees' reports, parents of the boys seemed to feel an obligation to have their sons become a bar mitzvah but felt no such obligation to their daughters.

Chapter 2

Searching, Finding,
and Making a Commitment

The foundation for the spiritual-religious transformation of Jews who become Orthodox is formed in childhood when experiences such as those portrayed in chapter 1 take place.[1] They lie dormant until circumstances in their adult lives spark latent and undeveloped impressions and animate a search process. This chapter illuminates the search process, the discovery and exploration of Orthodox Judaism, the initial learning process, and the progression to making a commitment. In most cases, the process is gradual. In later chapters, I describe the changes that occur after commitment.

Social scientists have given considerable attention to the process of religious change, particularly conversion. Beginning in the 1960s, sociologists drew attention to new religious movements (NRMs), which were attracting youth. In their seminal study, Lofland and Stark (1965) described seven conditions, built upon each other, that lead to conversion to a new religious group. These are: (1) subjectively perceived tensions, (2) a propensity to use a religious problem-solving perspective, (3) defining oneself as a seeker, (4) encountering someone from the group at a turning point in one's life (e.g., an illness, loss of employment), (5) forming an affective bond with one or more members, (6) absence of or neutralized attachments to others outside the group, and (7) intensive interaction with members of the new religious group. Recognizing the salience of social relationships in this model, Gooren (2007) characterized Lofland and Stark's approach as a "social networks model." A subsequent analysis of this model as it applied to other religious movements found overall support for it (Kox, Meeus, & 't Hart, 1991). In an analysis of conversion to ten religions (Eastern religions, groups that derive from Christianity, and "occult" groups), Greil and Ruby (1984) identified affective bonds and intensive interaction with group members as indispensable to religious conversion.

A couple of sets of authors have developed stage models that illuminate the religious change process for Christians (Batson, Schoenrade, & Ventis, 1993; Edwards & Lewis, 2001). Hay (2001) criticized these models for their inapplicability to diverse religious traditions. Rambo (1993), however, formulated a generic model that applies to different religions. His model consists of seven interacting stages—context, crisis, quest, encounter, interaction, commitment and consequences—which have some relevance to the study of BTs. Gooren (2005, 2007) described a dynamic model of "conversion careers" that consist of five levels of religious involvement—pre-affiliation, affiliation, conversion, confession, and (in some cases) disaffiliation—and five types of factors that influence all levels—personality, institutional, social, cultural and contingency factors. Among these, he considers social factors critical to conversion and institutional factors decisive in an individual's level of commitment to a religious institution. Consistent with Gooren (2007), as well as Lofland and Stark (1965), Greil and Ruby (1984), and others, the process of change of those who became Orthodox is social and relational, involving intensive interaction with Orthodox individuals and affective bonds.

Besides attempts by Rambo (1993) and others to develop generic models of conversion, little has been done to examine the conversion process in Judaism. Bockian, Glenwick, and Bernstein (2005) explored the applicability of Prochaska and DiClemente's (1992) Stages of Change model to conversion to Judaism. Used to assess and intervene with individuals receiving psychotherapy or treatment for addiction, this model consists of five stages—precontemplation, contemplation, preparation, action, and maintenance. The Stages of Change model is pertinent to the study of religious change because it examines the process of cognitive and behavioral change. Bockian et al. (2005) found some empirical support for the model among individuals in the process of converting to Judaism. Although it has not been applied to already Jewish individuals who intensify their adherence to Judaism, the model does show that the religious change is a process that requires thinking, preparation, action, and continuation.

Authors of previous studies of *baalei teshuvah* depicted the process of becoming Orthodox in a variety of ways. Aviad (1983) described four modes of *teshuvah*—search, external, internal, and community. The search mode entails a deliberate quest for a value or religious system that is a break with the past. With the external mode, an outside event such as an illness is involved. The internal mode is connected to the individual's inner world, and includes his or her personal identity and sense of harmony. The fourth mode, community, has to do with feeling socially and culturally connected to a religious community. Aviad found that the community mode was prominent for close to two-thirds of her study participants, especially for women.

Davidman and Greil (1994) described three pathways leading to involvement in the Lincoln Square Synagogue and a Modern Orthodox religious commitment. One is called "accidental contact," the result of a chance meeting that brought them to the synagogue. Another is a "casual search," in which the individual had become interested in Judaism and attended synagogue as a means to learn more. The third type, "committed search," applied to those who had been exploring religious alternatives for years and finally decided to examine their own religion. Davidman and Greil found that more women than men were accidental seekers, women's searches were mediated by relationships, and more men than women engaged in committed searches. Later in this chapter, I describe categories that have similarities to the first two pathways.

In her book on how *baalei teshuvah* learn the language and culture of the Orthodox communities they join, Benor (2012) described four stages of BT trajectories. The first, Interested Prospective, refers to non-Orthodox individuals who attend classes about Orthodox Judaism. Next are Peripheral BTs, who observe some religious laws and customs but affiliate only marginally with an Orthodox community. The third, Community BTs, refers to those who consider themselves Orthodox and move to Orthodox communities. Some BTs continue into the fourth stage, Yeshiva/Seminary BTs, which entails pursuing further education in intense, residential educational settings.

An entirely different approach to the study of religious change within and outside Judaism is to examine the structure and content of conversion narratives (Wuthnow, 2011). These narratives describe conversion to another worldview (such as adopting the ideology of Alcoholics Anonymous, Greil & Rudy, 1983) and from one religion to another. Several authors suggest that there is formulaic way in which converts describe their conversions (Beckford, 1978; DeGloma, 2001; Popp-Baier, 2001; Williams, 2013). For example, narratives based on the *Confessions* of St. Augustine describe youthful indiscretions, a search process, regrets, and later transformation through conversion. Another formula is for narrators to demonstrate the continuity between their unschooled childhood beliefs and their beliefs after conversion

(Johnston, 2013). In some cases, however, there is no known formula to follow (Davidman & Greil, 2007). The BTs interviewed for this study had a formula available to them that was known by BTs who preceded them and by those who were raised Orthodox.

In this chapter, I describe a process of change that was pervasive among the participants in the study. It is based on the narratives related to interviewers about their individual trajectories and the spiritual timelines that were part of the interviews (see the Introduction and Appendix A). As mentioned in the Introduction, the analysis of individual narratives resulted in what Richardson (1988) called a "collective story." The process that will be described in the rest of this chapter is nonlinear. As scholars of Erikson's theory have observed, when it comes to spiritual development (or "spiritual identity"), the stages do not necessarily unfold sequentially (Kiesling & Sorell, 2009). I am using the term *state* instead of stage to suggest fluidity. The sequence is not fixed and individuals can cycle back and forth and straddle different stages simultaneously. For ease in reading, however, I am describing the states in a linear form.

The Process of Change
of *Baalei Teshuvah*

The process of change was propelled by an inner need and an attraction to something that might fulfill that need. As Marilyn said about her life from the perspective of a middle-aged adult:

> Probably for most of my life, I saw myself as, yes, I was Jewish, whatever that meant, and having this internal tug that there was . . . that I'm missing something. Not being satisfied . . . Being satisfied but not being satisfied. (Having a) . . . good life, having fun, but knowing that there was something else.

This "internal tug" and consciousness of being Jewish and not knowing what that meant pulled the BTs in various directions, described in the various states.

In the previous chapter, I described elements within the first state, the foundation on which the other states developed. Besides the beginnings state, Table 2.1 portrays the processes that are discussed in this chapter.

Table 2.1. The Spiritual Transformational Processes: From Beginnings to Commitment

Processes	Definition
Beginnings (see chapter 1)	A variety of foundational experiences with Judaism, other Jews, and non-Jews that expose children and adolescents to ideas about God, spirituality, and religion; can block and/or support their expression of spiritual needs.
Random Exploration	Exposure to spirituality within other traditions and Judaism through an array of spiritual activities, course work, travels, and friendship.
Existential Vacuum	The feeling or perception that one's own life is empty and life is meaningless.
Spiritual Shock	Powerful transformative experiences, usually occurring while in the midst of an existential vacuum or random exploration, that provoke a deeper exploration of Judaism.
Active Exploration of Judaism	Deliberate searching and study of Judaism.
Transitioning	Gradually move toward commitment by incrementally adhering to commandments; accompanied with ambivalence and attempts to live in two worlds simultaneously.
Reversals	Return to a state of non-observance or non-observance of particular commandments (e.g., eating non-kosher food).
Commitment	The assumption of the responsibility of observing the commandments (i.e., to be *shomer mitzvot*); may be a conscious decision or the realization that one is observant after behaving in accordance with commandments.

Random Exploration

In an earlier book on *baalei teshuvah* who were studying in institutions in Israel, Aviad (1983: 5) observed the "happenstance nature" of the turn toward Judaism. It entails a search that occurs over a period of years in which people travel, engage in life experiments, and explore a wide range of religions, eventually discovering Judaism. This is what is meant here by random exploration. Here I extend Aviad's observation by stating that the happenstance events often occur during late adolescence or early adulthood when one separates from one's family of origin and seeks to find one's identity. In the process, one is exposed to frameworks that are different from those that were offered in their families of origin. Ruth explained how she became open to spiritual alternatives after she left her parents' home and went to college:

> I think the fact that I was starting to see that there were things out there, and there were things that people did, you know, (it) wasn't just like in my house as a kid. . . . I was beyond my parents' house, and I started to see that people really were living meaningful lives and spiritual lives, and that there were possibilities.

For three BTs, this recognition occurred while they were living at home and still in their teens. For everyone else, this came later, mostly during emerging and early adulthood, but for some, it was when they were middle-aged (see chapter 3). Some interviewees randomly explored other spiritualities before exploring Judaism. Others explored Judaism without delving into other religions or spiritualities. Those who explored other spiritualities spoke readily about their experiences.

RANDOM EXPLORATION OF OTHER SPIRITUALITIES

During and after college, the BTs encountered ideas about different religious systems and spiritualities, as well as people who practiced within these systems of meaning. These encounters seemed to occur when they were feeling adrift. As Sherry recalled, before she became observant, she was "a disoriented lonely person who was looking for something and not knowing what she was looking for. And not knowing where to find it. Sort of knowing the general direction, but not having the rootedness that I now have."

The BTs experienced the random encounters as accidental. As mentioned, Davidman and Greil (1994) used this term to describe one of their pathways to deeper involvement in Modern Orthodox Judaism and the synagogue they were studying. Annie, for example, spent her junior year at another university, where she became friendly with some Christian students who were on the path to becoming ardent believers. She saw them as having found "comfort" and "answers" in their religion. The next year, when Annie was troubled over her young cousin's sudden death, she wondered if perhaps Christianity had answers. She explained:

> I really didn't know what to do for myself. So I think at some point I must have gone to speak also to the rabbi back in my home town. And he said to me, "If you want things to be meaningful you have to start going to *shul*. If you don't make God a part of your life, then you aren't going to find any answers." I think that's when I started trying to find a synagogue where I was comfortable and that I could go to.

Another BT, Shifra, was also exposed to Christianity through her friendships with Christian friends she met during college. She celebrated Christmas with them and often accompanied them to church services. After graduating and moving to New York, where she felt isolated, she would go to St. Patrick's Cathedral and light candles. She recalled that when she did this, she wondered, "Why am I doing this?" but somehow she found it comforting.

Erica discovered Quaker meetings during college. As she explained to her interviewer, she found these meetings spiritually meaningful:

> It was a Quaker college and I ended up going to meetings many times. . . . (and) the thing I liked about the meetings is I felt like—well, a Quaker meeting is quiet. You close your eyes, if you want to. And you're just sitting in a very simple room with no carpeting and no draperies and everything very, very simple. And you just sort of relax. It's kind of like a group meditation in a way. But it's not guided at all. You just sit in your space. If the spirit moves you to speak, you speak. There was no Bible reading or anything like that. There was no cross on the wall. I really felt like it was definitely a universal thing. I didn't feel that it was un-Jewish at all. Yeah, so that's where I was at spiritually there.

Erica seemed to be attracted to the quiet solemnity of these meetings and conveyed positive feelings over their apparent religious neutrality.

A few study participants explored other spiritualities through college classes in philosophy and religion. This intellectual exposure stimulated their thinking about pathways to truth. Like Erica, Nora was drawn to a universal spirituality:

> . . . when I was in college, I was very much interested in philoso-
> phy and in . . . spiritual . . . concepts. But I wasn't relating them
> to Jewish concepts at that time. It was just a general universal
> spirituality, and reading books that were like spiritual books, like
> Eastern books and things like that.

Classes in women's studies raised awareness of patriarchy in Judaism, which
hindered some women from engagement with Judaism at the time and, as
discussed in chapter 6, was the subject of spiritual struggles.

During and after college, several BTs explored New Age spiritualities. A
few attended yoga ashram retreats, generally held in quiet, natural surround-
ings where they could experience calm and peacefulness. Everyone who spoke
of these retreats said that he or she attended them with others—a family
member, one or more friends, or a group of friends. Liora recalled how she
felt about going to an ashram:

> We used to go up to the ashram for a week at a time, and . . . that
> was really cool; it was a really special place. It was kind of like
> Taj Mahal-y. It was really beautiful; everything was just beauti-
> ful. It wasn't so much about God, wasn't about religion. It was
> about spirituality, and it was about having experiences that weren't
> grounded experiences; having transcendental experiences, feeling
> my body floating or whatever. It was about that kind of stuff.

At the ashrams and elsewhere, BTs learned about and engaged in a
variety of spiritual practices such as meditation and chanting. They explored
different types of yoga and meditation, as well as Buddhism, Taoism, Native
American religions, Wicca, paganism, taro, and astrology. Some delved into
and became practitioners of holistic medicine. The goal, which Ariella said she
was unable to achieve, was to "find completeness, wholeness, happiness, and
a spiritual level." At a later time, these spiritual seekers were able to channel
their spiritual longings into prayer.

RANDOM EXPLORATION OF JUDAISM

Baalei teshuvah explored Judaism in a casual way through trips to Europe and
Israel, volunteer work for Jewish organizations, reading on their own, attending
synagogues here and there, and participating in Hillel activities. As one focus
group member joked, he had planned to go to Indonesia, but his girlfriend of

the time said, "You should go to Israel. You don't need as many shots!" He, like others, found his trip to Israel an impetus to deeper exploration later.

A few participants spoke about traveling in Europe where they were not looking for but found sites that made them conscious of their Jewishness. For example, Zvi mentioned that he "stumbled across the Anne Frank house" in Amsterdam, went inside, and was "totally blown away by it." It made him think about the Holocaust and confirmed his plan to check out Israel.

Some BTs traveled to Israel with their families or youth groups when they were growing up, whereas others spent their junior year there, or they traveled to Israel on their own during or after college. Mark's mother sponsored his visit as a single young man, which turned out to be an illuminating experience:

> My Mom sent me on a singles mission with the (Jewish) Fed-
> eration to Israel. And while we were there we had an encounter
> with some Ethiopian Jewish immigrants. The adults decided they
> weren't gonna speak to the tours. They were angry about whatever
> it was, so we were out there talking only to the children. The
> children did not speak in English, we did not speak, most of us
> did not speak Hebrew. So we're out there, and all we could say
> to the kids was "shalom." And that was basically the end of our
> conversation. And I came back saying, I just went over to Eretz
> Yisroel, and I couldn't speak the language. A Jew should be able
> to speak Hebrew.

Erica developed a similar awareness of her limited knowledge of Hebrew in the context of a Friday night Sabbath get-together at college. Students were sitting on the floor with their candles in the middle of the circle when one of them said, "How do you say 'candles' in Hebrew?" The students knew how to say it in Spanish, but not in Hebrew.

Annie met Orthodox students at the summer program she participated in at an Israeli university. She met them through a budding friendship with an Orthodox suitemate with whom Annie made sandwiches for lunch. Sub-sequently the two of them invited some *frum* students to have meals together, expanding the network. Annie observed their washing their hands before meals and reciting *birkat hamazon* (grace) afterward. This sparked memories of what she had learned at Hebrew School and at Passover seders. As she explained, "I started, you know, kind of getting turned on and it was raising questions now like, 'Wow, these people knew so much. And this is part of my heritage and I don't know squat.'"

Several BTs found their ways to secular kibbutzes (*kibbutzim*) where they took classes in Hebrew (*ulpans*). While the language learning was helpful, they were disappointed in other ways. As Nora recalled:

> I went to the *kibbutz* and I stayed there. And then I said, I wanted to go to an *ulpan*. So I actually stayed in Israel for a year. But then I ended up just not really getting into anything spiritual, and I was still very confused because it wasn't what I was looking for. No one had, like I had gone to the *kotel* and no one said to me, "Do you want to come for a *Shabbos?*" Like I had been in non-religious environments in Israel! In irreligious environments in Israel! And I hadn't been in a religious community. And I just, like was very confused in Israel about what I was doing and what I was there for.

Nora's comment about her experience at the *kotel* (the Western Wall) referred to missing out at the common experience of being approached by someone from an outreach group who would have invited her to a Sabbath meal with an Orthodox family or to a class. Others who spent time on secular kibbutzes were surprised to find that the residents were anti-religious.

During her first visit to Israel, Batya had a variety of experiences. She lived in a secular kibbutz where she learned Hebrew, interned for an AIDS organization, lived with and worked for a family as a part-time au pair, and dropped in on classes at several yeshivas. From living with a Modern Orthodox family and meeting their friends, she changed her earlier impression that Orthodox people were "crazy" and recognized that that they were "reasonable, normal people." She explored different kinds of synagogues, including Orthodox ones, which became accessible to her after she learned Hebrew. She, like some of the BTs who had explored Israel in a random way, later returned to Israel where she actively engaged in serious learning in a seminary.

Some BTs worked or volunteered for Jewish organizations in the United States prior to becoming observant. Maya held the position of secretary to the Hillel director at the university where her husband was a graduate student. She also was active in a women's chapter of *B'nai B'rith*. Shifra volunteered for the Anti-Defamation League, an organization that combats bigotry against Jews throughout the world, and Sherry did fundraising for the Lubavitch organization, Chabad. These activities led to further involvement in Judaism and social networks that increased their contacts with Orthodox people.

Another way in which BTs randomly explored Judaism was through books. While active in a Jewish organization (the equivalent of Hillel) during college, Allen put himself on a self-directed reading program:

And then somehow I got the idea that I should read the Bible, and I began reading. I bought a JPS [Jewish Publication Society] Bible, and I began reading a chapter every night just starting with "In the beginning." This was a *Tanach* [Torah, Prophets, and Writings], I guess, because it wasn't just the five books of the *Torah* but was all of the Prophets and maybe even the *Ketuvim* (writings, such as the Psalms and the Book of Ruth), and whatever it was I started reading it. And I just would read one chapter every night. I didn't analyze it or get involved with [it], I didn't go to a rabbi and ask what it meant. I just thought it was like literature you should read. But I began to have more religious feelings between these things.

Similarly, Ezra studied *Tanach, Kabbalah,* and "everything I could lay my hands on" until he found a rabbi with whom he could study.

Random exploration also encompassed participating in Hillel activities and attending religious services. A few BTs engaged in Jewish political activities; others joined study groups. Paul came across a Bible study group, which he initially joined as a means to meet college women but later found inspiring. Some campus Hillel organizations ran Reform, Conservative, and Orthodox services, providing students with an opportunity to explore different branches of Judaism. Chabad, an Orthodox outreach-oriented group located near many college campuses, welcomed Jewish students to their centers for Sabbath and holiday meals, services, and special programs. Besides attending services offered on or near their colleges, BTs explored religious services at local Reform, Conservative, Reconstructionist, Jewish Renewal, Orthodox, and Sephardi synagogues, and at *havurahs* (prayer fellowships, usually egalitarian). These experiences helped them assess where they felt comfortable and where they did not.

Existential Vacuum

In his classic book *Man's Search for Meaning,* the psychiatrist Viktor Frankl (1946/1959/1984) reflected on the frame of mind of prisoners of Nazi concentration camps who were living in a terrifying, dehumanizing environment. He asserted that under these circumstances, one comes face-to-face with the

question of the meaning of one's life. To depict this frame of mind, he created the concept of an "existential vacuum," a state of inner emptiness and
purposelessness where one perceives that life lacks meaning. It is manifested
in boredom, depression, aggressive behavior, materialism, and/or frustration
(Frankl, 1946/1959/1984).

Although they were not in circumstances similar to Frankl's, most of
the interviewees spoke of times when they felt that life was meaningless and
felt disconnected from meaningful relationships or activities. They experienced
anxiety, depression, shame, and confusion. These feelings were prominent
around times of transitions—looking for but not finding a spouse, divorce,
thinking about moving to a new city, feeling uncertain about one's career
direction, and so on. Some acted out in response to these feelings by using
drugs, drinking, or engaging in a peripatetic lifestyle. They recognized that
something was amiss but were not sure what they needed.

Ezra recalled a period of time when he felt that his life was empty.
Although he earned a high income from his line of work and was active in
his Conservative synagogue, his marriage was falling apart and he felt that he
was at loose ends. Similarly, Shimon spoke of a time when he assessed the
previous ten years of his life and concluded that what he had done (about
which he did not elaborate) "was related to some pain" and that he wanted to
remake his life in a positive way. Annie was more direct about her existential
vacuum: "I needed something in my life. There was like a void, and I needed
something to give my life a purpose and meaning." Just about all the key informants interviewed for this study stated that *baalei teshuvah* had experienced
such a void and were seeking meaning and connection.

Consistent with previous research (Danzger, 1989; Kaufman, 1991), a
few *baalei teshuvah* spoke of being unhappy with the superficiality, materialism,
and immorality that surrounded them. Yossi decided to leave his West Coast
community because his life there seemed meaningless:

> And there was a certain feeling, I wanted out of there. . . . I was
> on the road to leading a very decadent life. And I thought . . . (this
> is) not really going to make it in the long run. . . . So there was
> this stirring, like, what am I going to do with myself now, you
> know? I've done everything that I've wanted to do. I had this really
> cool ten-speed bike, and I used to play tennis. And the women
> that I was meeting were all very shallow. And looking back, I
> was probably pretty shallow myself. (Laughs.) But, it just didn't
> seem to satisfy me. I wanted some more meaningful relationships.

Like Yossi, Susan wanted to avoid a similar community where she was surrounded by millionaires. "I wanted to get away from that. I wanted to look for a different meaning in life."

In contrast with participants who felt alienated from their communities, Marcia was satisfied with her life but did not feel that her accomplishments were enough:

> I would say that my life was [one] of high achievement. I focused on my career, I was independent, I lived on my own. And I functioned very, very well. At thirty I got married, and from thirty to forty-two was a very multi-faceted period. You know, with having kids and everything, and toward forty-two, I remember asking my husband, we were lying in bed and watching the news, and I said to him, [husband], what is my life all about? I mean, I know that we have, I knew he was gonna say, okay, we have children, you have your career, I have my career, but, there's something missing. There's something missing, I mean, what can we say that our life is worth? What can we really say that's valuable about our life? Like, he was gonna say, well you do, we do have kids and what else does anybody else do? You know, you get up, you go to work, and you send your kids to school. And we have dinner together, you know, I said, I knew you were gonna say that. . . . I said . . . [it is] like . . . when you think of a wheel and a tire, you think of the spokes and the hubcap. Now what's the center of our life?

At the time Marcia talked to her husband about her need for greater meaning, she did not associate her emptiness with religion.

BTs experienced a void at various points in their lives. Some were unhappy over their careers, whereas others were concerned about their single status, marital conflict, or their financial situation. Howard left his job amid political turmoil, leaving him with questions about the meaning of life. When Arthur arrived at the conclusion that his goal to become a Reform rabbi was not what he wanted or needed, he was at a loss about what he was going to do instead. Karen, who had a job working in England, was depressed over not meeting a man she would want to marry. For some, career issues coincided with financial and marital problems, which were followed by efforts to compensate for the emptiness they experienced. For example, Greg remained in an unfulfilling marriage eighteen years while trying other things ("politics, sports, drinking, you know, profession") to make himself happy.

The examples that have been given are consistent with what Steinsaltz (1982) identified as the first of two steps leading to turning away from one's previous way of life, or *teshuvah*:

> When a vague feeling of discomfort turns to clear recognition that something is wrong, and when that recognition is expressed in words spoken either to oneself, to God, or to another person, the first step in the process of turning has been taken, the part that relates to one's previous life and character. (p. 6)

(Steinsaltz's second step is resolve.) The BTs struggled with their unhappiness, using strategies such as immersion in work, drinking, and multiple geographic moves to escape from or numb the pain. As they were emerging from their depression and/or anxiety, they gained insights into themselves and their needs. According to the literature, it is common for people who later convert to experience tension prior to conversion (Greil & Rudy, 1984; Lofland & Stark, 1965; Snow & Machalek, 1984). For the men and women who later became observant, grappling with meaninglessness seemed to make them receptive to experiences that stimulated their thinking about Orthodox Judaism.

Spiritual Shock

The BTs reported powerful transformative experiences that occurred when they were experiencing an existential vacuum or during their random explorations. Denzin (1989) refers to experiences like this as epiphanies; Rambo (1993; Rambo & Bauman, 2012) speaks of crisis. According to transformative learning theory, which comes from the field of adult education, adults change their frames of reference in response to new challenges and reflection (Mezirow, 1997). The transformation process begins with a "disorienting dilemma," a challenge to one's usual methods of solving problems (Mezirow, 1978). The dilemma generates tension motivating one to look beyond past experiences and to ask questions about one's assumptions and beliefs.

In their retrospective verbal accounts, interviewees viewed these transformative experiences as emanating from a divine source. A few exclaimed, "Hashem gave me a *potch!*" (Yiddish for spanking) or spoke about the *yad Hashem* (hand of God) or *hashgacha pratit* (Divine providence) influencing their lives. The varied experiences they described jolted them, provoking a spiritual shock or awakening.

Erica, who had found comfort in attending Quaker meetings during college and subsequently explored a variety of spiritualities outside Judaism, described being spiritually shocked by a Hillel rabbi:

> He was saying that Judaism is as valid a spiritual path as Taoism, as Buddhism, as Native American religion, as anything else. And that was the thing that got me. That Judaism is not about "jappy, make-up, spoiled, rich, be ashamed of yourself, you don't get Christmas, and you all should have died in the Holocaust." That's not what Judaism is. Judaism is a valid, deep, spiritual path and a way to connect with God. And I had never really heard that. Because anything that I had done on my own, I had done in private. It was something that was just me and God. It wasn't that we have a huge, thousands-of-years-old system that we can utilize and that's part of our heritage; that we inherited this. That is who we are, and that I can be as proud of my ethnic heritage as anybody else. Not just my ethnic heritage, but also my religious heritage, [these] kind of go hand-in-hand when you're talking about Judaism. And that to me was a *huge* turning point. Huge.

Conversations with this rabbi led Erica to reexamine her understanding of Judaism and the stereotypes that she had internalized. Once she recognized that her notions were erroneous, she was able to affirm her ethnic and religious heritage and engage more deeply with Judaism.

Another BT, Jacob, had an interpersonal interaction that shocked him into exploring Judaism. During law school, he was seriously dating a secular Jewish woman. He described a "defining moment" during a conversation about circumcision with this woman and her father:

> I had this girlfriend, lovely girl, very nice girl, hugely secular, and came from a very secular family . . . her father was a professor . . . a real pipe-smoking, super bleeding-heart liberal Jew. And at some point, we just were having a literally an informal conversation about circumcision, a *bris*, having a kid, and having a *bris*. And . . . my girlfriend said something like, "Ooh, that sounds, oh really, you do that? That's terrible." And the father turned to me and says, "Oh we, we Jews, we don't do that anymore . . . that's defacing the

body" and all these kind of things. I never even thought about it. Maybe I was nineteen, twenty, twenty-one, twenty-two, I don't remember exactly what age I was. But I remember something inside of me saying, really? Gee, that just doesn't sound right. Just, something inside me, it just didn't, I had absolutely no ability to make an argument, religiously or otherwise, against it, just, the comment made by the father, and I guess seconded by the girl, about a baby boy not having a *bris*. I remember saying, "Gee, isn't that like just, doesn't that define you as being Jewish? Like isn't that the ultimate difference between being a Jew and not being a Jew?" To which the father responded something like, "What's the difference? I mean, nobody here believes in God anyway, so what's really the difference?"

This conversation provoked extensive soul-searching on Jacob's part. He was shocked that these people did not believe in God and pondered whether he believed in God. After this episode, he "just thought about it, thought about it, thought about it" and concluded that he did believe in God. That was a significant decision that became a turning point in his life. He broke up with his secular girlfriend and began to explore Judaism.

Sherry was also confronted with a parent's perspective that triggered her exploration of Judaism. The context of this experience was the death of a friend.

In my first year of college, a very close childhood friend of mine died of leukemia. And he died . . . after a bone-marrow transplant. . . . And his parents were atheists. And his girlfriend was an atheist. And he was an atheist. And I remember, I was very close with the family in the last two weeks after the bone marrow transplant and he started going downhill, um, we sort of lived in the hospital. And I remember saying to his mother after he died, "He doesn't feel pain anymore. He's in a better place." And she said to me, "I don't believe that. And if you believe in God, then God killed my son. And how does that make you feel?" And I think that was a pivotal moment for me, because I realized that either I was looking at nothingness, or I could look at everything. And I chose, I chose to look at it as if it was just the beginning of something for him.

This was also the beginning of something for Sherry. She concluded that she was "Jewishly illiterate" and needed to learn more. Before long, she enrolled in a seminary in Israel.

Several BTs spoke of serendipitous encounters with people who influenced their pathways to Judaism. Howard met a man on an airplane who introduced him to the writings of Dennis Prager on Judaism. Although it took a few years for Howard to read the material this man sent him, once he did so it proved to be significant in Howard's spiritual transformation. Zvi, too, had a chance encounter that turned out to be significant. During his random travels to Europe, Zvi learned that he could get a ticket from Greece to Israel for $100. He went to Greece where he met an Israeli man who not only advised him to enroll in a yeshiva in Israel, but also gave him some addresses of places to stay in the Old City of Jerusalem. Zvi ended up spending many years at a yeshiva. In a different vein, a *baalat teshuvah* friend of Greg introduced him to a cousin with whom Greg studied over the telephone. Subsequently this man insisted that Greg attend a seminar sponsored by the outreach group, Aish Hatorah, instead of attending a sports event:

> He said, "No, you can't, I made reservations for you at Aish Hatorah seminar." I said, "Wait a minute, I got to go to the game." He says, "I already paid for you, you got to go." So I said, "All right, I'll go for a couple of hours, right?" And then I figure I'll get back to see the game. So I went down to Manhattan, and I went in and it was riveting, electrifying, it was unbelievable. And it showed that I was ready to accept Orthodoxy, 'cause I knew God existed and I knew that there was a revelation and by inspired people. . . . But from this seminar, I learned that the Torah is the actual word of God, and when you realize that it's not from messengers but it's the direct word from God, and it's not historically or culturally relative but it's the absolute truth, and that Hashem wants us to do certain things, it gives you a sense of urgency, where you don't pick and choose what you want. And that . . . was the point of no return.

Although the man who enrolled Greg in the Aish Hatorah seminar appears to have been aggressive, Greg responded to being pushed. His existential vacuum associated with his being separated from his wife at that time may have made him particularly receptive to the message that contradicted his prior learning.

Tzirel, a member of the second focus group who also attended an Aish Hatorah Discovery seminar, spoke of the leap she took because of arguments presented at this seminar:

> I remember the leap. I remember the moment was, I was at an Aish Hatorah Discovery, and I was listening to these proofs . . . how the Torah could not have been written by people, and at the time, that intellectually finally made sense to me. Something clicked and I said, well, I was so relieved that there really is a God in heaven, and for some reason for me, being a God in heaven meant that Mount Sinai happened. Like, I never got into, well, there's God but I could do what I want. I, for some reason, that was not an issue for me. So it became clear that this was truth, and that this is what my soul longed for.

During the first focus group, participants identified particular mitzvahs (*mitzvot*, commandments) that they tried out that gave them a jolt. Chaya, for example, went into a mikveh on the advice of a rebbetzin, who suggested that she do this as a way of thanking God for her infant child's recovery from strep. When she returned home, her husband told her that he saw something intangible about her that made her glow. This was Chaya's first conscious mitzvah.

In chapter 1, I pointed out that, during their childhood years, those who later became Orthodox had been socialized to identify ethnically with being Jewish. While searching as adults, some experienced a reawakening of their ethnic or Zionist consciousness that was communicated to them in Hebrew School, Jewish camps, and/or in their homes. They experienced these spiritual shocks in relation to wars that involved Israel. They expressed worry, concern about relatives who lived there, and awareness of antisemitism. Allison, who was a member of an Israel action committee and marched in Israel Independence Day parades when she was growing up, explained how Zionism brought her and her husband toward religion:

> And what happened was the 1982 War. In Lebanon. And that's what brought us back to religion. Zionism, ironically. And it was how the world completely turned on Israel. And we were just horrified and we just, we wanted to do something. And a friend said, you really should be coming to the *havurah* up at _____.

One of the key informants pointed to something like a spiritual shock when *baalei teshuvah* meet religious persons to whom they are attracted during times of "latent searching" or "emptiness." "They were not necessarily thinking about Judaism" but after becoming further acquainted with religious persons, they say, "Ahah! I would like to be like that." Some experienced dramatic spiritual shocks through encounters with charismatic Jewish religious figures. In chapter 1, I described the impact that Shlomo Carlebach's Yom Kippur service had on one *baal teshuvah*. Other charismatic leaders whom the BTs pointed to as having a significant impact on them were the Bostoner Rebbe, Rabbi Shlomo Riskin, Rabbi Ephraim Buchwald, Rabbi Avi Weiss, Rebbetzin Esther Jungreis, and Rabbi Shlomo Twerski. Encounters with these dynamic figures shook people up, increasing their desire to engage in an active, deliberate exploration of Judaism.

Active Exploration of Judaism

The previously discussed states of random seeking, existential vacuum and spiritual shock set the stage for *baalei teshuvah* to increase their knowledge of the Jewish religion and an observant way of life. Even those who had attended Jewish day schools and camps that stressed learning realized that they needed more education and textual skills than they had. Eighteen of the forty-eight interviewees (37.5 percent) enrolled in yeshivas or seminaries, mostly in Israel but also in the United States. Israeli institutions geared especially for *baalei teshuvah* have curricula designed to transmit foundational knowledge that includes the Hebrew language, the Pentateuch, the prayer book (*siddur*), and basic norms (Aviad, 1983; Danzger, 1989). Most are gender-separate, with men given exposure to the Talmud and women to the Hebrew Bible, the Prophets, and practical laws (Danzger, 1989). There are some yeshivas that are for both men and women and that teach Talmud to women. Two of the men who attended Israeli yeshivas remained there about a decade, eventually receiving *semikhah* (rabbinic ordination) at their institutions. One woman who studied at a seminary said that she solidified her connection to God after exposure to the atmosphere at the seminary and in Israel:

> I grew a greater understanding of what God means in your everyday life. I certainly started *davening* there. That's just a natural in Israel, just to go to the *kotel* and *daven*. And then you're there and you see everyone *davening* around you and you want to understand

why they're crying and whatever their emotions are and whatever they're doing. (Lauren)

Another study participant, Tamar, seemed to concur that the ambiance of being in Israel made her learning "come alive." Moreover, she was able to get specific answers to her questions.

Those who did not study in Israel attended classes (*shiurim*) led by rabbis or other learned teachers; studied with a study partner (*chavrutah*); or attended classes held by outreach (*keruv*) organizations in the United States. In the process of becoming Orthodox, Allison attended a *shiur* in her community. Consistent with the nonlinear sequence of phases, she had a "spiritual shock" when she learned in class that Orthodox people believed that the Torah came directly from God at Mount Sinai. As she explained:

> I can't remember which Torah portion it is but the one where they get the Torah from *Har Sinai* (Mount Sinai). And this is the first time I'm hearing the concept, *Torah MiSinai*. The very first time. Because Conservative theology had taught us, man wrote this. He was influenced by God certainly, but that it was direct from God, and that's why we're supposed to observe everything. And that's why it's law and it's written in stone, as the rabbi liked to make fun of. You know, he says those words every week. And a Jew should not break the laws of Shabbos, or *kashrut* or anything. I'm like, I come home and, and every week (husband) would say, "So, how was it?" . . . I said, "Do you know, do you want to hear something?" like I had a big dark secret. I go, "This whole neighborhood thinks the Torah is straight from God." And he didn't say anything; he was just listening. I don't know what he was thinking at the time. But I thought this was like, I'm walking around, I had this revelation. So I went to *shul* that week and I was thinking, all these people believe this. I was in shock.

Even though Allison was astonished to learn that Orthodox people had a belief that the group with which she used to affiliate considered unreasonable, she continued to learn and enact some of the *mitzvot*, learning from doing.

A few *baalei teshuvah* in this study participated in the beginner's *min-yan* of the Lincoln Square Synagogue in New York City, where they learned about the prayer service, or participated in Sabbath weekends in the Lubavitch community (see Davidman, 1991). While actively exploring Judaism at these locations and in classes elsewhere, they gradually took on some *mitzvot* such as observing the Sabbath and keeping kosher.

It was especially challenging for those BTs from Minimalist families and others who had limited Jewish education growing up to engage in the active exploration of Judaism. They had to acquire sufficient language skills to pray in a synagogue and to obtain knowledge of Jewish laws about how to observe the Sabbath and festivals and how to keep kosher. They developed beginning knowledge by finding people who knew more than they did and were willing to instruct them. A few rabbis of small congregations mentored them one on one. Other rabbis offered classes on particular texts or on special topics. A number of *baalei teshuvah* found FFBs in their communities who gave them informal instruction and advice about how to maintain a Jewish home. They also sought advice from longtime BTs.

Several interviewees spoke about the families that they informally adopted (or who adopted them), who guided them during the early phases of their journeys. They met members of these families through synagogues, classes, or outreach organizations. These experiences sometimes led to invitations to attend a Sabbath meal at the families' homes where they could observe ways in which these families live as Orthodox Jews. Some BTs used these occasions to ask questions about practices or words that they did not understand (cf. Benor, 2012). The families provided informal socialization in a comfortable setting. One of the key informants we interviewed, the wife of an outreach rabbi, mentioned that she frequently hosts some fifteen people for Sabbath meals. Although she sometimes finds this exhausting, she enjoys having them. She commented on the emotional neediness of the guests and said that she tries to be supportive. It appeared to her that *baalei teshuvah* were looking for community and a feeling of belonging. Another key informant, also the wife of an outreach rabbi, said that the key to growth had to do with the extent that "people felt totally embraced by someone on the inside, making them able to grow." This supports the idea put forward in the conversion literature that an affective bond is a key influence on religious change (Greil & Ruby, 1984; Lofland & Stark, 1965).

Karen was invited to a Sabbath meal with a "black hat" family that she met through the outreach organization Hineni. She explained how involved with this family she became:

> I actually met them even before I became *shomer Shabbos* (Sabbath observant). . . . So, it's just a family that I got introduced to and I became very close to them. . . . I was at their house every

day. . . . I went to them every single *Shabbos* that I was in New York. Every meal . . . I would say that this woman, who is only a few years younger than my mother, is like a mother to me and like a best friend. I mean, I'm still so, so close to her.

Elsewhere in the interview, Karen mentioned that she was not close to either of her biological parents, who divorced when she was a child. The family she embraced functioned as both surrogate parents and a conduit to Orthodox Judaism.

The organization that referred Karen to this family, Hineni, was one of a number of *keruv* organizations that reached out to adults who were interested in exploring Judaism. Others include Aish Hatorah, Etz Chaim, and Chabad. These organizations offered instruction, support, and religious services. Some synagogues also held classes that attracted BTs while they were in the process of seriously exploring Orthodox Judaism. In addition, seminars and classes offered in the Discovery program, Gateways retreats, and Project Identity were available to people who were interested. These *keruv* organizations, synagogues, and educational programs also facilitated linkage to a network that enabled *baalei teshuvah* to identify people in their Orthodox communities who could serve as role models and develop a support system of peers who also wanted to increase their knowledge. As a participant in one of the focus groups said, "The process of becoming *shomer mitzvos* (observant) was one of enjoying the outreach programs and the camaraderie and the friendship." *Keruv* organizations and programs were not, however, available where some participants were living when they were searching.

Through recommendations of rabbis and friends, and their own explorations, *baalei teshuvah* educated themselves further through books. Table 2.2 is a list of books that participants identified as influential. They addressed issues around faith and gender and provided explanations and guidelines for practice. A few of these books continued to be helpful after they committed to being observant.

The process of active exploration of Judaism took different forms depending on whether one was in a formal learning environment, studying on one's own, taking classes with a rabbi, or living in an Orthodox community. Their engagement with Jewish texts, knowledgeable individuals, synagogues, and religious practices propelled *baalei teshuvah* to remain adrift without knowing where the current was pulling them. Danzig and Sands (2007) used the term "spiritual canyoneering" to convey BTs' willingness to explore vast, unfamiliar territory without knowing where they were going. Journeying without a map,

Table 2.2. Influential Books

Dimont, M. I. (1962). *Jews, God and history*. New York: Signet, 1962.

Dresner, S. H. and Siegel, S. (1959/1966). *The Jewish dietary laws: Their meaning for our time and a guide to observance*. New York: Burning Bush Press. See also https://www.massorti.com/IMG/pdf/kashrout_anglais.

Greenberg, B. (1981). *On women and Judaism: A view from tradition*. Philadelphia: Jewish Publication Society.

Grunfeld, I. (2003). *The sabbath: A guide to its understanding and observance*. New York: Feldheim.

Herberg, W. (1951/1959). *Judaism and modern man: An interpretation of Jewish religion*. New York: Meridian Books.

Lamm, M. (1992) *The Jewish way in death and mourning*, rev. ed. New York: Jonathan David.

Pliskin, Z. (1983). *Gateway to happiness*. New York: Aish HaTorah.

Telushkin, J. (1991/2008). *Jewish Literacy*. New York: William Morris Press.

Wouk, H. (1959/1970). *This is my God: The Jewish way of life*. New York: Dell.

Wilson, R. (2002). *The Shabbat seder: The family guide for and welcoming the Sabbath*. Woodstock, VT: Jewish Lights.

---

they plunge in blindly. As Brian said of himself, "I'm the kind of person that doesn't like to walk into cold water; I like to jump. . . . I jumped deeply into it before I really knew what it was all about or what I was going to experience." At the time the *baalei teshuvah* jump in, they do not realize how much knowledge they must attain, what former pleasures they will have to give up, and the consequences for themselves and others.

Once they plunge in, however, they begin to experience the depths. Danzig and Sands (2007) described the process of learning about Judaism, taking on commandments, and social networking as "cascading" because it rushes forward like a waterfall. Caught up in an intense experience, the BTs feel excited and energized—an experience some described as the "BT high." A common statement made by *baalei teshuvah* engaged in learning was, "The more I learned, the more I wanted to learn." Mark described a similar cascading process in relation to performing *mitzvot*:

> I would describe it almost like the commercials about potato chips. You can't just eat one. You can't just do one *mitzvah*. You start

doing one, and probably one of them triggers (others). . . . Because I wanted to learn to read from the Torah, I started to go to *minyan*, and I started putting on *tefillin* (phylacteries). And then I started going to Shabbos services, and because I was going to Shabbos services I started feeling I really couldn't do other activities on Shabbos. And little by little, as I was doing more, the other things just didn't seem right anymore.

In keeping with Mark's metaphor, it appears that one starts the process with an appetite for learning and once one feels partially satisfied, one realizes that there are many more chips to consume. So one continues in this expanding pattern. Yet the process does not necessarily go smoothly.

Transitioning

As indicated, the *baalei teshuvah* gradually took on mitzvahs as they learned what they were, what they meant, and how to perform them. This process entailed some struggle, as they had to relinquish activities they previously enjoyed in exchange for religious practices that they had not fully embraced. The struggle was particularly trying to the women who had considered themselves feminists. They found some of the mitzvahs they learned about incompatible with their values, raising questions whether they wanted to pursue Orthodox Judaism any further. (For more about the challenges for feminists, see chapter 6.) *Baalei teshuvah* who were transitioning expressed their ambivalence as "living in two worlds," which Dov described as having "one foot in the (Orthodox) Jewish world and one foot in the secular Jewish world." Aviad (1983: 110) portrayed this as a painful process of "push and pull—back and forth from the past and the present, from the secular to the sacred."

One arena in which they engaged in transitional behavior was kosher food. For example, while Ruth was transitioning to Orthodox Judaism, she had roommates whom she knew from her yoga ashram activities who were not Jewish but "were willing to do this kosher thing." In her retrospective account, she commented that this was absurd, explaining that she was trying to bridge worlds that were incompatible. Other participants spoke of keeping kosher in their homes but eating in non-kosher restaurants. Deborah stopped this practice after her child, who was attending an Orthodox day school, commented that he found this confusing. Nina described a process in which the family first stopped eating meat, next ate only chicken, and then ate only fish in non-kosher restaurants. Finally, they decided that when they went out, they would eat exclusively in kosher restaurants.

While transitioning to keeping kosher, they unlearned previous ideas. Some had erroneously believed that Jews ate kosher meat for health reasons. This may be because trichinosis is associated with pork or the belief that kosher meat is safe because it is inspected by religious authorities. As Allen said:

> I had always grown up thinking that kosher was strictly a health code. That's the Reform party line; it's strictly a health code. The government keeps kosher for us today because they check all the animals and it's not important. . . . So I read this (book) and part of what it said was that at every meal you should be thinking about where the food comes from and that eating should be a holy experience. And that made a lot of sense to me. The book made a lot of sense to me. I mean it didn't try and argue that it was bad for you in some scientific way to eat meat and milk together or to eat things that weren't properly *shechted* (slaughtered) or the lamb's toe. All right, so I began keeping a kosher style. It was really, I think, quite comical. I was eating in a law school dormitory so if I would get chicken and peas and mashed potatoes, I would eat the mashed potatoes with the butter first and then I would eat the chicken. Of course, it wasn't kosher chicken anyway.

During his transitional period, Allen unlearned previous ideas and learned from a book on Jewish dietary laws that the purpose of being kosher has to do with acknowledging holiness in everyday life (Dresner & Siegel, 1959/1966). Prayers recited before eating contain variations of the Hebrew word for holiness (*kedushah*). Expressing gratitude for the food one eats elevates the consumer so that one is functioning on a higher level than lower animals (Dresner & Siegel, 1959/1966). Allen's transitional form of keeping kosher, however, shows that he had not fully grasped the application of the kosher laws to daily life.[2]

Other BTs struggled over keeping Shabbat during this phase. Before Eli became observant, he was a Grateful Dead groupie, following the band around the country. While transitioning, he thought he could combine Judaism with his previous lifestyle. He spoke of one concert that was near a Chabad house where he was going for Shabbat:

> The show was in the afternoon so I . . . went (to the concert) after lunch. . . . I went over, like I was wearing a suit and everything. I met my non-Jewish friend who had the ticket, went to the concert, and I got back in the middle of *shalosh seudos*[3] (laughs). Seems like a lot of weird stuff went on, because you know I was sort of

like trying to make things fit into my plan. You know I wanted everything to fit together.

A number of BTs drove to synagogue during their transitional period. One woman described an incremental process in which she and her family gave up driving. At first they drove. Later they rented a small apartment that was walking distance to an Orthodox synagogue where they stayed for Shabbat and holidays. Eventually they bought a home and moved to the Orthodox community. Others spoke of driving for distinct purposes (dinner at their parents' home; attendance at a friend's concert) on Shabbat.

Some participants had little mentoring while taking on the various mitzvahs. For example, Howard and his wife learned about the Friday night Shabbat meal from a book.

> So we were reading about this thing called Shabbat. We didn't know what it was. We read a little bit, I got a book on the Shabbat called *The Shabbat, How to Do the Shabbat Seder.* It was a Conservative book. And we decided that we would light candles on Friday night without particularly having much meaning, so we lit candles. I didn't know . . . how to say anything in Hebrew, didn't know any *brachos* [blessings] and whatever, and so we lit candles. And then we basically went our way. And then we decided we would make a meal. *Treif* [non-kosher] as it was, we lit candles and had a *treif* meal. And then we would go upstairs and watch television.

After learning more, they raised the level of their observance, but they were not yet fully observant. Howard went on to say:

> We continued in celebrating Shabbat and so, as we moved forward, we started to want to recognize the *kedushah* of Shabbat, so while we would drive to *shul* and drive home[4], we did nothing else. We didn't stop in between, we didn't, we didn't go to restaurants on Shabbos, we didn't go get gas, we didn't go to the store. We drove to *shul* and we drove back, and we didn't listen to the radio. At home, we did use electricity, and I can't even remember if we cooked or not. We probably did.

Facing a different challenge, Yossi struggled with giving up Israeli dancing during his transitional period. From his description, he had been an accomplished folk dancer who was invited to be a member of a folk dance troupe in the United States prior to his enrolling in a yeshiva in Israel. After arriving in Israel, he participated in folk dancing at Hebrew University while attending the yeshiva. The folk dancing was co-ed and at times required that men and women hold hands, which is not accepted by strict Orthodox communities. As Yossi explained, "After doing that for about two weeks, I said, 'This is not really working out. It's either one or the other.' "

Coming to a decision helps resolve ambivalence, at least temporarily. Still, the awareness of "two worlds" remains. Most of the BTs work in the secular world and continue to have family members and a few friends who are secular. Uri, for example, spoke critically about his wife's happiness being "encapsulated in an Orthodox cocoon," in contrast with his enjoying interacting with worldly people through his work. Despite ambivalence, however, he did not suggest a desire to leave his Orthodox community. When another BT, Karen, was transitioning, she would leave the home of her Haredi "adopted family" in a skirt and change into pants at a friend's house afterward. Marcia expressed her continued ambivalence after she committed to Orthodox Judaism by keeping her blue jeans in the back of her closet, as with the bride depicted at the beginning of the Introduction who also had jeans in the back of her closet. For Marcia, the blue jeans seemed to represent the option of reversing her course and returning to secular life.

Reversals

Struggles over living in two worlds do not always result in a decision to be consistently observant. Frequently BTs revert to non-observance or relinquish one or more *mitzvot* that they were keeping. Reversals can occur while transitioning, earlier in the process, and even after making a commitment. They may be prompted by disappointments, stress, or experiences of existential anxiety that are similar to those that led to their initial interest in Orthodox Judaism. They may question whether this is the direction they wish to pursue.

Two women participants underwent reversals after getting divorced. Maya reported that she became lax in her observance of modest dress (began to wear shorts) and kosher food (ate dairy in non-kosher restaurants). Considering divorce a "social embarrassment," Marilyn withdrew from active participation in activities of her synagogue and stopped attending services. Although she described this as turning her back on religion, she said, "I never gave up having a kosher kitchen." During college, another woman returned to her former affiliation with Conservative friends after breaking up with an Orthodox boyfriend. After making mistakes in her kosher kitchen, Susan temporarily gave up on *kashrut*, but at a later time she redid the process.

While Erica was transitioning, she became uncomfortable at a particular rabbi's *shiur* because of comments he made about someone he knew who thought she was Jewish but was not because her mother had a Reform conversion. This caused Erica to be self-conscious and to doubt her ability to go through an Orthodox conversion. She thought she "would sort of try not being Jewish for a while" and went out with a non-Jewish man. Her reversal was partial, however, because she "couldn't stop keeping Shabbos." Subsequently she broke up with this man and switched to another rabbi's *shiur*. An Orthodox conversion followed.

All the reported reversals quoted thus far are from women. A couple of men described reversals following study in an Israeli yeshiva. Zvi left his yeshiva in Jerusalem, went to Eilat for a vacation, and returned to non-observance and his non-Jewish girlfriend in the United States. Another man, Eli, spoke about "being a little down on the Jewish thing" after a negative experience at a yeshiva. One man spoke of interrupting his spiritual journey by marrying a Christian woman whom he later divorced.

A couple of BTs used special terms to describe their temporary reversals. Maya spoke of going "off the *derech*" (off the road or path) for a while. This term, also known by the acronym OTD, is a commonly used in the Orthodox community to depict the disaffiliation by already Orthodox individuals (see Margolese, 2005).[5] Cheryl described her reversal as having "a little bit of a '*chozer bishiayla*' phase of life." This term, which means return to asking questions, is used to describe people who shift from observance to non-observance. In our study, we interviewed only those who stayed with the process, at least up to the time of the interview. Because so many of them (16) described reversals, it is likely that others depart from the *derech* without returning to the spiritual path they were on.

Commitment

After exploring the terrain, acquiring basic knowledge, and returning to the path after a reversal, a time arrives for one to decide whether one wants to make a commitment. This may be a conscious decision or one that was developing prior to awareness that one has already changed (Becker, 1960). Although many religions have rituals for receiving newcomers into the fold (Rambo, 1993), Judaism does not have such phenomena except in the case of converts, who engage in a ceremony involving circumcision for men and immersion in a ritual bath (*mikveh*) for men and women.

Ariella, who had explored other spiritual systems before reclaiming Judaism, said that she was ready to make a commitment when she realized that she could have a deep spiritual life within the framework of Orthodox Judaism. Previously she thought that Judaism consisted primarily of

> things that you had to do, and physical things that you did, that was just a set of rules and regulations. And it took a long time to understand that within that framework, the framework is established to bring out and enhance the internal spirituality. That was kind of the "ah-hah." Once I understood that, that's when I committed. And then, once I did, then my spiritual life became organized, and I felt complete . . . and at peace.

Ariella's "ah-ha" experience was not unusual. Others felt ready to make a commitment when their questions were answered and issues they struggled with were settled.

As discussed by Becker (1960), making a commitment entails being consistent in one's behavior, assuming obligations, and being persistent in the line of activity that one has espoused. Accordingly, BTs who are keeping kosher at home but not when they eat out must relinquish eating in non-kosher restaurants so that they are consistently kosher. Those who were driving to synagogue on the Sabbath will have to walk or stay home, as driving is forbidden on the Sabbath. Those who were holding onto other practices that violate Jewish law will give these up.

At this point, the *baalei teshuvah* recognize that they can no longer live in two worlds simultaneously; that they have to choose one. Marilyn recalled being confronted about her inconsistency by her Conservative rabbi, who said, "You've got to make a decision. You're either Conservative or you're Orthodox. Make your decision." She responded to him with, "You know what? You're right." After she returned home and parked her car, she concluded, "That is the last time. I won't be driving on Shabbos." Eli, the former Grateful Dead follower, explained his decision to give up living in two worlds as follows:

> Before that period . . . [I was] trying to work things into my life. And now, I was just you know, okay, what's the *halachah* [law], and you know, I'll just work my life around what the *halachah* is instead of working the *halachah* around what my life is.

Many of the BTs displayed religious behavior publicly, demonstrating their commitment symbolically. The men wore *yarmulkes* (skullcaps or *kippot*), and married women covered their hair with *tichels* (fitted scarves), hats, or *sheitels* (wigs) at work and in the community. Others switched synagogues or moved to a new home that was close to an Orthodox synagogue. Some told work colleagues that they kept kosher and thus could not go out for lunch with them. Joshua described this process as "coming out of the closet" or "living openly . . . as a Jew should live."

As indicated earlier, some people were gradually taking on religious behaviors without acknowledging that they were Orthodox. Like Joel, who was attending the Orthodox *minyan* at his college daily, wearing a *yarmulke* all the time, and "hanging out" with an Orthodox crowd, actions sometimes preceded the recognition of one's transformation. Batya was more deliberate in her process. As she explained, she proceeded slowly and purposefully, making sure that she was comfortable with each step:

> I remember being a vegetarian. Like there was like six months to a year I didn't eat meat and people would say, "Are you a vegetarian?" And I would say, "No, I'm just cutting back on my meat intake." "Are you Orthodox?" I'd say, "No. I'm just observing Shabbos and *kashrus*." You know, I didn't feel comfortable with the label until I knew that I could observe it and could live it. You know, I don't know what to call it but to say that I am a person who prefers to live it and later call it than to call it and then try to live it. So, you know, I was going to an Orthodox synagogue and observing Shabbat and *kashrus* for probably at least a year before I would even say that I was Orthodox.

Becker (1960) maintained that commitments could be ensured by linking them with "side bets" on other interests. By staking "something of value to him, something originally unrelated to his present line of action" (Becker, 1960, p. 35), the individual strengthens his or her resolve to be consistent. A number of interviewees made side bets that involved people and places that were important to them. They enrolled their children in Orthodox day schools, sold their homes and moved to new neighborhoods, broke off inappropriate romantic relationships, and made other life decisions that were linked to making a commitment to being Orthodox. Clearly, they were staking valued entities on the decision to become *frum*.

Moss Kanter (1968, 1972), who examined the commitment processes of nineteenth-century Utopian communities, proposed that there is a reciprocal relationship between the individual personality system and the group whereby the individual is willing to give what the group needs to maintain its social order. She identifies three aspects of the personality system that support the social system: the cognitive, cathectic, and evaluative. Among these, the cognitive aspect, in which one assesses the costs of leaving against the benefits of staying, best supports continuance; the cathectic aspect, which involves affective ties to the community, supports group cohesion; and the evaluative aspect, which is related to morality and values, supports social control. At the time they made their commitments, the *baalei teshuvah* were convinced cognitively that Orthodox Judaism was the right path and beneficial to them. They expressed their convictions behaviorally by keeping the *mitzvahs* that they knew about to the extent that they understood them. They formed affective ties (cathexis) with rabbis, families that hosted them, and others they met in educational programs and synagogues, including other BTs. They were willing to follow the laws and community norms they learned about, the evaluative aspect. By then, they had acquired some knowledge about how to be an observant Jew, but had only partly changed their worldviews. Commitment is only the beginning of a radical process of undoing prior ideas and behaviors associated with being an assimilated Jew and taking on a new belief system and set of obligations. Much academic and social learning loomed ahead of them.

The Place of *Teshuvah* in the Process

As discussed in the Introduction, *teshuvah* refers to repentance. Even though none of the participants spoke directly about engaging in a process of introspection, self-examination, and remorse, their interviews were infused with allusions to a past life about which they felt guilty or ashamed. Such references were made in relation to every state. Some of the references are oblique, such as Shifra's response when the interviewer asked if the invitation to be interviewed raised any issues for her. Shifra said that she was concerned that she would be asked to provide information about her pre-Orthodox life. Later she expanded on this but was not specific:

> I know supposedly *Hashem* takes away the things from your pre-life, pre-Orthodox life, there are a lot of things that I did that I feel bad about, not that I hurt anybody, but that I hurt myself, that I put myself in positions that it was only from God watching over me that I survived them. As a girl in college, as a young person in the secular world, you try things and you do things. . . . A lot

of experimenting that, you know, I'm lucky that I'm around. I'll put it to you that way, *Baruch Hashem*.

One can speculate that Shifra was drinking and driving or that she experimented with drugs, but she did not share the details.

Speaking about the past to an Orthodox interviewer, they expressed shame about past activities that are no longer acceptable. They referred to sexual relationships with nonmarital partners, romantic relationships with people who are not Jewish, dressing immodestly, violating the Sabbath, leaving for a vacation on Passover night, and not observing other holidays. They alluded to past drug and alcohol problems. One man spoke of having sired an out-of-wedlock child with a woman who was not Jewish and his subsequent rejection of that child (although he said that he did provide child support). Another was critical of himself for not speaking up when members of a political organization in which he had been active maligned Israel.

After revealing some of his pre-Orthodox indiscretions, Greg used his newly acquired knowledge to forgive himself. He said:

> It was beforehand. That was a different person. And you know, the word for sin is *aveirah*, and *avar* means past. So you're a different person then. That's why I don't mind [speaking about the past]; I'm not that same person anymore. I'm a different person.

Greg went on to say that shame is beneficial as it motivates you to change. That is as close as anyone got to stating that he or she had repented. Another BT, Ruth, used the term *teshuvah* to depict a lesson learned from conflict in her extended family that was disruptive and painful. She said that she would do her best that this does not happen in her life, that she would forgive and let things go. *Teshuvah* is an open-ended and continuous undertaking. It can occur any time during the process of spiritual transformation and persists as a religious obligation.

Diverse Pathways

Although the process leading to commitment was similar for all forty-eight interviewees, the circumstances in their lives were different. Some started to become *frum* during high school or college; others when they were older. Several were recruited by outreach organizations that helped them get oriented to traditional Judaism and whetted their appetites to learn more, whereas others had no contact with such organizations, finding their way on their own. Some participants engaged in their journeys together with a spouse or potential spouse. Almost everyone became friends at some point with Orthodox individuals who opened them up to a web of relationships with other Orthodox people.

Furthermore, the *baalei teshuvah* faced different challenges, depending on their starting point. For example, the seven individuals (three women and four men) who came from Minimalist families began their journeys aware of being Jewish but feeling disconnected from Jewish communities and Judaism as a religion. They had to more or less start from scratch in learning basic information about Judaism and struggled to acquire at least a reading knowledge of Hebrew by studying in Israel or taking classes held in the communities in which they lived. They had a long learning curve because they were also disadvantaged in their beginning knowledge about Jewish holidays, keeping kosher and observing the Sabbath. The ten individuals who grew up Reform (six women and four men) reported feeling connected to their Jewish communities. All but two came from families that had strong ties to their synagogues. These BTs attended Reform supplementary schools and Jewish camps and were active in Jewish youth groups. Most of them had close relationships with their rabbis while growing up and three aspired to be rabbis themselves. On the other hand, their competence in Hebrew was weak and knowledge of Judaism as a traditional religion underdeveloped. Accordingly, they were further along and had more familiarity with Jewish cultural life than those from Minimalist families, but they still had a long way to go in learning how to live as Orthodox Jews. Those who grew up in Modern Traditionalist homes and in Mainstream families that affiliated with Conservative synagogues and sent their children to Hebrew Schools knew more Hebrew and were more familiar with traditional practices; this knowledge was helpful in the beginning but insufficient for full participation in an Orthodox community. The *baalei teshuvah* who attended Jewish day schools while growing up had advantages that the others had to acquire through hard work.

It was normative for the process leading to commitment to occur gradually over a period of years. Four participants in this study were exceptions, reporting that they became *frum* in less than a year. Three of these were involved with outreach organizations or rabbis associated with them when they made their commitments. The fourth had been exploring synagogues with her husband prior to attending a human potential training program where the group was asked to commit to making a change in their lives. The couple made a sudden decision to observe the Sabbath. After following through on their pledge, they kashered their home, located an Orthodox synagogue they liked, and rented a Shabbat apartment within walking distance to that synagogue. Passover was a few months later, necessitating that they buy Passover dishes and make their home kosher for Passover as well. This *baalat teshuvah* spoke about how stressful this process was. Several of the key informants we interviewed expressed concern over rapid transformations and asserted that the change process and integration into Orthodox communities take time.

Summary

This chapter identified and provided illustrations for the various states that *baalei teshuvah* experience in their spiritual transformational journeys. The model presented is predicated on prior exposure to Judaism during childhood, whether this experience was rich or minimal, positive or negative. The nonlinear states that were discussed are called Random Exploration, Existential Vacuum, Spiritual Shock, Active Exploration of Judaism, Transitioning, Reversals, and Commitment. For some individuals, the sequence may be different or two states may occur simultaneously. *Teshuvah* infuses the process but also is a life-long obligation. From the perspective of participants, the random search and discovery of traditional Judaism reflect the operation of divine forces leading them to Orthodox Judaism.

Although these states are particular to *baalei teshuvah*, they have some commonalities with stages depicted in sociological models of conversion. Interpersonal relationships and affective bonds, identified as critical in many conversion models (e.g., Greil & Ruby, 1984; Lofland & Stark, 1965), are integral to most states; during the existential vacuum the lack of meaningful relationships is critical. Rambo's (1993) model includes the stage of crisis, which is similar to the existential vacuum, which could turn into a crisis; and encounter, which parallels spiritual shock. Rambo and I acknowledge the importance of commitment. Rambo has an additional stage, consequences, that follows. In later chapters, I describe the consequences as a prolonged post-commitment period. With respect to previous studies of *baalei* and *baalot teshuvah*, the searching of BTs described in this chapter is similar to Aviad's (1983) internal and community modes. The random searching in this chapter resembles Davidman and Greil's (1994) "accidental contact" and "casual search" and their "committed search" is similar to active exploration of Judaism, described in this chapter. The participants in my study were similar to Benor's (2012) Peripheral BTs in their early states and Community BTs after they moved to an Orthodox community. Those who attended yeshivas or seminaries could be characterized as Yeshiva/Seminary BTs.

As a whole, the states constitute an extension of Erikson's (1959/1980) psychosocial stage of identity versus identity diffusion, applied to their spiritual identity. During the identity stage, individuals explore and try to come to terms with who they are. They waver between the two poles (such as having wanting to live in two worlds and having reversals) until they are able to make a decision and move on. Making a commitment is an indication of identity consolidation (Erikson, 1959/1980). More about the developmental trajectories of *baalei teshuvah* is provided in the next chapter.

Chapter 3

Developmental Trajectories

In the previous chapter, I described the process that leads to a commitment to Orthodox Judaism, building on beginnings in childhood. While the transformation process was similar for all the interviewees, there were patterns common to individuals in a particular developmental stage. In this chapter, I examine the biopsychosocial developmental stages at two periods—at the time of commitment to an Orthodox life, and at the time of participants' interviews. In the third section, I present findings from a quantitative inventory that assessed participants at the time of their interviews according to each of Erikson's developmental stages.

Developmental theorists who examine the biological, psychological, and social changes that occur during the life cycle have described the characteristics and normative tasks of different stages. When it comes to adulthood, biological changes are less prominent than they are during childhood and adolescence (Arnett, 2001), whereas psychological and social changes are important. Although theorists attach a variety of labels to the adult stages, roughly speaking they portray emerging adulthood, early adulthood, middle adulthood, and older adulthood, with age groups associated with each stage.

Development Stages at Time of Commitment

The search process described in the previous chapter varied depending on where participants were in their psychosocial development at the time they made a commitment to be observant. Their stages suggest psychological needs and social situational issues that underlay their decisions to become Orthodox

Table 3.1. Age of Commitment to Observing *Mitzvot* (N = 48)

Age of Commitment	Interviewees in Age Range	Developmental Stage
15–19	3	Late adolescence
20–24	9	Emerging adulthood
25–29	12	Emerging adulthood
30–34	9	Early adulthood
35–39	5	Early adulthood
40–44	7	Middle adulthood
45–49	2	Middle adulthood
50–54	0	Middle adulthood
55–59	1	Middle adulthood

at the time they decided to do so. Table 3.1 depicts the ages of the interview participants when they made that commitment and a general description of their developmental stage at that time. Of the forty-eight interviewees, three reported that they became observant (*shomer mitzvot*) in the teens; twenty-one in the twenties; fourteen in the thirties; nine in the forties; and one in the fifties.

Late Adolescent Committers

The three BTs who became *frum* while teenagers—one man and two women—were actively involved in Jewish activities. All were in Jewish youth groups, with two participating in NCSY, which is affiliated with the Orthodox Union, and one was active in USY, a Conservative youth group. Two of the three attended Jewish day schools; the third continued his Hebrew School studies through high school. Two attended Camp Ramah. Two families were Modern Traditional and one was Mainstream. All of their families belonged to synagogues and conveyed positive attitudes toward Judaism. The three early committers studied in Israel after they became *frum* and two attended Orthodox-affiliated universities in the United States.

From their descriptions and their ages at the time, having an observant peer group and being in an exuberant Jewish environment were crucial to their early decision making. They found others like them who were enthusiastic about Jewish learning. The youth groups generated friendship and feelings of community. The Sabbath weekend programs (Shabbatons) of these groups were spiritually uplifting and inspiring. Summers at Camp Ramah were characterized similarly.

The early committers went through most of the states described in chapter 2, sidestepping some. None of the adolescent committers appeared to have had an existential vacuum prior to seeking an alternative religious path, but two expressed dissatisfaction with public schools and one with his extended family. No one explored other spiritualities. One had a short-lived reversal during college when she became less intense.

Erikson (1959/1980, 1968) speaks of *identity vs. role confusion* (also called identity diffusion and identity confusion) as a psychosocial conflict or crisis that is precipitated by physical changes of puberty, becomes a crisis during adolescence, exists in some form prior to adolescence, and continues throughout life. During this crisis, one explores possible roles, occupations, political ideologies, religious beliefs, values, and other areas and gradually tries to integrate various identifications. One tries to understand oneself and decide on the kind of person one wants to become. The crisis involves reflection on the various options and experimentation with possibilities. The exploration is influenced by opportunities in the environment and the historical period in which the person lives, including available role models and prototypes (Erikson, 1968). It can be a period of anguish and confusion.

Although *identity achievement* is the goal (Marcia, 1966), there are alternatives associated with this stage. One is *identity diffusion*, the negative pole of the identity crisis. This refers to the inability to settle on an identity (Erikson, 1959/1980) or a lack of commitment to an occupation, ideology, or anything else (Marcia, 1966). Alternatively, one may circumvent anxiety over potential choices by over-identifying with a particular ideology. Another possibility is to form a *negative identity*, the adoption of an identity based on qualities that had been portrayed by significant others as undesirable, such as such as delinquency (Erikson, 1959). An additional route is *identity foreclosure* (Marcia, 1966), making a commitment, usually consistent with parents' goals, without experiencing a crisis. Identity can also become foreclosed by making a decision that limits other possibilities such as becoming pregnant as a teenager. Another option is the *psychosocial moratorium*, the postponement of making a commitment because one is not able to decide (Erikson, 1959/1980; Marcia, 1966).

The three early committers interviewed for this study seem to have come to terms with their religious identity earlier than the other participants have, but because they had not made other commitments, this choice was revocable. They made decisions about marriage and their careers around the time they completed college. None of them expressed regrets about his or her early religious commitment and all remained with the same marital partner.

One switched careers in her thirties. Accordingly, their religious commitment seems to have been based on being informed about traditional Judaism, feeling passionate about it, and being confident that they wanted to take this path. They did not take psychosocial moratoria, yet their identities did not appear to be negative or foreclosed.

Emerging Adulthood Committers: Twenties

Twenty-one interviewees, almost 44 percent of the forty-eight, reported that they had become observant in their twenties. Of these, thirteen were men and eight were women. Nine of their families were Mainstreamers, seven were Modern Traditionalists, and five were Minimalists (including one Minimalist Plus family). At the time of their interviews, eighteen of the twenty-one had been observant thirteen or more years whereas three were observant a shorter period. During their twenties, they explored and came to terms with their Jewish identities, launched their careers, and married. Association with peers who were observant facilitated this process.

Most of those who committed to Orthodox Judaism in their twenties became *frum* prior to meeting their spouses, with their religious orientation informing the kind of person they wanted to marry. Shifra asked her prospective spouse to attend a yeshiva prior to their marrying so that they both would be in a similar place, while Baila was asked to study at an Israeli seminary before her prospective husband would marry her. For three men who were on the path but not yet Orthodox, meeting a prospective spouse who was further along encouraged them to increase their level of observance. Where the couples were married and moving toward observance together, having children influenced them to become more observant. Having a baby motivated one married woman and her husband to discuss how they would raise the child religiously, inspiring them to look into Orthodox Judaism.

Seventeen of the twenty-one in the "twenties" group spent time in Israel prior to or while they were increasing their level of observance. Several had extended stays when they attended one or more yeshivas or seminaries or lived in a kibbutz. A few met their spouses in Israel. Other couples met in college, graduate school, or through a network of friends. Two BTs mentioned meeting their spouses in the kosher dining room at college. Another became part of a religious peer group through friends made in the kosher dining room.

Erikson (1959/1980, 1968) associates the period following adolescence with the crisis of *intimacy vs. isolation*, highlighting the desire to find a life partner. Still, Erikson allows for continued work on identity issues during the twenties and beyond. Levinson (1978), whose major interest was in middle adulthood, called the period that begins at seventeen or eighteen and ends no later than age forty-five early adulthood. During this period, when men (the focus of his 1978 book) are ordinarily physically vigorous, they struggle to establish their place in society. Levinson calls the early adult period that corresponds to the twenties the "novice phase." During this period young adults usually separate from their parents, obtain an advanced education, form ideas about the kind of life they want to live (their Dream), and explore relational and occupational options—which are foundational to forming their first life structure. The life structure includes a pattern of intimate relationships (e.g., marriage and children), a way of relating to one's parents, work, residence in a particular community, and involvement with religious, political, and/or other groups. Individuals who have difficulty separating from their parents, making a commitment, or forming love relationships experience special challenges during this period (Levinson, 1978).

The men and women who became *frum* in their twenties explored their ethno-religious identities during this phase. This included an investigation of other spiritualities and Judaism, discussed in chapter 2. They reflected on their Jewish ethnic identity through affiliation with Hillel during college and graduate school, travel to Europe and Israel, and political activities. Simultaneously they pursued advanced secular education and began to work in their chosen occupations. A few took psychosocial moratoria (Erikson, 1959/1980, 1968), delaying decisions about their careers, marriage, and religion. By the time they reached thirty, most were married to the same person they started with, one was separated, three were divorced, and two remained single. For the most part, there was a convergence in their commitments to Orthodox Judaism, a career path, and marriage. Consistent with Levinson (1978), those who became Orthodox in their twenties were novices in their careers, romantic relationships, and religion. In chapter 4, I describe the experiences of novices in Orthodox Judaism and Orthodox communities.

In Table 3.1, I refer to the twenties as "emerging adulthood," the label the developmental theorist Jeffrey Arnett (2000, 2004) applies to the period from late teens through the twenties. (I also adopt Arnett's term "early adulthood" for the thirties.) Noting that this is a distinct period in industrialized society, Arnett characterizes it as a time of "profound change and importance" (Arnett, 2000, p. 469) in which one perceives oneself as neither an adolescent nor an adult, but both. During this period, young people engage in identity exploration in relation to work, love, and worldviews. They begin this process by seeking exposure to a range of life experiences, becoming more purposeful as they move along. Those who attend college explore a variety of possible majors, with a focus on preparing for a career through a major and/ or graduate education. They take jobs that will prepare them for the future, and their relationships become more serious. They examine the worldviews of their parents, including their parents' religious beliefs and values, and arrive at their own beliefs (Arnett & Jensen, 2002). The adults in this study who became observant in their twenties engaged in such exploratory processes. They lived in and worked in different cities in the United States, and they studied and traveled in Europe and Israel. Although they did not elaborate on their explorations of relationships and career options, they did address the outcome (marriage, completed graduate school, took a job in their field). All of them diverged from their parents' level of religious observance, but for the most part they were continuous with their parents' affirmation of their Jewish identity.

Early Adulthood Committers: Thirties

Fourteen of the forty-eight interviewees (about 29 percent) became observant in their thirties. They were predominantly women (nine women compared with five men). All the men and six of the women had been *frum* fewer than thirteen years when they were interviewed. Thus, at the time of their interviews they had less experience as Orthodox Jews than the twenties group. The families of origin of the BTs who became *frum* in their thirties were predominantly Mainstreamers (n=10); the others were Modern Traditionalist (n =3) and Minimalist Plus (n=1).

The men and women who were thirty through thirty-nine who went to college had, by that time, completed college and advanced professional degrees. Most were working. Many of them, however, lagged behind their peers in their psychosocial development. Some were spiritual seekers who had explored other spiritualities prior to finding their way to Judaism. Several described psychological issues that they struggled with, such as emotional or physical abuse by a parent or step-parent, low self-esteem, and a poor relationship with a parent. Two spoke of receiving therapy to help them with these issues. Because of the psychological issues these BTs described, it is likely that they took psychosocial moratoria (Erikson, 1959/1980) in their twenties, delay-ing their decision making. Most of those who became *frum* in their thirties were married in their thirties or were on second marriages. Although it was typical to become observant before meeting the person they married, a few went through this process while married. In some cases, one partner (either the man or woman) was the prime mover who encouraged the other to follow. These couples were challenged to achieve a comfortable balance in their practices and their relationship. In other cases, the couple explored Judaism together, moving incrementally toward Orthodoxy. One BT hurried his process because a prospective spouse expected him to be observant and knowledgeable.

During their thirties, the BTs were reworking their Jewish identities, deepening their intimate relationships, and dealing with Erikson's crisis of *generativity vs. self-absorption* (Erikson, 1959/1980). Generativity refers to giving to the next generation, whether it is through nurturing children, meaningful work, service to others, or creativity. The men and women who became observant in their thirties were working and, if married, raising families. Some were generative in their religious lives by transmitting their newly acquired knowledge to their families and supporting religious schools and synagogues.

Levinson (1978) calls the thirties "Settling Down." During this stage, one builds a second life structure, one that encompasses forming and living out one's dreams. This life structure "gives certain relationships, aspirations, and aspects of the self a prominent place in one's life while requiring that others be made secondary or put aside altogether" (Levinson, 1978, p. 139). Those in their thirties establish roots in their families, work, and community and work toward improving their skills and achieving their ambitions. They form mentoring relationships, usually with a senior colleague who offers guidance. The equivalent of the mentoring relationship in the religious sphere is the spiritual guide, discussed in chapter 4. Adults in their thirties take pride in having a better idea of who they are, their abilities, and how they are valued by others. Levinson did not have much to say about settling down with respect to one's religious orientation. For the *baalei teshuvah* who made a commitment in their thirties, being an observant Jew became central to their life structure. Family was also central, with career and community life taking on some importance.

In Levinson's (1978) schema, the period from thirty-six or thirty-seven to forty or forty-one is called "Late Settling Down: Becoming One's Own Man"; in the book on women, this phase is called "Becoming One's Own Woman" (Levinson, 1996). This period is characterized by increased autonomy and endeavoring to speak with one's own voice—at the same time one needs affirmation from others. As one increases one's authoritativeness as a parent and worker, one runs into conflict with one's mentor, breaks away, and moves toward becoming a mentor to others (Levinson, 1978). "Becoming One's Own Man" (or Woman) may work in the work world, but applied to the religious sphere autonomy is difficult for *baalei teshuvah*, especially in the early years of their involvement with Orthodox Judaism when they need a great deal of guidance.

Middle Adulthood Committers: Forties+

Ten individuals, five men and five women, committed to Orthodox Judaism during middle adulthood (almost 21 percent). All but one were in their forties, with one in the fifties. Of those who committed in their forties, most were forty to forty-three. Relative newcomers, the Middle Adult Committers, had been *frum* from three to ten years at the time of their interviews. Of the ten individuals, six were from Mainstream families, one from a Modern Traditionalist, and three from Minimalist.

The Middle Adult Committers fell into two categories—those who had been gradually moving into Orthodox Judaism over a long period and those who sought a life change. Those in the former category were previously involved with non-Orthodox Jewish organizations as members of Conservative synagogues, students in adult religious education classes, and volunteers. The BTs who sought a life change had embarked on a new marriage, had children whose Jewish education was to be decided upon, and felt that something was missing in their lives. Those who were married experienced a need for more Jewish content in their family lives. After enrolling their children in yeshiva day schools, they concluded that they should be consistent in their lives with what the children were learning. As one woman said, "The children pushed us along." Several of those looking for a lifestyle change were single or divorced. Around the same time they were attending educational programs sponsored by outreach organizations, they were seeking (and found) a spouse. A few newly married couples embarked on a religious quest together, creating a bond that was centered on their joint desire to learn more about Orthodox Judaism.

The BTs who made a commitment in their forties and fifties were continuing to address Erikson's psychosocial crisis of *generativity vs. stagnation*. Some were still dealing with issues around intimacy and their Jewish identity in their forties, but most were focused on nurturing the next generation, primarily their children. During Levinson's stage that corresponds to the 40s, one builds a middle adult life structure. This is preceded by a transitional period in which one examines and reflects on one's life and ponders what one wants to do in order to make life more fulfilling. Levinson's mid-life transitional period can be experienced as a crisis in which parts of the self that had not been lived out seek expression (Levinson, 1976). This appears to be the case with these "late bloomers." For adults who become Orthodox during this period, the crisis ushers in the development of a life structure that gives primacy to religion. As I show in later chapters, when religion becomes central, one's work life, family relationships, and community life are affected.

Evaluation

Half of the interviewees made a commitment to Orthodoxy before they reached age thirty. Late adolescence and emerging adulthood are life stages when one explores one's identity, the values and beliefs one holds, and the kind of person with whom one wants to share one's life. During these stages, one is receptive to the example of peers and the opinions of authority figures such as rabbis who may influence decision making. In addition, one is anxious to come to a decision about one's education and career direction during this period. Making a commitment to become Orthodox relieves some of the decision-making pressures that emerging adults experience and creates parameters for other decisions made around the same time, such as finding a marital partner who is observant.

Those who became Orthodox in their thirties had spent their twenties searching and dealing with psychological wounds from childhood. Before or during their thirties most of them were married, had children, and were working in a chosen field of endeavor; they settled down. The added responsibility of keeping the *mitzvot* disrupted their routines and, as explained in chapter 4, increased their anxiety over new knowledge they needed to acquire and new religious obligations.

The BTs who became Orthodox in their forties and, in one case, fifties, sought a life structure that would stabilize their family lives. For some, it was the outcome of years of involvement in Jewish activities; for others, it was a decision that had to do with their children's education, a new marriage, or the dynamics of an existing marriage. Those embarking on a new marriage or changing an existing one seemed to want to create a new life structure that was an improvement over the previous one. The timing of becoming Orthodox did not appear to be related to whether their families of origin were Minimalist, Mainstream, or Modern Traditionalist.

Developmental Stages at Time of Interview

At the time of their interviews, the participants were older than they were when they first committed to being Orthodox. Table 3.2 shows how old they were at the time they were interviewed. In contrast with Table 3.1, which showed that twenty-four individuals became *frum* before they were thirty, none of the interviewees were in their twenties or teens when interviewed. Thirteen were in their thirties, nineteen were in their forties, and sixteen were in their fifties at the time of their interviews. There was a statistically significant positive correlation between their ages and the number of years they had been Orthodox at the time they were interviewed ($r = .43$, $p < .01$), that is, the older they were when interviewed, the longer they had been observant. Nevertheless, as noted in the section on Middle Adulthood Committers, some middle-aged adults were newly Orthodox.

The psychosocial issues related to the various developmental stages of Erikson, Arnett, and Levinson were described in the previous section. Here I add to that portrayal to convey where the interviewees were developmentally at the time of their interviews. Their retrospective accounts of their spiritual journeys were influenced by their current developmental stage. Moreover, they were able to reflect on issues they were dealing with at the time of their interviews.

By the time one reaches *early adulthood* one usually develops a life structure that includes work, intimate relationships, and community participation. Erikson identified the psychosocial crises of *intimacy vs. isolation* and *generativity vs. stagnation* as the key developmental issues associated with this period, whereas Levinson focused on settling down. *Baalei teshuvah* interviewed at this stage spoke of the tension they were experiencing between the requirements of Orthodox Judaism and their developing careers. Trying to work and succeed in their careers, they struggled to find a work-family-religion life balance. Furthermore, they felt challenged in their relationships with their spouses and children, their families of origin, and friends as they tried to conform to the norms of their religious community. They also felt pulled away from heightened spiritual feelings by the demands of parenting young children. BTs who were single while in early adulthood sought partners who shared the same

Table 3.2. Age and Stage at Time of Interview (N = 48)

Age at Interview	Interviewees in Age Range	Developmental Stage
15–19	0	Late adolescence
20–24	0	Emerging adulthood
25–29	0	Emerging adulthood
30–34	3	Early adulthood
35–39	10	Early adulthood
40–44	8	Middle adulthood
45–49	11	Middle adulthood
50–54	9	Middle adulthood
55–59	7	Middle adulthood

religious values. Divorce occurred for those whose initial choices proved to be mistaken, with remarriage an attempt to reconstruct their life structure.

Exemplary of participants in early adulthood is Uri, a thirty-two-year old male, who became *frum* ten years prior to his interview. He met his wife-to-be in Israel, where both were in junior-year-abroad college programs. She was already a Sabbath observer when they met, and he soon followed. A turning point for him came later, when he interviewed for a job in the finance field with high work demands. He realized that he had to tell his prospective employer that he needed to leave early on Fridays and would not work on Saturdays. He and his wife had three small children at the time of his interview. Self-described as "open Orthodox," he was struggling to find his place in the religious community.

Middle adulthood encompasses the forties and fifties. Close to 73 percent of participants in this study were in that age group when they were interviewed. During this period, Erikson's *generativity vs. stagnation* is the prominent developmental crisis and the next stage, *integrity vs. despair*, is anticipated. As described earlier, during *generativity vs. stagnation*, individuals seek to nurture the younger generation, usually their children but sometimes their students, clients, patients, or workers they are mentoring. They also may generate ideas through creative activities whether this is in the arts, scientific endeavors, or the business world. They modify their life structure (Levinson, 1978) to account for their children's moving into adolescence, leaving home, and/or producing grandchildren.

Exemplary of BTs whose focus is on generativity is Annie, a forty-nine-year-old married woman who had been *frum* for twenty-four years. Her generativity has entailed nurturing her children and engagement in community service. Her Mainstream family of origin was peripherally involved in Judaism but did send her to an intensive Hebrew school. She was a high achiever in her secular studies and attended a prestigious college and law school. During a summer at Hebrew University, she met Orthodox students who reignited her latent interest in Judaism. After completing law school, she took a position in a city where she became acquainted with an Orthodox family who became her "adopted family." Moving toward Orthodoxy at that time, she was able to make a commitment after questions she asked this family were answered. Before long, she became acquainted with other *frum* families, one of which introduced her to her husband-to-be, a widower. Since marrying, she has been raising three children, one from her husband's previous marriage. Initially, she focused on being a stepmother and mother, but she also became involved in a Jewish communal organization in her new community, where she assumed a leadership role. In recent years, she has returned to working in law, but she did not discuss her career very much. She reported attending *shiurim* where she has filled in gaps in her religious knowledge.

Paul, fifty-eight at the time of his interview and *frum* for thirty-eight years, was the only participant who addressed issues consistent with Erikson's stage of *integrity vs. despair*, but he was also dealing with *generativity vs. stagnation*. During *integrity vs. despair*, one comes to terms with and accepts the life one has lived. The individual assumes responsibility for his or her life without falling into despair (Erikson, 1959/1980). Paul was an only child, whose parents gave him little religious education but insisted that he have a bar mitzvah. He learned about religious observance during and after college from rabbis and peers and gradually took on *mitzvot*. He recalled a childhood in which he had little responsibility but an adulthood in which he became a parent to several children and a caregiver of his aging parents. Now that his parents are deceased and he approaches retirement age, he is reflecting on the past and concerned about the future. He questions the way his children have turned out—too *frum*—and worries about them. He is also concerned about his future financial situation considering the help he continues to provide for his adult children and the potential for illness after retirement. He expressed some disappointment that he has not achieved the heights he thought he might reach in his career when he started out. He was also critical of the hypocrisy he has observed in individuals in his own and his children's Orthodox community. He does appear to be dealing with both poles of the two developmental stages, without clear resolution. Nevertheless, he seems to have a stable life structure, having been married to the same woman over thirty years, having launched most of his children, holding a tenured position at a prominent university, and established as an active member of his synagogue.

Other BTs who, like Paul, had been *frum* for a long time and were in middle age at the time of their interviews, were seeking changes in their lives. A couple of interviewees spoke of their participation in a men's group where they reflect on their lives. Several spoke about increased self-confidence as they have learned their way around the Orthodox community and raised children in that environment.

Quantitative Findings on Erikson's Stages

In order to obtain an external quantitative measure of where the interviewees were developmentally, we asked each participant to complete the Modified Erikson Psychosocial Stage Inventory (MEPSI; Darling-Fisher & Kline Leidy,

1988). The MEPSI is an outgrowth of an earlier instrument that measured the first six of Erikson's stages (Rosenthal, Gutney, & Moore, 1981). Darling-Fisher and Kline Leidy's modified scale covers all eight stages. The MEPSI was developed on an American sample of 168 men and women whose age range was nineteen to eighty-six (*mean* = 47.0 years, *SD* = 15.5). The inventory consists of eighty questions, the responses to which are indicated along a five-point scale from "hardly ever true" to "almost always true" (of you). This pencil-and-paper inventory was administered to participants after the formal interview was completed. We followed instructions by the authors of the MEPSI and reversed certain items and computed the mean scores of items related to each of Erikson's stages (Darling-Fisher & Kline Leidy, the Modified Erikson Psychosocial Stage Inventory [MEPSI], n.d.). In our analysis of the reliability of the scale and each item, the Cronbach alpha for the total scale was 0.96 and all subscales were between 0.69 and 0.88.

In Table 3.3, the mean scores, standard deviations, and range of responses on each of the stages are shown. The mean scores are mostly in the positive range (4.0 and above) or close to that. The lowest score was for *integrity vs. despair*, which is the stage associated with older adulthood. The score for *generativity vs. stagnation*, which is the age-related stage for most of the participants, is in the positive direction. The mean of the total score was 3.98 (*SD* =.45). All scores are close to those found by Darling-Fisher and Kline Leider (1988).

Table 3.3. Scores of Interview Participants on the Modified Erikson Psychosocial Stage Inventory (MEPSI) (N = 47[1])

Stage	Mean	Standard Deviation	Range of Mean Scores
Trust vs. mistrust	3.92	(.57)	2.30 – 4.70
Autonomy vs. shame and doubt	3.92	(.56)	2.00 – 5.00
Initiative vs. guilt	4.01	(.53)	2.90 – 4.80
Industry vs. inferiority	4.12	(.67)	2.30 – 4.90
Identity vs. role confusion	4.14	(.55)	2.60 – 5.00
Intimacy vs. isolation	3.86	(.54)	2.80 – 4.90
Generativity vs. stagnation	4.09	(.49)	2.60 – 4.80
Integrity vs. despair	3.77	(.55)	2.20 – 4.90

[1]One interview participant did not complete the MEPSI.

Note: According to the developers of the MEPSI, scores of 1–2 are considered low, reflecting the predominance of the negative side of the scale, whereas scores of 4–5 indicate the predominance of positive attributes (Darling-Fisher & Kline Leidy, 1988).

For this study, the interview sample consisted of twenty-four participants who had been *frum* for two to twelve years and twenty-four for thirteen years or more; and twenty-four men and twenty-four women. A man who had been observant fewer than thirteen years did not complete his form. In order to determine whether there was a difference in developmental stage achievement between that those who had been *frum* for shorter and longer periods, I conducted *t*-tests, which compare the means. I found that the differences between the two groups on each of the eight stages were not statistically significant. Accordingly, length of time with Orthodox Judaism is not associated with greater psychosocial development.

When I compared the men and women, however, I found a few significant differences. These can be seen in Table 3.4. This table shows significantly higher scores for women in *trust vs. mistrust, intimacy vs. isolation,* and *integrity vs. despair*. It is not surprising that women scored higher on intimacy considering their gender role. In their developmental work on the inventory, Darling-Fisher and Kline Leidy (1988) found gender differences only in *integrity vs. despair*, with women scoring higher. The gender difference for the total means for the BTs is close to significance, considering 0.05 the conventional cut-off point for statistical significance. It is notable that women had mean scores of 4.0

Table 3.4. Comparison between Men and Women on Erikson's Stages of Development, based on the Modified Erikson Psychosocial Stage Inventory (MEPSI) (N =47)

Stage of Development	Male Mean (S.D.)	Female Mean (S.D.)	p-value[1,2]
Trust vs. mistrust	3.67 (.58)	4.15 (.46)	.003
Autonomy vs. shame and doubt	3.86 (.63)	3.98 (.48)	.46
Initiative vs. guilt	3.95 (.50)	4.07 (.56)	.46
Industry vs. inferiority	3.98 (.72)	4.24 (.60)	.17
Identity vs. role confusion	4.13 (.58)	4.15 (.53)	.90
Intimacy vs. isolation	3.67 (.47)	4.05 (.55)	.015
Generativity vs. stagnation	4.02 (.43)	4.16 (.55)	.31
Integrity vs. despair	3.51 (.53)	4.03 (.44)	.001
Total	30.78 (3.48)	32.83 (3.53)	.052

1. Tests of significance are based on *t*-tests, 2-tailed

2. Statistical significance was evaluated at the 0.05 level. Thus, those less than 0.05 are considered not statistically significant.

and above (high range) for every stage except *autonomy vs. shame and doubt*, for which their score was close to 4. Men's scores were 4.0 and above for only two stages—*identity vs. role confusion* and *generativity vs. stagnation*. Overall, it appears that women scored relatively high in all stages and had a higher level of psychosocial development than men.

After completing this analysis, I returned to the interview data of those individuals whose scores were between 2 and 3. (No one had any scores between 1 and 1.9.) The two with scores hovering in that range had reported mental health challenges. On the other hand, a few participants who mentioned past depression or anxiety had relatively high scores. More is said in a later chapter about the healing effect of the *baal teshuvah* experience.

Summary

The decision to become Orthodox occurs in the context of individuals' psychosocial development. In this chapter, I have examined the participants' religious-spiritual change in relation to developmental theories that describe changes that occur at different periods in one's life. There are, of course, individual differences, with some people making a commitment while they are in their late teens and others in their forties and fifties. Still, it is significant to acknowledge that becoming Orthodox when one is a teenager or young adult is different from a middle-aged person who has raised his or her children and may even have grandchildren. In this examination, I observed that half of the interviewees became observant during late adolescence or emerging adulthood (before age thirty); others did so in early and middle adulthood.

Several theories were used to depict the psychosocial processes that occurred when participants became Orthodox. Erikson's theory encompasses the entire life span, with individuals facing developmental crises at certain normative ages. These stages can be revisited later on when, for example, individuals reconstruct their Jewish identities—in this case, their spiritual identities—when they become Orthodox. Arnett gives particular attention to the period he calls "emerging adulthood," in the twenties or earlier. Levinson's "seasons" of a person's life describe changes in life structure that characterize each decade, with transitional periods in between. *Baalei teshuvah's* religious/ spiritual change—whether it occurs in late adolescence or emerging, young or middle adulthood—constitutes in change in life structure. It is continuous with their Jewish ethnicity, but for some it may be radically different from their Minimalist or Mainstream upbringing, and for those who were previously Reform, Conservative, or Reconstructionist, it is more intense and demanding than their prior religious orientation.

At the time of their interviews, interviewees were in a different place than they were when they committed to Orthodox Judaism. Most were married and had children, and all had a religious community. They had settled down or were reorganizing their lives in relation to a spouse, family, work, and religion. Their psychosocial development was within or close to the positive poles within Erikson's developmental theory, with women having a higher level of development than men. Still, they were to face new life changes as they integrated into pre-existing Orthodox communities. The next five chapters deal with challenges occurring post-commitment.

Chapter 4

Challenges of Novices

Learning and Adapting

When Allison left the beautiful home she loved and moved to an Orthodox neighborhood, she thought that she had resolved her indecision and found what she had been looking for the previous seven years. What she did not realize at the time was that it would become

> the beginning of a journey, you know, that I can see is going be lifelong, to be honest. And I very simplistically thought that by moving to the neighborhood it would end and that all my spiritual questions would be done. Not understanding, because I had no idea, not understanding that it was just the beginning. . . .

In chapter 2, I described the various states that *baalei teshuvah* go through in the process of becoming Orthodox up to and including making a commitment. As Allison indicated, commitment is the beginning of a long process. In order to function adequately in an Orthodox community, BTs need further education and socialization. Members of the Orthodox communities they join become socializing agents who directly and indirectly provide instruction on living a communal Orthodox Jewish life. In the process of being socialized, the BTs struggle to acquire new knowledge, experiencing feelings of inadequacy as they do so.

In this chapter the focus is on the post-commitment *novice state*, which occurs when *baalei teshuvah* connect with an Orthodox community, further

109

their knowledge, and learn how to participate in a religious community. As noted in the previous chapter, Levinson (1978) used the term *novice* to describe the beginning phase of adulthood, in the twenties, when one creates an initial adult life structure. According to *The New Oxford American Dictionary* (McKean, 2005), the word *novice* refers to "a person new to or inexperienced in a field or situation" (p. 1165), such as a beginner or neophyte. A novice is in the process of acquiring skills or experience needed for a profession, career, or sphere of life but has not yet achieved mastery. No matter how old they are at the time they commit to being Orthodox, *baalei teshuvah* start out as novices and, to a great extent, remain as such because of deficits in their backgrounds and the fact that they continually face new experiences that require further socialization.

After commitment, *baalei teshuvah* usually join and immerse themselves in an Orthodox community. The immersion is physical, social, cultural, and moral. Typically, they move to a new neighborhood, attend services at one or more Orthodox synagogues, and, if they have children, enroll them in an Orthodox yeshiva day school. In the United States, most neighborhoods are neither exclusively Jewish nor Orthodox, but there are sections in which substantial numbers of Orthodox Jews reside. Orthodox Jews tend to cluster in locations that are within walking distance to their synagogues. In such areas, it is likely that they have neighbors who share a religious outlook, observe Shabbat and religious holidays, keep kosher, dress modestly, and send their children to religious schools. *Baalei teshuvah* meet their Orthodox neighbors on the street and through their children, and become acquainted with other Orthodox people at synagogue, in classes, at their children's schools, at the kosher butcher or kosher department of the grocery store, at the *mikveh*, in certain barbershops, in Jewish bookstores, and other places where Orthodox Jews congregate. A move to a new neighborhood or synagogue may prompt invitations for Shabbat or holiday meals, where they meet more Orthodox people. Their new acquaintances may be people who were raised *frum* (FFBs) and/or other BTs. As they become increasingly involved in the community, they learn the ethical conduct, norms, and behavioral standards that are expected of them.

The socialization process that unfolds post-commitment entails academic and social learning. *Baalei teshuvah* become exposed to new information and cultural practices in formal classes and informal gatherings, where they absorb knowledge, observe what others are doing, and consider how their learning applies to their lives. They also become aware of community expectations around appropriate dress, participation in religious rituals, and Torah study (described as "learning"). They may once again experience "spiritual shocks," described in chapter 2, when new ideas contrast sharply with their previous beliefs. Novices may struggle with ideas or practices that they initially find objectionable or difficult to integrate into their lives. For example, Elliot described feeling overwhelmed with the discipline he had to maintain in order to be observant:

> Growing in *Yiddishkeit* [Jewishness] requires discipline as an absolute prerequisite. So being a not disciplined person, and to grow in *Yiddishkeit*, it's difficult, because there's a lot to keep (unclear). . . . When you're not used to that, you're used to doing what you want when you want, you can't do that.

Five years post-commitment and forty-seven years old, Elliot found it difficult to anticipate and maintain the routine practices of religious life, such as saying one *bracha* (blessing) after washing his hands, another prior to eating bread, and still another after a meal; and planning his day around prayer times.

In this chapter, I describe some of the challenges novices faced as they gradually learned what they needed to know to navigate successfully in their new communities. The topics to be addressed include spiritual guidance, language literacy, learning, *davening* (praying), and the holiness of the Sabbath. I begin with a discussion of spiritual guidance and then will move into language literacy. Where the experiences of men and women, and those committed to Orthodox Judaism fewer or more than thirteen years, were different, I describe the divergences.

Spiritual Guidance

It is difficult to move into a new situation without assistance from someone in the know. Many of the interviewees had spiritual guides prior to their making a commitment and continued with these individuals and/or others afterward. A variety of terms has been used to depict the relationship between a person with knowledge, experience, and expertise and a novice. In *The Seasons of a Man's Life*, Levinson (1978) discussed the mentor relationship as a significant early adult developmental experience for men, but less common and significant for women (Levinson, 1996). Narrowly, the term mentor refers to a "teacher, adviser or sponsor" (Levinson, 1978, p. 97) particularly in a work setting. Levinson (1978) describes the role further:

What are the various functions of the mentor? He may act as a *teacher* to enhance the young man's skills and intellectual develop-ment. Serving as a *sponsor*, he may use his influence to facilitate the young man's entry and advancement. He may be a *host and guide*, welcoming the initiate into a new occupational and social world and acquainting him with its values, customs, resources and cast of characters. Through his own virtues, achievements and way of living, the mentor may be an *exemplar* that the protégé can admire and seek to emulate. He may provide *counsel* and moral support in times of stress. (p. 98)

The mentors of the participants in this study performed all these functions but, in particular, served as teachers and exemplars.

Oman and Thoresen (2003) used the term *spiritual model* to describe a person who serves as an exemplar on living a holy life and demonstrates how to perform an array of complex behaviors and skills. Biblical and historical figures as well as individuals one may meet in one's daily life can serve as spiritual models. Spiritual modeling is based on Bandura's social cognitive theory, which emphasizes learning through observation (Bandura, 1977, 1996). The BTs in this study used the terms mentors and role models. More often than not, they had one or two mentors and many role models all of whom served as spiritual models.

The individuals who served as spiritual models were rabbis, rebbetzins (wives of rabbis), teachers, and friends. A member of the first focus group, Leah, spoke of how inspiring it is for her to have a rebbetzin, her teacher, as a role model. She said that every woman who learns with this rebbetzin "is lifted off the ground by the time they walk out of her house and want to do more." Arthur, thirty-six years old and *frum* for twelve years, views the rabbi from his *shul* as a role model and guide, but not as an equal or as a friend:

He is someone that is a role model to me, someone . . . who will remind me of the things that I have to do, so that ritualistically, where I have to sort of be a little bit more observant and more careful in what I do. And when you look at him, at times in our life when we've needed him, he's always been there for us. My wife thinks he's a very caring person. But it's definitely, I think, a very kind of student/teacher relationship.

Arthur portrays his rabbi as an expert on ritual observance. By bringing in his wife's perception of his support, care, as well as the rabbi's reminding

Arthur of his obligations and the rabbi's availability when they needed him, Arthur suggests that he views the relationship as parental. Several others who described their mentors conveyed a similar impression.

Brian was forty-seven years old and observant twenty-five years when he recalled his feelings about the rabbi who was his spiritual guide for a brief but significant period:

> Meeting Rabbi ___ was certainly a watershed moment for me in terms of my relationship with Judaism, because I was meeting somebody who was certainly, was definitely an authority in Jewish issues, whether it was Jewish law or deeper spiritual issues in *kabbalah* and mysticism. And yet I was meeting somebody who wasn't afraid to tackle modern life head on. And that was a very special and unique attitude that I felt he had. That he wasn't a person who insulated himself from the modern world, which I judge a lot of Orthodox people do, or would like to. . . . And I also felt that he could see through me, see through my shortcomings and see through my . . . into my shadow, into the spaces where I wasn't even aware of, of myself. And that feeling convinced me I needed to be around him and learn from him. And even though it was a short-lived affair, it was a very powerful transformation for me to be around somebody like that.

Other BTs, however, had ordinary relationships with rabbis, who were informal teachers, advisors, and friends. Nora, fifty-five years old and a BT for twenty-two years, described her relationship with a rabbi and rebbetzin from her neighborhood whom she and her husband regarded as models:

> They invited us a lot for *Shabbos* and used to spend a lot of time, we used to spend every day together, and they answered all our questions and they were very wonderful people to ask questions to when we wanted to become observant. And they basically taught us, were good examples for us and taught us like how to be an observant family.

Chani, a member of Focus Group 2, said that she and her husband, as well as other *baalei teshuvah* that she knows, attach themselves to a particular rabbi who, they believe, helps them in their spiritual growth.

More men than women spoke of their relationships with rabbis who were their mentors and role models. Several women spoke of wishing they had had a special rabbi who could guide them; instead, they obtained advice from a variety of people. A few of the women talked of obtaining guidance from a rebbetzin or through a network of women whom they met at classes at the home of a woman teacher. Through these networks, they made friend-ships that reinforced their learning and found out about other educational resources.

Language Literacy

Knowledge of Hebrew is integral to life in an Orthodox Jewish community. Hebrew is the language of prayer, recited upon rising and going to sleep, before and after eating and other activities, and in communal prayer settings. In Orthodox communities, men are expected to pray three times a day, in the morning (*shacharit*), afternoon (*minchah*), and evening (*maariv*), either at home or in a *minyan* (prayer group with a quorum of 10 men) at a synagogue or alternative location. There are differences of opinion on women's obligations in daily prayers because they are mostly exempt from time-oriented com-mandments (Berman, 1973); moreover, they are not obligated to *daven* with a *minyan*. The Torah and other holy texts, such as the Mishnah (a compendium of rulings of the Oral Law), are written in Hebrew.

Most of the participants in this study had some childhood Jewish edu-cation. All but two of the twenty-four men and eighteen of the twenty-four women interviewees had, during their growing up years, some supplementary religious education, whether it was Hebrew school, Talmud Torah, Reform Sunday school, or day school. One of the two men who lacked formal reli-gious education came from a secular, unaffiliated family; the other's family thought that their son, who had a learning disability, was not capable of learning enough to have a bar mitzvah. (He had a bar mitzvah later as an adult.) Those women who had no formal Jewish education during childhood came from families that were very secular or did not think their daughters needed a Jewish religious education, in contrast with their sons who, they believed, need to be prepared for a bar mitzvah. Two men and four women had attended Jewish day schools.

A few of the men and women who went to Hebrew or Sunday school said that despite attending classes, they did not learn Hebrew. Allen, fifty-four years old and *frum* for twenty-six years at the time of his interview, offered this description of his Reform Hebrew school and temple:

Well, let's not exaggerate. It wasn't a Hebrew school. The only Hebrew that was spoken there was the *Shema*, meaning, until I became much more observant later on, I thought the *Shema* consisted of one line, *Shema Israel*, that one line, which I never understood anyway. But other than that, there was no Hebrew spoken even during the services.

Although many, like Allen, were critical of their Hebrew and Sunday schools, a number of them were grateful that they had learned how to read Hebrew and that they had been exposed to the *Chumash* (the Pentateuch; the Five Books of Moses) and some prayers. With a few exceptions, however, the BTs were taught to decode the Hebrew words, enabling them to participate orally in religious services. Those preparing for a bar or bat mitzvah learned to read a portion of the Torah and/or the *haftarah* (reading from the Prophets) or memorized their readings from a recording.

When they moved into adulthood and were exploring Judaism, ten men and eight women studied in yeshivas or seminaries. The shortest stay was one woman's four days at a Lubavitch seminary in the United States; most varied between a month and a year; and the longest was for ten years. Most of the institutions they attended were designed to fit the learning needs of *baalei* and *baalot teshuvah* and were in Israel. Learning in men's yeshivas entailed learning *Chumash*, the *mitzvot* (commandments), the *siddur* (prayer book), Jewish ethics, and the *Gemara* (part of the Talmud that includes in-depth discussions of the Mishnah) (Aviad, 1983; Danzger, 1989). The curriculum in traditional women's seminaries covered similar ground but excluded study of the *Gemara*, although some modern schools teach *Gemara* to women (Danzger, 1989). Hebrew language classes are available in these institutions (Aviad, 1983). Students increase their knowledge of Hebrew by studying Hebrew texts and learning new words with the help of dictionaries and from the context in which they appear, and those who study *Gemara* learn Aramaic in a similar way (D. Moskoff, personal communication). In these yeshivas and seminaries, learning is typically undertaken with study partners (*chavrutahs*) who have a similar level of competence.

Aside from those who went to yeshivas or seminaries, some learned Hebrew elsewhere. Six men took Hebrew classes at *ulpans*, language learning programs, in Israel or classes in the United States.[1] Two women took what they called "crash courses" in the United States, one studied Hebrew more intensively at a synagogue, and two attended ulpans in Israel. Several men reported that they were taught to read Hebrew and recite prayers by rabbis who mentored them. Men and women spoke about how helpful they found their ArtScroll[2] prayer book, which has word-by-word/line-by-line translations from Hebrew to English.

The men and women who reported that they attended Jewish day schools when they were young or had a year or more of advanced study in a yeshiva or seminary in Israel, or classes in the United States were better prepared to participate in Orthodox religious services. Those who achieved a good grasp of Hebrew through their own efforts expressed pride in their accomplishments. Ben, whose Modern Traditionalist family observed Shabbat to some extent and kept kosher, had some prior knowledge of Hebrew gained from Hebrew School and the Conservative-affiliated Camp Ramah. Although he did not attend a yeshiva or go to an *ulpan*, he said that he has benefited from working at advancing his Hebrew skills:

> Since I've worked on it, it's good enough now; enough, where I can ask questions. I think I understand this, but I don't understand what this word means, and how does it fit in. . . . And plus . . . I can ask questions of why is this, this, this. Because there's people you can ask these questions to. And I can feel part of that question and answer thing. Trying to really understand something that's meaningful to yourself that you can convey to other people—that's exciting to me!

Ben, who had been *frum* for ten years and was forty-one years old at the time of his interview, seems to be gauging his progress with Hebrew through his increased ability to participate intelligently in classes he is taking.

Among the women, Batya, whose Mainstream family was affiliated with Reform synagogues, had no supplementary school education. *Frum* for four years and thirty-one years old, she worked on her Hebrew by attending an *ulpan* in a kibbutz. As she explained, being able to decode Hebrew opened up the possibility of becoming Orthodox:

> At this point I had for the first time the most freedom in my Jewish explorations that I'd ever had because I could read Hebrew and speak somewhat, but read. So this, I would say, was the opening to my Orthodoxy possibilities, that any synagogue became accessible to me. I was no longer relegated to the transliteration, to the Friday night service. I could go on Saturday now because I could

follow where they were. It was like *nirvana*, like, "Whoa!" Like if anybody ever says to me, "What was the difference between being Orthodox and not Orthodox?" it was reading Hebrew. Because I just never felt comfortable, never felt like (it was) accessible.

Despite the achievements of BTs who were better educated, the interviews were permeated with expressions of inadequacy. With respect to language literacy, the men focused on deficiencies in Hebrew and Aramaic—even men who had been Orthodox thirteen or more years. Most of those who knew how to decode Hebrew spoke about not being able to understand what the words meant. The few who comprehended Hebrew spoke about not understanding the *Gemara*, which is written in Hebrew and Aramaic. Mark, who grew up in a Mainstream family and was five years post-commitment, had attended a Reform supplementary school, and took Hebrew classes later as an adult in the United States, reflected on how little he knew after he moved to an Orthodox community. In his previous Conservative setting:

I had been one of the best-educated people in the group, and all of a sudden . . . it's like being a hutch on a Little League, and then you go to the next level and all of a sudden you discover you're playing in the Yankees with the all-stars. Wait a minute. I thought I knew what I was doing and now I'm an ignoramus again.

Like the men, many of the women with limited prior Jewish education expressed feelings of inadequacy over their deficiencies with Hebrew (but not Aramaic). This includes women who had supplementary education when they were growing up and further education afterward. For example, Deborah, who said that she was in Hebrew school through her bat mitzvah and confirmation and had some post bat mitzvah education, disclosed that she could not read Hebrew. After attending an *ulpan* in Israel, she was able to speak but not read. When she goes to synagogue, she feels like a "child that's lost in a classroom." Others spoke of feeling "ignorant," having "gaps" in their Jewish education, being "illiterate," and having deficits in "textual knowledge."

One woman, Cheryl, *frum* for eighteen years, appeared to have an exceptional grasp of Hebrew. She had the advantages of a day school education, summers at Camp Ramah, and study at a seminary in Israel. She had learned how to lead prayer services in day school and Ramah and led Orthodox women's *davening* groups after she became *frum*. This woman was sufficiently competent in reading and understanding text that she was teaching others.

She was the only woman who spoke about the *Gemara,* noting that she can gain access to it with the help of her husband.

Some men who had worked hard at learning Hebrew commented on their progress with *Gemara.* Uri, thirty-two years old, *frum* for ten years, and from a Modern Traditionalist family, explained that although he took Hebrew in college and spent his junior year at Hebrew University, he did not have the kind of education one gets from a yeshiva:

> I was at Hebrew U., and if you kind of look at the curriculum, it was all learning Hebrew, which is the fundamental building block of being able to learn on your own. . . . I did my first *chavruta* at Hebrew U with someone who I was set up with and made phenomenal progress just going through *Tanach,* learning *Rashi* script, getting some basic education. And I've basically done a *chavruta* [in] . . . every city I've gone to. . . . But at the end of the day, you know, it's pretty weak. So now I'm studying *Gemara* with someone locally . . . [and] just because of how strong my Hebrew skills are, I make rapid progress versus other people; [I've] done a lot of independent reading. But I haven't kind of had that formal education process.

Uri represents a best-case scenario of men who have not studied in a yeshiva yet are able to learn Hebrew and, to some extent, Aramaic. Despite his efforts, however, he cannot bridge the gap. Two men who studied for eight to ten years in yeshivas in Israel, eventually receiving ordination as rabbis, attained these skills. Except for those men who were fewer than five years post-commitment, the others were learning Gemara at *shiurim* or with *chavrutahs.* Some picked up Aramaic by attending *shiurim* in which the instructor went through a text line-by-line translating the line into English and expanding on its meaning, or by working one-on-one with a knowledgeable *chavrutah* or teacher.

Learning

Before they make a commitment and join an Orthodox community, *baalei teshuvah* engage in a process of learning, which is primarily academic but also encompasses social norms. As they become socialized to community norms, they discover that learning is an ongoing, never-ending endeavor that, in their case, is a necessity. In order to "make it" in their adopted communities, they have to enhance their knowledge and upgrade their skills. In table 2.2, I listed the books BTs told the interviewers that they had found informative prior to their making a commitment. Post-commitment, they delved into some of the same books and some additional ones that would help them enhance their lives as observant Jews. These included Rabiat's *The 39 Melachos* (1999; 4 volumes) on prohibitions related to observing the Sabbath; Steinsaltz's *The Essential Talmud* (1976), an introduction to study of the Talmud; Twerski's *Living Each Week* (1987), about the Torah portion for each Sabbath, and the Schottenstein edition of the Talmud (in Hebrew/Aramaic and English).

Allison, forty-seven years old and observant ten years, spoke about the books she accumulated soon after she became *frum*. She and her family were living in small temporary housing while waiting for their new house to be in move-in condition. She spoke of the books[3] she received by mail from a Jewish bookstore:

> Every week there was a drop of books from Eichler's. Like this library that I'll show you in the next room. . . . we had put . . . most of our belongings in storage. 'Cause it was a teeny little row house where we were living. And we came from a four-bedroom house. . . . But the books! The books! The books! The *seforim*, *seforim*, and bookcases were lining up. We had never moved in with that. By the time we left the house nine months later, the walls of the dining room and the living room were ceiling to floor books.

Besides purchasing books, the BTs borrowed books and other learning resources from outreach organizations and mikvehs. Some listened to audio recordings, which they also accumulated. Eliza, fifty-six years old and *frum* for nineteen years, said:

> [I] listened to a lot of tapes from a lot of different personalities. Rabbi Twerski, Noach Weinberg, Manis Freidman, etc., etc. Different perspectives, *chassidish* [and] more traditional. [I] listened to a lot of tapes on a lot of different subjects. On *midot* (character traits), and on ritual, and on theology. . . . I read quite a few books very avidly. And still do. . . . *parshah* tapes, and every topic imaginable. So we have a tape library. . . . we must have two or three thousand tapes in this house. No kidding. . . . And we've given plenty of them away to different synagogue libraries.

Several other women were also avid listeners of tapes.[4] They spoke about the convenience of listening to tapes while cleaning the house, driving, or walking to the train station on the way to work, and men listened to audio recordings as well. Others spoke about the help provided in these tapes to solve moral, spiritual, parenting, and personal problems. Baila, age fifty-one and *frum* for twenty-four years, said that the Torah tapes help her gain clarity in issues with which she is struggling.

Besides reading and listening to audio recordings, the BTs learned through classes offered at their synagogues or elsewhere in the community. According to two key informants, taking classes fits in with the intellectual needs of *baalei teshuvah*. As a rebbetzin who does outreach work explained (paraphrased by the interviewer), "The main things in the beginning BT's mindset was reflective of their learning styles, that they wanted to study and 'go to classes.' So, classes in Torah were similar to taking yoga or other similar pursuits." (Considering that most of the BTs in this study were college graduates, taking classes was a familiar experience.) Equally important, the rebbetzin said, are the sense of family and friendship and the feeling of being loved that they experience in the process. Coming from a personal perspective, Saul, shared with others in Focus Group 2 that having come from a family of high achievers, he wanted to establish "an expertise in *frumkeit* as I had in other things."

Because men and women differ in the kinds of Jewish learning in which they engage and have different attitudes toward it, men's and women's learning are discussed here separately, beginning with the men. Most of the male interviewees expressed feelings of insecurity about the level of their Jewish knowledge. As Chaya commented in her focus group, the expectations for men are different from those for women:

> You don't have to have a degree of mastery in learning and pro-
> ficiency to feel like a *mentsch* that a man has to have. And for a
> man, it's very important to feel like he knows what he's doing. It's
> very injurious to a man's self-esteem to feel suddenly when you're
> used to being an [MD?] and respected, you know, that all of a
> sudden now you're a neophyte.

As suggested by Chaya and others, the men felt deficient in their language competence and were self-conscious about their *davening*. However disquiet-ing, their anxiety served as an incentive to further their knowledge and skills so that they could hold their own in the synagogue and other settings where their performance is visible. They developed a variety of strategies to do that including taking classes, working on a particular text with a study partner, learning on their own, studying with a rabbi, studying with family members, and learning from books and audio recordings.

The classes the men spoke of attending were on the week's *parashah* (Torah reading; sometimes pronounced *parsha*), the Mishnah, the *Shulkhan Aruch* (code of laws), and the *Gemara*. Classes were given by rabbis and other learned members of their communities and through outreach organizations. The BT men varied in the frequency of their attendance at classes. One spoke of going to a class one day a week, on Shabbat afternoon, whereas another was running to classes nine times a week. Some took classes on *Gemara*, which was a challenge because most of them did not have sufficient background to untangle the meaning of these texts on their own. One man described spending years studying with a rabbi who took "the scenic route," slowly walking him, his father-in-law, and his brother-in-law through the *Gemara* volume they were studying.

The men experienced community pressure to learn *Gemara*, a norm for men who were raised Orthodox.[5] Nevertheless, *Gemara* was not everyone's cup of tea. Ben, mentioned early in relation to his love of learning and pride in his accomplishments, asserted that the *Gemara* does not appeal to him. Rather than arguing with others about the meaning of a text, he likes to read "*droshim*" (stories with a moral lesson). Like a number of other men, Ben prefers to learn on his own but he, like others, participates in an array of activities such as attending *shiurim* and working with a *chavrutah*.

The women described learning formally in classes, informally by observing or asking questions of others, studying with a *chavrutah*, and by reading books and listening to audio recordings. They attended classes offered by learned men and women on topics such as Shabbat, *taharat hamishpachah* (family purity),[6] *challah*, keeping kosher, the Torah portion of the week, *shmirat haloshon* (guarding your tongue [from gossip]), and *halakhah*. In contrast with many men, who portrayed learning as arduous and obligatory, the women expressed a great deal of excitement about their learning (Sands, Spero, & Danzig, 2007), regardless of their background and years *frum*. For example, Maya said that she goes to as many women's classes as possible "so that it keeps me . . . revved up and in the right direction," and Marcia remarked, "I hope and I pray to Hashem that I continue learning for the rest of my life." At the times of their interviews, Maya, whose background was Minimalist and had been *frum* for thirty years, and Marcia, from a Mainstream family, who had been *frum* only seven years, continued to experience a "BT high" from learning. Frequency of class attendance for women ranged from three times a week to not at all. Those who were not learning spoke of having learned in the past and expressed hope that they would get back to it when their family responsibilities lessen.

Also in contrast to the men, the women emphasized learning through observation and interactions with neighbors and friends. Shabbat meals to which they were invited provided opportunities to observe and ask people who were more knowledgeable than they about particulars of being *frum*. Some women deliberately sought out people who were raised Orthodox as role models and information sources. Women who had developed close relationships with FFBs were able to ask them questions that may have embarrassed them in larger settings in a safe environment. Allison reported that a neighbor gave her "a crash course in *bishul*," referring to the Shabbat prohibition against cooking and how to avoid it while making tea.

Allison's course on *bishul* is an example of one of the ways in which BTs learned cultural practices. They learned through observing FFBs' practices, asking questions, and informal instruction. When they practice learned behaviors and are corrected, they learn from their mistakes. In her book on how BTs learn the language and culture of Orthodox Judaism, Benor (2012) describes how newcomers learn about the accepted dress codes, hair and head coverings, preferred foods, and home decorations of the Orthodox communities they join. Like the BTs in my study, her participants learned from interactions with FFBs and adopted prevailing cultural practices. Through these interactions, BTs become socialized as Orthodox community members.

As they engaged in a process of learning, men and women acquired more specific and nuanced information about living a religious life, and translated this into their practices. Some of what they had learned or thought they knew prior to making a commitment had to be unlearned as they took on more practices.

A few men and women who considered themselves committed had been making exceptions to their observances. For example, Seth and his wife had been driving to his mother's house for Friday night Shabbat dinners and allowed their son to watch cartoons Shabbat afternoon. With increased learning and socialization to community norms, they gave up these practices. Similarly, those who had made the exception of eating fish or dairy meals in non-kosher restaurants decided that they would eat only in kosher restaurants. Other BTs added to their repertoire practices that they had previously found objectionable. These included women who began to cover their hair and dress modestly and men who wore their yarmulkes to work. With respect to keeping kosher, some switched to milk and milk products that were certified as *chalav Yisrael* (or *cholov Yisroel*), which ensures that the milk came from a Jewish-owned farm where non-kosher animals are not on sight, or came from a non-Jewish owned farm where milking was performed under the supervision of an Orthodox Jew ("Cholov Yisroel," n.d.) One woman who had kept kosher her entire adult life took a rabbi's advice and submerged her dishes in a *mikveh* (a practice known as *tevilah, toveling*, or *toiveling*). The purpose of this process is to confer holiness to the dishes and utensils ("Immersion of Vessels," n.d.). In order to uphold commandments of *taharat mishpachah*, those who previously slept in double beds switched to twin beds. As a gesture to please his wife, one man (Allen) put on *tefillin* more frequently than he had before. Subsequently he studied a mishnaic text on *davening*, which led to his gaining a deeper understanding of this practice. At the time of his interview, Allen was donning *tefillin* daily with his morning *davening*.

Davening

Davening (praying) is integral to Orthodox life. As mentioned, men are obligated to *daven* three times a day, whereas the expectations for women are less clear (Berman, 1973). Women are expected to *daven*, but not according to specified times during which men are obligated and are given leeway because of childcare responsibilities (D. Moskoff, personal conversation). Although some *baalei teshuvah daven* in English initially, they are encouraged to use Hebrew as soon as they learn the language. The ability to read, follow others' reading, and chant in Hebrew is necessary for participating in group *davening* in a synagogue (*shul*). Novices with little Hebrew education struggle to keep up with the service, experiencing embarrassment over losing their place.

BTs whose families of origin were affiliated with Reform or Conservative synagogues were in atmospheres that did not address this illiteracy[7]. When many of the BTs in this study were growing up, services in Reform synagogues were conducted almost entirely in English, with the few Hebrew prayers transliterated. In Conservative synagogues, in which more prayers are recited in Hebrew but also include some in English, page numbers are usually announced from the pulpit, helping participants to keep up with the service. In Orthodox environments, pages are not usually announced and praying tends to be rapid, making it difficult for those who are weak in Hebrew to follow. Furthermore, Orthodox synagogues in the United States tend to use the Ashkenazic pronunciation of Hebrew, whereas Reform and Conservative synagogues usually use the Sephardic pronunciation, contributing further to the difficulty of following the prayers.

Baalei teshuvah are encouraged to *daven* with *kavanah* (concentration, intention). As the late Rabbi Zalman Schachter-Shalomi explains:

> Jewish prayer begins with *kavanah*. To *daven* with *kavanah* means to pray with focus, intention, meaning. It means praying from the heart, rather than prayer centered solely in the mind. Celebrating a Shabbos or a holiday with *kavanah* gives that day a deeper, richer texture. *Kavanah* gives meaning to our rituals of marriage and birth and death. It inspires us to perform a mitzvah on a more conscious and ultimately more rewarding level. *Kavanah* lies at the heart of Jewish devotional life. That one word encompasses an entire body of inner work necessary to live consciously in the presence of God. (2014, pp. 5–6)

Accordingly, one does not simply recite or chant the prayers. One needs to bring one's total being into the experience.

Men and women interviewees portrayed *davening* as a spiritually uplifting experience. It draws them close to God and is a way for them to express gratitude for the blessings they have received. Seth, *frum* for fifteen years, spoke of *davening*, along with learning and performing mitzvahs, as a means of elevating the soul:

> I do think that behind it all there is this God, there's this spiritual force that does have meaning in the world and that we have to . . . *daven* to, that we have to direct ourselves to, and just be thankful for our good health and anything good that comes to us.

In a similar vein, a more recent BT, Batya, said that *davening* was about her relationship with God, which she works on by being mindful of what God expects of her and by being thankful.

One way the *baalei teshuvah* experienced a spiritual connection with God was to concentrate on the prayers they uttered. Schachter-Shalomi (2014) suggested that "meditating on key verses that express the situation we are looking to create" or "the spiritual understanding that we hope to merit" (p. 15) is one pathway to *kavanah*. Some BTs had favorite prayers during *davening* as well as on other occasions. For example, Jacob, *frum* for 22 years, said that the *Ashrei* prayer (a twenty-four-line chapter from Psalms beginning "Happy is the one who dwells in God's house") is important to him:

> I remember feeling, in my room . . . when I said that first *Ashrei*, I remember feeling like tingling. Which I still feel today. . . . When I go on vacation, and I'm all alone, and I'm staring at a mountain or a river. And I'm just by myself, it's me and God, and I say this *Ashrei*, slowly, every word, I will sometimes read it in English (and) as I'm reading, it'll take me a half-hour to say *Ashrei*.

Deborah, *frum* for 25 years, said that early in her spiritual journey a rabbi advised her to concentrate on particular words. The words she focused on were "*poteach et yadecha,*" from Ashrei, which refers to God opening His hand to humanity. This was meaningful to her because at the time she learned these words, she was experiencing family problems. Ben mentioned that he underlines passages of the *siddur* that are important to him and recites them with special *kavanah*. A number of the participants spoke of reciting prayers consciously rather than zipping through them mindlessly. In making statements like this, the BTs were distinguishing themselves from FFBs, whom they viewed as *davening* perfunctorily.

Several *baalei teshuvah* spoke about making a spiritual connection with God through the musicality of prayers (cf. Schachter-Shalomi, 2014). A few expressed enthusiasm over Carlebach-style Friday night *davening* in their communities. Others had their own ideas about prayer. Brian, Orthodox for twenty-five years, responded in this way to the interviewer's question out how his praying has changed over the years:

> It's much simpler now. I kind of have a little disdain for the quantity of words that we say in our prayers. So I don't always say a lot of words, but the words I do say I try to be aware of what I'm saying, and I try to be more present and conscious. Rather than valuing my prayer based on the quantity of prayer, [I focus] on the quality of the prayer. And also, sometimes, the absence of prayer. Because I want my whole life to be a prayer. Even my work I want to be a prayer. And sometimes it doesn't have words. Sometimes it's just getting up and doing something for somebody, and often myself; and that's a prayer.

Three men reached a level in which they could assume leadership roles in religious services. They spoke with pride about leading the prayers and serving as a *gabbai*, who manages the internal functioning of the religious service. Mark, who gave up acting in a community theater after he became Orthodox five years before he was interviewed, found leading the service a way of redirecting his acting and singing skills. Jacob, whose love for *Ashrei* was mentioned earlier, found that serving as *gabbai* for the High Holidays enabled him to learn the service:

> I knew nothing, and I took a *machzor* (holiday prayer book), and I remember going through it page by page looking at the English, looking at the Hebrew, and I bought a little *luach* [calendar] in English, so I would go through the *tefillah* (prayer), you know, and know what to say and try to figure out why to say it, and it was an incredible thrill for me to be a *gabbai*, and I took it very seriously and I worked very hard. And of course, when you're involved in something you learn it the best. 'Cause I believe being active as opposed to being passive is the way you really internalize.

Jacob's active role as *gabbai* for Rosh Hashanah and Yom Kippur led to his becoming *gabbai* in the main services of his congregation on Shabbat and to his increased feelings of competence.

The *davening* for men tended to be synagogue-centered, where there were opportunities for leadership. Cognizant that the preferred context for men is with a *minyan*, three times a day, men who did not meet this ideal explained how barriers such as work obligations, travel, and childcare responsibilities limited their participation. Several men spoke of difficulties they had *davening* in a *minyan*. Allen, who progressed from *davening* in English to Hebrew, found himself falling behind the others. Others struggled with the Hebrew words. Women who *davened* tended to do so at home, where they recited all or part of the morning service if they had time and other prayers on different occasions. They attended *shul* on Shabbat and holidays, if at all.

Women whose *davening* was minimal or not at all offered several reasons for this. As stated previously, women are not obligated to *daven* with a *minyan*, nor do they count in the quorum. This, combined with the ambiguity over how often they should *daven*, left them free to *daven* where and as often as they liked. Those who were parents of small children found it difficult to find time to pray. Others, like Karen, *frum* for eleven years, were apologetic over their inability to meet expectations over *davening*:

I don't *daven* as much as I feel that I should. I have a real trouble. I mean, just like I told you, I don't *daven* formally. Okay, let's put it this way. I talk to Hashem all day long. But it's talking to Hashem, it's not saying *Shemoneh Esrei* . . . so, just like I said, I'm not from the big *shul*-goers.

Shemoneh Esrei ("*Eighteen*"), is the colloquial name for a set of blessings (originally eighteen for weekday prayer services) that constitute the *Amidah*, the silent prayer that is recited while standing. It is a key component of the daily and Sabbath services. Another woman, Shifra, mentioned that her rabbi told her to *daven* at least one *Shemoneh Esrei* a day.

Regardless of whether they were caring for young children, a number of women found it challenging to incorporate *davening* into their lives. Allison, Orthodox for ten years, said:

I wish I *davened* every day. I don't. When I make the time, and I do Shabbos, I'm so thrilled. And for me, this is something that's taken a lifetime to appreciate, *davening*. And my friend who was the Hillel rabbi then, I remember saying to him, you know, I'm just not interested in the *davening* piece. And he used to say to me, that comes last . . . And so it did for me. And now I just love poring over that *siddur*.

On the other hand, some women found it meaningful to pray daily. Liora, who used to meditate, chant, and do yoga, recognized at one point that since becoming *frum* and having children, something was missing in her life. As she explained:

One of the things that came out of that time for me was how much I missed my meditating, my chanting, my prayer time. I felt like it wasn't enough for me to see God, be with God, recognize God, and relate to God through my daily thing. I wanted prayer time, more than just going up to *shul* and trying to keep the kids quiet, and packing the food, and just the race of it, and then getting home to serve the meal. And I felt like I needed to institute my prayer time, and guard it. And I did. . . . And I found that there was a real opportunity and a real channel for me to connect and plug into spiritually on a daily level.

Liora was thirty-nine and *frum* for six years when she said this. She, along with others, also recites *tehillim* (psalms) occasionally. Four other women spoke about the importance of daily *davening* in their lives. Nora spoke about spending forty-five to fifty minutes each morning *davening*: "Davening is a big part of my day. It's like the most important part of the beginning of my day." Those who found *davening* satisfying spoke of occasional *kavanah*.

Several women found other activities that they considered substitutes for daily *davening* and the spiritual experience that they associated with praying. A six-year BT, Sherry expresses her spirituality by reciting *Shema* every night, lighting the Sabbath candles, and blessing her children at the Sabbath table. Susan, *frum* for eight years, reported a longtime interest in spirituality:

> [There are] many *brachos* you could say every day, hundreds of them. So even if you just say a couple, it's a good thing. So, you know, that's something that's very positive. It's a very positive thing in life, in general, to be able to wake up and say thank you, you know, to be appreciative, it makes you appreciate things you have.

When they prayed, women prayed for themselves and others. *Frum* for twenty-four years, Lauren takes *davening* more seriously since she enrolled in school, as this gives her time for herself and keeps her from being "crazed." A therapist who has been Orthodox for thirteen years, Ruth prays for patients she considers in need of healing. Allison includes family members in her prayers:

> I have a cousin who got married at the age of thirty-nine. And we kept trying to fix him up, trying to fix him up, and I would *daven* for him every Friday night. And, he got married last February, and I made the match actually. And then she wasn't pregnant and I was *davening* for that, [and] now she's pregnant, thank God.

It is striking, however, that many women expressed displeasure with *davening* at their synagogue on Shabbat. A few remarked that their current *shul* does not elicit the spiritual feelings that they experienced at a previous synagogue or prayer group. Others admitted that their poor command of Hebrew made synagogue attendance unpleasant. A couple of the women referred to health problems that interfered with their walking to *shul*. Sherry attributed her *shul*-avoidance to the patriarchal environment of the *shul*:

I really can't stand going to *shul*. I'm not into the collective prayer thing. Partially, because I'm illiterate, I think . . . but, somehow or other, it just doesn't do it for me. I see the prayer environment as a very male environment, and I think that's the way it should be because I think there are very few outlets for healthful male bonding. And women do things face to face, 'cause they have that intimacy, and that need for intimacy. And men do things side by side. And they don't have to look at each other when they're *davening* . . . they just have to be doing the choreography of prayer together.

Sherry seems to be critical yet tolerant of the synagogue as male space. Having grown up in a Modern Traditional Conservative family, she was accustomed to mixed seating in the synagogue. In chapter 6, I discuss struggles some of the women had in adapting to the patriarchal environments they encountered as Orthodox Jews.

The Holiness of Shabbat

While moving toward commitment, the BTs learned about the rules of Sabbath observance and were guests of Orthodox families for Shabbat meals. They picked up a great deal of cultural knowledge on these occasions. They learned that it was common to shower before the onset of Shabbat; to tape down the light switch in the refrigerator beforehand; and to keep some lights on and others off or use a timer. They also learned that they could not write, drive, use the telephone, or watch television during Shabbat, activities they had engaged in previously. The invitations to Sabbath meals persisted post-commitment, as did their learning. After commitment and, especially, after creating a religious home with a spouse, they furthered their knowledge of Shabbat by learning additional rules and, importantly, trying to create an atmosphere of *kedushah* (holiness) in their home observances.

Preparation for the Sabbath tends to fall primarily on women. They plan the meals and cook food that is sufficient for their families and their guests over three Shabbat meals: Friday evening, Saturday mid-day, and Saturday evening. They need to cook the food prior to Shabbat so they do not violate the Sabbath by lighting the stove or oven during the Sabbath. (They could, however, keep food warm by placing it on a metal sheet over the stove for the duration of Shabbat if the stove is left on low.) Women either bake their own challahs (Sabbath bread, traditionally braided) or purchase them at a kosher bakery or food store. If they make their own challahs, they have the opportunity to fulfill a mitzvah of breaking off a small piece of dough, reciting a special blessing, and burning the dough in remembrance of a gift made to the priests in Temple times.

Women usher in the Sabbath by lighting candles. This must be done before sundown by a specific time, which changes every Friday. Women interviewed for this study found that candle lighting was an especially meaningful experience for them. Allison, for example, described taking her time lighting the candles as follows:

> Candle lighting for me is a whole spiritual experience. I mean I take a good fifteen minutes to light candles . . . that's my time. You know what it's like. You're racing around, everything, and then, ah, it's done! Right. And you make the *brachah*, and I cover my eyes and then I'm just talking to Hashem the next ten minutes easily. And, I'm thanking Him.

Allison was explaining how candle lighting helps her transition into Shabbat. There is a prescribed prayer to be said after lighting the candles, but some women add personal prayers during this time. Once the candles are lit, Shabbat begins for the family. The men and some children usually go to *shul* to recite the *Kabbalat Shabbat* (welcoming the Sabbath) service and then *maariv* (evening service) prior to dinner.

Traditionally, the meal is preceded by the song "Shalom Aleichem," a song of peace. In some homes, the husband recites or sings "*Eishet Chayil*," a chapter from the book of Proverbs honoring his wife as well as the Sabbath Queen. Then a blessing is said over each child ("May you be like Ephraim and Menashe," two of Jacob's grandsons; or "May you be like Sarah, Rebecca, Rachel, and Leah," the matriarchs), an experience participants also described as spiritually elevating. Next is the recitation of the kiddush (a prayer sanctifying the Sabbath over wine), and, after ritually washing hands, recitation of a blessing prior to eating the challah. The Sabbath meals are usually eaten at a table set with a white tablecloth and fine china. The meals have several courses in which special foods are served. Some families sing *zemirot* (or *zemiros*, songs) during or after the meal. Annie said, "I feel particularly connected to *Hakadosh Baruch Hu* (the Holy One) when we're singing *zemiros*." At the conclusion of the meal, the group recites *birkat hamazon*, a prayer of thanks over the blessing of having food.

For the BTs, Shabbat (or Shabbos) was meaningful to themselves and to their families, and important for their connections with others in the community. Ruth, observant thirteen years, described Shabbat as "probably the most nourishing spiritual thing that I feel." It is also a time when families spend time together eating, going to synagogue, talking, and learning. Some discuss the week's Torah portion and give a *d'var Torah* (lesson drawn from the Torah). Just as they were Shabbos guests of others when they were exploring Orthodox Judaism, they often invite guests for the Sabbath meals.

Considering the centrality of Shabbat and the need for advance planning, *baalei teshuvah* anticipate this day with great excitement. Sherry spoke of the evolution of her appreciation for Shabbat from the time she was becoming observant to the present:

> I saw people who love *Shabbos*. And, you know, I was into it while I was in their houses but it just wasn't for me. And so, one day I had decided, all right, we'll try it. We'll see what it's like. And it just grew, from one week to the next week to the next week, now I live for *Shabbos*. I live for *Shabbos* now.

In contrast, Baila said, "I don't get the spiritual high on Shabbos that I'm supposed to be getting." In a different sense, Allen, an academic, spoke of Shabbat as beneficial to him but not in the way he thinks it should be:

> Now what I worry about religiously is I think that, in many respects, I see *Shabbos* in particular as good for my work because it rests me up so that I can really go back into the work world. And I wonder whether I will reach a point where . . . I can really enjoy *Shabbos* because *Shabbos* is really the focus of the week. I think I've still got it backwards. I think to me work is the focus of the week and on *Shabbos* I rest up for the next [work week].

Neither Baila nor Allen, both *frum* for over twenty years, made the shift from their secular concerns to making Shabbat a central spiritual experience. Each sees this as a shortcoming.

Regardless of their ability to appreciate Sabbath, the BTs were observing it at home and in the community. Almost everyone spoke of Sabbath as significant. It brought their families together in a meaningful way and, they said, it brought them closer to God. As Zvi, observant fifteen years, remarked, observing Shabbat, as well as daily engagement with Orthodox people and Judaism, keeps you connected to Judaism:

> I eat kosher, and pretty much the only people I talk to . . . are *frum* people . . . my kids are in Torah schools, and all the books are Jewish. So, I mean, my daily life expresses itself in a religious way all the time. I'm always running into it. Got to *daven*, got to put the *tzitzis* on, got to make sure the *mezuzah's* up, you know. Friday afternoon you got to stop painting the house. So . . . you keep running into ways of having a relationship with God, because, that's what the *halachos* do to you. Can I do this, can I not do that? And, you're constantly in somewhat of a religious state even when you're not.

Summary

After making a commitment to be Orthodox, *baalei teshuvah* have additional hurdles to overcome. They are novices, lacking deep knowledge and experience about living out their commitment. Although they did acquire some knowledge while they were seriously thinking about becoming *frum*, they needed to know more about the religious practices, laws, and religious culture they have joined. They also needed to know how to apply the knowledge they had attained. This required socialization by insiders within Orthodox communities.

Many of the BTs were able to obtain spiritual guidance from rabbis, rebbetzins, teachers, and members of the community they met and befriended. Some of these individuals gave classes and/or invited the *baalei teshuvah* to their homes where the BTs could observe the living out of Orthodox Judaism and ask questions. Still, the men and woman needed to improve their mastery of Hebrew, and the men wanted to learn Aramaic. Hebrew is the language of prayer and some sacred texts. The Talmud (*Gemara*), which is venerated by those who were raised Orthodox, is in Aramaic as well as Hebrew. Both men and women expressed feelings of inadequacy in their knowledge of Hebrew, but more men than women felt pressured to be knowledgeable. Men were expected to pray three times a day, preferably with a *minyan*, leaving them in a situation in which their deficiencies in Hebrew could be observed by others. Women expressed both positive and negative feelings about praying privately and at synagogue. It appeared to be less significant to them than to the men. Besides improving their language skills, the BTs furthered their education by attending classes, studying with a study partner, reading books, and listening to audio recordings.

Most of the BTs found mentors, role models, and others in the Orthodox community who served as socializing agents or spiritual guides. They answered the BTs' questions, invited them to their homes for Shabbat meals, and directed them to resources that could help them remedy their deficiencies. Still the novices, especially the men, appeared to find the demands from their new environment stressful. They encountered norms they had not anticipated, such as the emphasis on lifelong study, and were frequently in environments in which they felt lacking in knowledge and skills. Although they may have been experts in their chosen professions, they were neophytes as Orthodox Jews.

Chapter 5

Marriage, Parenting, and Relations with the Family of Origin

In addition to increasing their knowledge and skills in the practice of Judaism, discussed in chapter 4, the *baalei teshuvah* become socialized to new norms about marriage and family, another paradigm shift. In this chapter, I focus on their family lives. Whether they were single, already married, or previously married when they did *teshuvah*, their religious-spiritual changes became particularly salient in their lives as single and married individuals, as parents, and as adult children of their own parents. They found that they could not follow the example set by their non-Orthodox parents and thus had to find new role models and acquire new knowledge about marriage and parenting. In addition to struggling with incorporating religious practices into their lives, they had to consider others whose lives they affected and the norms of their religious communities. This chapter discusses the challenges the men and women who became Orthodox faced in relation to marriage, parenting, and family relations.

Marriage

For Orthodox Jews, marriage is a central aspect of life and a key context in which to live out the commandments and further spiritual growth. Developmentally, marriage is associated with Erikson's stage of *intimacy vs. isolation* and Levinson's "settling down."

The BTs in this study grew up in a society in which practices around dating and marriage that are common in the secular world conflict with teachings of the Torah. With contraceptives easily available and the fear of unwanted pregnancy diminished, some young people have brief "hookups" as recreation (Taylor, 2013), casual and extended affairs, or non-marital, live-in relationships. Increasingly, marriage between same-sex partners has become accepted. Many Jews are married to non-Jewish partners. All these practices—birth control, sex outside of marriage, cohabitation, same-sex marriage, and interfaith marriage—are objectionable in BTs' new communities. Some interviewees had had casual and extended non-marital sexual relationships in the past that caused them shame.

In Orthodox communities, dating is a serious matter, pursued for the purpose of marriage. Early in the dating process, the individuals discuss what they are looking for in a marriage partner, the kind of home they would like to establish, how they want to raise their children, and their life goals. For example, they might talk about the level of stringency they want to maintain, their attitude toward higher education in secular universities, and the kind of community in which they want to live. Marriage is the pathway to fulfillment of one's mission in life as well as the structure within which to raise children (Ner le-elef, "The Jewish View of Marriage," n.d.).

Traditionally it is believed that God decides who will marry whom. One marries one's *beshert* (predestined partner) or *ezer k'negdo* (soul mate) with whom one builds "an eternal soul connection" (Ner le-elef, "The Jewish View of Marriage," p. 1). In practice, a matchmaker (*shadkhan*) or another intermediary who is acquainted with eligible individuals and their families introduces potential partners and monitors their process of meeting each other and deciding whether they are interested in pursuing the match. Lebovits (1987) draws a distinction between *shidduch* and *zivug*. The term *shidduch* (plural, *shidduchim*) is used to describe the process of introducing two people for the purpose of serious dating that has the potential to lead to marriage, whereas "*zivug* is Hashem's assignment of a specific mate to a person" (Lebovits, 1987, p. 2). God is regarded as the matchmaker-in-chief but the parties to a match need to be receptive to prospective candidates. Lebovits (1987) recommends that the parties, families, or intermediaries investigate the backgrounds of prospective matches to assess their character and that of their respective families.

Study participants who were single when they became *frum* sought marital partners who were similarly oriented toward Orthodox Judaism, with most marrying other BTs. Marriage to another Orthodox person was an expression of one's commitment to be *frum*. Besides considering the religious orientation of a prospective partner, some BTs had to come to terms with personal issues that entered into their wish to get married. As Dov said:

> My parents are divorced. . . . They weren't the best role models
> for me. Am I gonna make the same mistakes in marriage or am
> I gonna be a good husband, a good father, a good provider, and
> learn from the past and break a bad cycle? And I think . . . a
> man who comes from a divorced background, parents divorced
> background, sometimes will question that. And I definitely am
> somebody who . . . fit into that category of somebody who said,
> you know, I want to change the past, I want to . . . do better in
> raising my own family.

In addition to coming from a divorced parents background, his family fell
into the Minimalist Plus category. Dov began his journey of changing the
past when he insisted on attending a Jewish day school.

Most of the *baalei teshuvah* interviewed for this study met their partners
in Jewish contexts or through friends. The Jewish contexts included synagogue,
Hillel, Israeli dancing, Jewish summer camp, and a university's kosher dining facility. They met during college, in Israel, or at work. A few referred to
a match made by a friend as a *shidduch*. Some of those who were involved
with outreach organizations or attended a yeshiva or seminary at the time
they were looking for a spouse met prospective partners through the "*shidduch*
system," in which they were matched with pre-screened individuals.[1] Several
people who worked through this system describe their experiences as "hard,"
"horrible," "unpleasant," or "rough." A few mentioned that they found the rule
about *negiah* (physical contact) challenging during the dating and courtship
period, as touching is barred. It was difficult for some to find an appropriate match because criteria such as secular higher education and professional
standing that are valued in the secular world were no longer important. As
Ben, who had a Ph.D., said about his experience dating within an Orthodox
Jewish community:

> Dating was a hard thing about being religious, because it was a
> different paradigm. [I was] set up on dates, and I wasn't used to
> that. And plus, your résumé's not as good anymore. When I wasn't
> religious, my résumé was pretty good. . . . But now, once you're
> religious, things that you felt were high points were no longer
> your high points anymore [laughter].

Like Ben, some of the men found that their lack of a yeshiva education,
deficiencies in Hebrew, and *baal teshuvah* status were disqualifiers for some

prospective partners. Other participants were turned off by potential spouses whose religious comportment was alien to them. Sherry, who was studying in a women's yeshiva in Israel at the time she experienced a strong desire to marry, described her experience thus:

> I decided at that point that I wanted to get married. So I just told everybody I wanted to get married, and did they know anybody for me? And all my friends from Habonim [youth group] thought that was intensely uncool, 'cause you don't tell people that you want to get married . . . but that's what I did. And I went to the rebbetzin of the *yeshiva*, and I said to her, "Rebbetzin _____, I'd like to get married." She said to me, "How old are you?" I said, "I'm 23." She said, "Well, you're no spring chicken but we'll see what we can do." And so I dated one of her sons and I remember going out to the hills of Jerusalem with him and . . . he sat on one rock facing the other way. And I sat on the rock facing nothing. And we had this conversation; he wouldn't even look at me. And I'm sitting there saying to myself, "What am I doing here? This is not for me." So we had one date [and] that was it.

This story is atypical in that it is required by Jewish law that a man see his bride before marrying her (B. Moskoff, personal communication), but it is possible that the boy had already decided that he was not interested in marrying her and thus looked away. Regardless, this is an example of a poor cultural match between a Haredi youth and a modern American woman. Shortly thereafter Sherry found her *beshert* in a man from her hometown who was in Israel the same time as she.

An unmarried interviewee who talked about her dating experience explained how difficult it was for her to find a suitable cultural match. When asked how she relates to people who were raised Orthodox, Batya, 31, said:

> Well, that's a real challenge I find. And I can speak mostly of it through dating. That I've dated FFB boys and they just come from a totally different world and a totally different mindset. I just feel like by coming from such a secular background, by really valuing a lot of things in the secular world like art and theater and a lot of different things, and choosing to give up so many things puts me in just a completely different place intellectually and developmentally.

For the most part, the BTs in this study married other BTs. This is partially due to attitudes of those who were raised Orthodox and partly the cultural similarity between *baalei* and *baalot teshuvah*. *Baalei* and *baalot teshuvah* are subject to criticism within the *frum* community for lacking *yichus*, an esteemed family lineage of observance, such as having a parent who is a well-known Orthodox rabbi or community leader. Several BTs spoke of marrying someone whose background was similar to theirs. Nora, for example, married a man whose parents, like hers, were Hungarian. She described having "a very strong affinity to him as if like he was my soul mate." A woman who had been active in a Jewish youth organization during high school married a man who had been active in the same organization.

Marriage provided an incentive for some participants to become Orthodox. Impressed with Orthodox families and individuals they met at Shabbat dinners, they saw opportunities to meet single men and women through these connections. For example, Ariella was so impressed with dinner guests of her BT brother that she wanted to follow suit:

> And to be perfectly candid, I think some of it, some of my motivation for becoming *frum* was in order to find a partner. Because I saw what was happening . . . in the general community and it was nothing. And also . . . my brother . . . he always attracted men who had values and were stable and intelligent, and I thought, "Oh, I want one of those."

After moving to her brother's community and making friends, several people recommended that she meet a particular man, whom she would eventually marry. A rabbi was the intermediary. Other BTs for whom marriage was an inducement had met potential spouses who were more observant than they before becoming a *baal teshuvah*. Uri, for example, met his future wife in Israel where both were spending their junior year abroad. He gradually followed her into Orthodoxy. Another participant, Dov, met his future wife at the home of Orthodox friends. Although he was moving toward keeping Shabbat and kosher when he met her, she wanted him to do more learning before she would marry him. Eager to marry her, he moved ahead with his learning and increased his observance.

The preferred Orthodox Jewish pattern is to have a short courtship and a short period between the engagement and marriage (Lamm, 1979). This is to prevent premarital relations. Among the interviewees who were *frum* when they married, a few became engaged after a couple of weeks and were married a few months later, whereas others waited a year or more. Those with relatively long engagement periods were guided by practical considerations such as completing college or graduate school. A few who had asked their prospective marriage partner to study in an Israeli institution before they would consent to the marriage were wed soon after he or she returned.

During the course of courtship, engagement, and preparation for marriage, some BTs came to realizations that something about their behavior or history was not acceptable. Ezra, who was cohabiting with his fiancée while they were in the midst of their journey, moved out of their shared residence after being told that this was not appropriate. Another man, Allen, realized that his circumcision, performed at a hospital after he was born, was not a religiously sanctioned *bris*. Because he was already circumcised, his case involved only drawing a little blood. A couple of weeks before he was married, a *mohel* (officiant for the *bris*) performed the procedure.

Of the 44 BTs who were married at the time of their interviews, thirty-five (79.5 percent) were in first marriages and nine (20.5 percent) were on their second or third. Those who were divorced from a Jewish partner were required to obtain a *get*, a Jewish divorce, before they could remarry in a religious ceremony. This necessitated the consent and cooperation of a former marriage partner, an appearance before a religious court (*bet din*), and a waiting period. Obtaining a *get* can extend the length of the courtship period.

In many Orthodox communities, engaged couples separately take *kallah* (bride) and *chosson* (or *chatan*, groom classes [B. Moskoff, personal communication]). These classes address the laws of family purity (*taharat hamishpachah*), referring to the requirements of separation when a woman is menstruating, and immersion in a mikveh seven days after she ceases having any bloody discharge, after which they can resume relations. The classes also cover other topics, such as marital harmony, sex education, and modesty. It is notable that none of the participants in this study mentioned taking *kallah* or *chosson* classes prior to getting married, although one said that she learned about going to the *mikveh* before she was married. Several women, however, said that they attended classes on *taharat hamishpachah* after they were married.

It is customary for Orthodox couples to have an engagement party, usually an informal celebration known as *L'chaim* (to life) a few months prior to the wedding (B. Moskoff, personal communication). A formal betrothal ceremony is incorporated into the wedding ceremony (Lamm, 1979). The traditional Orthodox wedding consists of several components (Lamm, 1979). The bride and groom, who usually fast on their wedding day until after the ceremony, greet guests in separate areas of the wedding hall. The bride sits on a throne, where she may recite psalms and give and receive blessings. The marriage contract (*ketubah*) is signed at the groom's table in front of two observant witnesses. After the signing of the *ketubah*, the mothers of the bride and groom (or a substitute if the mother is absent or deceased), partake in a ceremony in which they hold a plate together and break it—a way of affirming the commitment. Subsequently the groom, followed by a procession of men, enters the bride's section of the wedding hall. Here the veiling ceremony (*bedeken*) takes place. Reminiscent of the biblical story of Jacob unwittingly marrying the veiled Leah instead of her sister Rachel, the groom lifts the veil from the bride and then returns it to cover her face. Afterward, the wedding party proceeds to the wedding canopy (*chuppah*) where the formal ceremony takes place, while the guests move to seats set aside for them. It is customary for the bride, her mother, and the groom's mother to walk around the groom seven times before any blessings are recited. Then blessings over wine are recited, and the bride and groom sip from it. Next, the groom places the wedding band on the bride's finger and says in Hebrew, "Behold you are sanctified (betrothed) to me with this ring, according to the Law of Moses and Israel." Then an honored guest reads the *ketubah* aloud. This is followed by the recitation of the seven blessings (*sheva berakhot*) and the bride and groom's drinking of a second cup of wine. At this point, the groom steps on and breaks a glass wrapped in a cloth napkin, marking the end of the formal ceremony. Traditionally the guests then shout "Mazal tov!" The newly married couple then leaves the *chuppah* and proceeds to a special room (*cheder yichud*) where they are alone. Besides having a quiet moment to be alone together, they also break their fast. When they return, the guests greet them with excitement. As illustrated in the vignette opening the introduction, the traditional Orthodox wedding has men and women seated in separate sections divided by a *mechitzah*, a partition between the men's and women's sections. Except for certain dances involving lifting the bride and groom on chairs, the men dance with men on the men's side and the women dance with women in the women's section. It is considered a great *mitzvah* to entertain the bride and groom, and the guests do so enthusiastically. Marilyn, a relatively recent *baalat teshuvah*, portrayed the Orthodox weddings she attended as follows:

> When you go to a normal wedding, a Jewish wedding, in a Conservative or a Reform or whatever . . . and there's a wonderful party, and people are happy . . . it does not have the spark that an Orthodox wedding does. Even though, in most cases, men are

sitting separately from women, and the dancing is separate, men and women do not dance together . . . the electricity is there. It's unbelievable! It takes your breath away! It absolutely takes your breath away!

Although most of the married participants recorded their marriages on the timelines they constructed during their interviews and discussed growth that followed, they devoted little attention to the wedding. One man, Paul, mentioned that his wedding had separate seating for men and women, which his mother enjoyed but a relative found objectionable. Another man, Seth, said that his wedding had separate dancing but no *mechitzah*. Three participants mentioned having celebratory dinners during the week following the wedding, which traditionally conclude with the same seven blessings (*sheva berakhot*) recited at the chuppah. (The meals are in fact referred to as "sheva berakhot" or "sheva brachos"). One BT mentioned that he did not know about this practice until after they had made plans for their honeymoon, whereas another spoke of complications—her father's death two days after the wedding—that interfered with this process.

Being Married

Regardless of the length of their courtship, marriage was a major life change. Those who had been spiritual wanderers or married late spoke of being more content now that they had settled down. Thirty-seven years old and a relatively new BT, Erica, who experienced a great deal of upheaval during her childhood and struggled during her spiritual seeking, enumerated aspects of her new life that have helped her attain a satisfying life structure (Levinson, 1978), that is: "being in a relationship, being in this community . . . and having the time and energy and resources to take advantage of a lot of what we have here. For example, the *shiurim*, community involvement, our wonderful *shul* that has really done a lot for (for my husband ane me)." Like others, Erika found that being married in an Orthodox community helped her "settle down" (Levinson, 1978), offering her the structure, security, and predictability that she lacked in the past.

Susan, who also experienced instability in her life as a single woman, and was newly Orthodox when she got married, spoke of marriage as a "fresh start":

When I was 32, we got married. And I wanted to bring whatever I was learning with me into . . . my marriage, into my house. So I had somebody come to this house and *kasher* the house and help me with the *mezuzos* and everything like that. And I wanted to get a new start, a fresh start, and I knew what I wanted.

Marilyn characterized her relationship with her husband as "best friends." Remarried and newly Orthodox late in life, she described a mutually supportive and growth-enhancing marital relationship. Their relationship is in keeping with the idea that the Jewish marriage is "a way to take two mature human beings and perfect them through a relationship of committed benevolence over the course of their life together" (Ner le-elef, "The Jewish View of Marriage," p. 18). Cheryl spoke of marriage generating "religious zeal," while Adam said that he is beginning to see his relationship with his wife as "my primary way of relating to God."

Whereas some couples began their marriages committed to being *frum*, others became observant in the course of their marriages. For example, Marcia and her husband began to explore Orthodox Judaism after they married, had children, and had successfully launched their careers. As they moved along in their journeys, Marcia and her husband were in different places. One day, Marcia came home wearing a *sheitel* (wig), shocking her husband, who insisted that she return it, as he was not ready to have her cover her hair in the way many Orthodox women do. Reflecting on this event, Marcia said, "My family thought I was really getting overboard, and I probably was." This woman was in the midst of what some BTs called the "BT high," when they become very excited over their new learning and want to apply it to their lives. At the time of her interview (five years after this event), she and her husband were seeking a comfortable balance in their learning and observances. Her husband was then *davening* every morning and attending *shiurim* twice a week.

Some couples began their marriages while in different places in their religious orientation and struggled with maintaining a balance. Susan, who spoke of her wanting a "fresh start," was studying with a Chabad rabbi when she got married in her early thirties. More interested in observance than her husband, she pulled him along. For a while, however, they backtracked. Yet when their children were school age, she talked her husband into enrolling them in a religious day school. Once her husband consented, he joined her in her journey. Reflecting on this, Susan said, "I created a monster!" Similar to Marcia's husband's reaction to her wearing a *sheitel*, Susan described her husband as going "overboard." At the time of Susan's interview, she was losing interest while her husband was spending a great deal of time at their synagogue:

> It caused a lot of problems with *shalom bayis* [peace in the home].
> You know, it still is at this point causing some problems, see,
> because he seems to be, for somebody who didn't want to do this
> at all, he is now going crazy and I'm going back, I'm not liking
> it as much anymore. I'm, at this point, I'm getting bored with it.

Frum for eight years, Susan seems to have had fluctuations in her religious enthusiasm. As her statement suggests, it is sometimes difficult for couples to remain in the same place with regard to level of observance.

Others, too, reported strains related to different orientations. Arthur, *frum* for twelve years, said that his wife is more to the right than he is. He has some ideas that are left over from his Reform upbringing that sometimes clash with hers. Eliza, *frum* for nineteen years, remarked that for a long time she described her relationship with her second husband as an "intermarriage," as she leaned toward Conservative practices and he toward Orthodox. A rabbi advised her husband to slow down so as not to rush her. Eliza has gradually taken on mitzvahs and now describes herself as a *baalat teshuvah*.

When a spouse takes on increased religious responsibilities, family roles are affected. Liora, who had been observant six years at the time of her interview, discussed how her husband's changes have affected her:

> He really got that he needed to *daven* with a *minyan* three times
> a day. This is a major family person, didn't work that many hours,
> loved to cook and shop and to be with the kids. So I was used
> to him getting up; I slept in, he would be making breakfast for
> everybody, and getting the kids off in school, and playing with them
> before work, and I would sleep in. All of a sudden, I've got to get
> up because he's not around. And I've got to feed them and all this
> other stuff. It made a lot longer day for me, so it was more work.

In keeping with secular, egalitarian norms, Liora and her husband had flexible family roles prior to their becoming BTs. Because her husband's religious activities took him away from home at times when he was taking care of the children in the past, their relationship became gendered. In contrast, Ben and his wife shared family roles even though he did not think this was "the traditional *frum* model." Several BT women said that they were affected by a spouse's absence because of extensive learning activities. Allison, for example, had to adapt to her husband's "running out of the house going to *shiurim* constantly." On a visit after this began, Allison's mother, who saw how frustrated her daughter was, advised her to leave her husband alone because he needs this. Eventually, Allison became more tolerant. At the time of the interview, she was supportive of his meeting with four or five *chavrutahs* a week.

A key informant, a marriage counselor, said that he has known married couples in which one partner was becoming more observant than the other was and wanted the partner to follow. In counseling such a couple, he told the more observant partner, "You changed the marriage contract; you had a secular contract; therefore you should accommodate." The marriage counselor's use of the term "contract" refers to the verbal understanding the couple had before they got married about their religious observance. He commented that couples like this rarely break up but they do "live with the pain of compromise." However, one interviewee, Shimon, did separate from his wife over her giving up some religious practices. When he spoke to a rabbi about this, he was told, "Well, she's your wife. You married her, right?" "Yeah." "Okay. So, what's the question?" They did reunite but later separated again.

When asked how their partner's journey affected them, most participants spoke of differences between them at the same time they acknowledged mutual influence. Several men described their wives as more spiritual than they but they did not find that problematic. In contrast, several women portrayed their husbands as rigid, but this was not universally the case. Nora described her husband as a moderating influence on her tendency to be headstrong and emotional. Yet, she said:

> I never felt like I was in the same place as my husband at the same time. Or like I wanted him to be where I was. But at this point, that's okay. It's okay. I got over that. And I realized that it's okay and it's good, I mean, the way it is.

Nora came to accept differences between herself and her husband as the "new normal." One couple, in which the woman was pushing the man to be more observant than he wanted, had pre-marital counseling where they discussed their differences. As Uri explained:

> The rabbi who married us . . . insisted on doing marriage counseling where we kind of vetted out these issues and he said, "Look. You know, you have to do what you want to do, and you have to let him here do what he wants to do," and she's like, "Oh. Okay. Good idea." And . . . from then on . . . she's been accepting and I've been accepting and we've both . . . come closer to a middle ground.

Other participants who, like Uri, described themselves and their spouses as differentiated spoke of having different personalities but similar ideas about the kind of community they wanted to live in and how they wanted to raise their children. Some had different goals and means of achieving them. Ben, for example, saw himself in a "growing mode," needing to learn more, whereas his wife was satisfied with where she was. Maya, who connects with God through music, recognized that she and her husband had different means of achieving a spiritual connection, but there is a meeting ground:

> So it's interesting that he's very spiritual but he doesn't, I guess music isn't just spiritual for everybody. So he doesn't get that. So we do that separately. But he's much more . . . he's a regimented person. He likes schedules, and . . . I think that's why he connected well to *davening* three times a day and all that. . . . I don't do that well. I'm not a very scheduled, regimented person. So sometimes he pulls me along and that helps me, and sometimes it's a conflict. But . . . I'm influenced by the way he sits and learns the *parshah* [weekly Torah portion] every day, to prepare, and gets excited about things that he reads, you know, so we're starting to share that.

Several members of Focus Group 1 spoke about having shared the journey of becoming a *baal teshuvah* with a spouse. As one man said, "The fact that my wife was on the path with me made all the difference" because if one was slowing down, he or she was inspired by the other to push ahead. Overall, there was mutual influence between the married BTs and their spouses. Although they were not always in the same place and they were uncomfortable when one partner wanted to take on more *mitzvot* than the other, the couples were willing to find a middle ground. They accommodated to each other by slowing up, speeding up, or accepting the other's need to pursue separate goals. They faced further challenges around accommodation as parents.

Parenting

Parenting beliefs and practices are strongly influenced by the cultures in which parents were raised and in which they live (Bornstein, 2013). These cultures provide norms, values, behaviors, practices, and symbols that are shared by a collectivity and transmitted to the next generation, that is, "cultural scripts" (Bornstein, 2013). When *baalei teshuvah* become parents, they face the challenge of learning about, internalizing, and transmitting norms of their adopted culture to their children. For American Jewish parents whose own parents and culture have emphasized achievement, individualism, and secular learning, taking on new norms that put Torah in the center is a difficult transformation.

The BTs in this study felt disadvantaged because they were not raised in homes in which their parents transmitted Orthodox Judaism to them from an early age, and thus they did not know the cultural scripts, the ways insiders communicate norms (Goddard & Wierzbicka, 2004). Lacking early socialization and role models, they did not know what to teach, when, and how to convey these practices to their children. Still learning themselves, they felt inadequate to perform the job of parenting. As Karen, who had her child at age forty, said when her son was a year old:

> My biggest concern right now is my child. Neither one of us grew up with role models that we would want our child to grow up with. And it's really hard. And I'm really scared about that, and making sure that . . . he's learning what I want him to learn. And what I feel he should be. . . . I don't [know], just the stupid little things. When do you start teaching a kid *brachos*? Okay, so I can read in a book, when they start to talk, or whatever. But you know what I mean; I don't have that real life experience.

As Karen suggests, she is at a loss on how to raise a child to be *frum*. What comes naturally to those who had Orthodox parental role models is a daunting responsibility for her.

Regardless of one's religious orientation, becoming a new parent is stressful (Stamp, 2003). Parent education is not a usual part of elementary, high school, and college curricula. Suddenly one is responsible for a human life! New parents learn how to care for children from what they have observed in their parental homes, media representations, and advice from family and friends (Bornstein, 2013). They also learn from observing parents of friends. According to attachment theory, individuals draw from such sources to develop internal working models or images of how to parent (Sroufe & Fleeson, 1986). Parents also learn by doing—enacting the role and examining the consequences.

In reflecting on their journeys, participants in this study asserted that Orthodox Judaism was attractive to them because it provides a good framework, meaning system, and structure for raising children. Joshua, who objected to Hebrew School when he was a child, said that after being Orthodox for twenty-five years and seeing how well his children are developing in an

Orthodox religious environment, he is convinced that the decision to become Orthodox was correct. Nora, who became *frum* after she had a couple of children, said regretfully:

> I wish I hadn't been a *baal teshuvah* as a mother. Because . . . I feel like I was learning on my children to become *frum*. Now that they're older [21 and 18] . . . I feel like, I wish I knew then, when I was raising them, what I know now about giving and kindness and . . . what really Torah teaches.

Nora seems to be wishing she had known about *chesed* (acts of loving-kindness), *midot* (good character traits), and performing *mitzvot* (commanded actions), which she could have incorporated into her parenting had she known about them. There are, however, resources, such as parenting classes, experts in the community such as rabbis and rebbetzins, and books that provide guidelines for raising *frum* children.

Miriam Levi's (1998) *More Effective Jewish Parenting* is an example of a book that explains how to convey Torah teachings through parenting. Levi gives emphasis to the parent's ability to control her/his emotions and model Torah values. Only if parents achieve emotional control can they focus on the child's welfare and apply Torah teachings. Parents who lose control and do something they later regret or experience unhelpful negative emotions such as guilt over being a working mother are encouraged to do *teshuvah* and correct themselves. They may even apologize to their children. Levi further stresses that parents train children in *mitzvah* observance, convey love and reverence for God, protect children from harmful environmental influences, and provide moral training. She recommends teaching children to help their parents as a way of honoring them and being considerate. She also deals with special problems such as jealousy, fighting, and learning disabilities.

Many of the teachings suggested by Levi and by other sources are transmitted in the religious or yeshiva day schools that most of the BTs' children attend. Besides conveying traditional Jewish values, the schools provide a didactic education in sacred texts that were not part of the BTs' background. By grounding children in Torah from an early age, the schools prepare them for a *frum* life—socially, intellectually, morally, and behaviorally. As Jerry, who had been observant only three years, said, "We needed a school to give it to them because we didn't have the tools." The schools, then, serve in part as surrogate or supplementary parents.

The BT parents spoke of giving serious thought to decisions around their children's schooling. Some enrolled them in Orthodox-run schools when the children started school. A few of the parents switched their children from day schools run by the Conservative movement to schools under Orthodox auspices, whereas others moved them from public schools in conjunction with a move to an Orthodox neighborhood. In a couple of cases, the children asked their parents to move them to religious schools.

Allison switched her children from a Conservative school (Schechter) to an Orthodox one (which I call here "HI," for Hebrew Institute) after her son asked her to move him there. Reluctant to make the switch from a school system with which she felt comfortable, Allison discussed her feelings with her husband and parents. Her husband was ready to move all their children, and her mother said she should move only the child who asked to be moved. Allison and her husband decided to switch the child who asked for one year "as an experiment" and then decide on the others.

> And then the following year, I actually asked my European father, "Daddy, what should I do?" I presented to him the two situations. And I go, "This is what Schechter's like and this is what HI's like." And his answer to me, I will never forget, is, "They should be educated." So, what does that mean? Right? I still don't know. So I went, "Well, what do you mean by that, Daddy?" "Hebrew Institute. Send them to Hebrew Institute." So he said, "You and [husband] can always do, they're in a special kind, a certain kind of home," he said, "but the other stuff, you won't be able to do. Send them to Hebrew Institute."

Her father, who later became *frum*, seems to have grasped the source of her ambivalence—her desire for her children to have both a secular ("the other stuff") and a religious education. Allison and her husband took her father's advice.

Several interviewees asserted that enrolling their children in yeshiva day schools affected them and their families. Parents whose practices were not on the same level as that observed at the school became more observant so that their children would experience consistency and not be ashamed. Shifra stopped watching television to be in line with the level of religiosity her son learned at his school. Maya, who had lost religious fervor after her divorce and contemplated reversing her path, found herself being pulled back by her children:

I was 34, something like that. But, what I noticed was that my children, and who they were becoming religiously, because of being at [Hebrew Institute], they were a grounding and an anchor, so that no matter where I went, if I started to go off the derech, I was pulled back for them. I would never, you know, change anything for them, and I don't think they ever knew that I went through that.

Parents who moved their children into an Orthodox environment after the children had been in public school or a Conservative day school for a number of years faced resistance from their children. One mother reported having conflicts with her daughter over the dress code observed in Orthodox communities and school. Her daughter wanted to wear blue jeans and objected to wearing skirts. The timing of parents' becoming *baalei teshuvah* has an impact on their children. A member of Focus Group 1 who, together with his wife, became Orthodox after two of their children were living independently, said that they raised their first set of children as non-observant, left-wing Zionists and the later set as *frum*.

Early in the process of becoming Orthodox, Liora and her husband experienced a "spiritual shock" (see chapter 2) when they learned that they were supposed to raise their children with Torah learning at the center. Liora recalled:

We spent a lot of time over *Shabbos* reading, and some things we read said that boys really are supposed to learn and not have a job. We shouldn't be encouraging them to think about a profession. Not having been raised *frum*, this isn't something that comes second nature to us. We're always thinking about, oh, he'd be good doing this, this would be natural for him, he could make a lot of money doing it, it wouldn't be a lot of hours. . . . So . . . as we were reading [we realized] that's not the way we should be looking at them. We should be looking at where they're going to learn, and we should be doing everything now to prepare them so that they don't have these other things that they're thinking about. They shouldn't be thinking about making a living, they shouldn't be thinking about a video game. . . . We should give them the environment of Torah.

Raising children in a Torah-centered way is an enormous challenge to *baalei teshuvah* who have been molded by the secular world and its educational and occupational status system. It means turning away from goals that they had for themselves (most of the participants are accomplished professionals or business people) and instilling their children with different values and goals. This process entails a radical shift in a parent's thinking and actions.

Several parents reflected on how meaningful it was for them to learn with their children. In keeping with Erikson's (1959/1980) concept of generativity (from his stage of *generativity vs. stagnation*), they were giving to, guiding, and nurturing the next generation. For these parents, generativity had a Jewish character, transmitting Jewish knowledge to their children and potentially their grandchildren. *Frum* for three years, Jerry said, "If I can provide the right foundation for my children and they could teach their children and other people, then I've done my job."

The parents also learned *from* their children. Their children brought home ideas and practices with which the parents were unfamiliar. Considering that the children were absorbing so much knowledge at their religious schools, most of the parents were behind them in learning. This inequality in knowledge motivated some fathers to move rapidly ahead in their Gemara studies so that they could study with their sons. Eli, the father of two sons, said:

> I really want to know, be more involved with learning. . . . I feel like this [is a] big thing . . . now [that] I have these sons, and . . . it was always like . . . some idyllic picture of father and the son learning together. I mean, like now we do that . . . with *parshah* and stuff, but you know I want to be . . . prepared by the time they start learning *gemara* [so] that I'll be like right there with them.

Another father, whose son is learning in a kollel, an advanced yeshiva for married men, said that when they study together over the phone, his son "can learn rings around me."

Despite the pride parents took in their children's knowledge, some parents expressed concern about their children's moving too far to the right. This created anxiety for parents who had advanced secular education, saw themselves as Modern Orthodox or right of Modern Orthodox, and wanted their children to espouse some of the same values. Shifra, for example, wants her son to be open-minded, as does Lauren, who would like her children "to know what's going on in the outside world" and for "them to experience what life has." Sarah, whose son was studying to be a Torah scholar in Israel, said, "To be honest, I would prefer that he did have a trade, a profession." These parents were concerned about the insularity of the children's schools and the emphasis on Torah learning over secular studies that would prepare them for a profession or field of work that would produce a higher income. In an earlier chapter I pointed out that Orthodox Judaism in the United States has moved to the right (Heilman, 2005, 2006; Soloveitchik, 1994), which is reflected in the religious day schools the children of BTs attend and the goals some of the graduates pursue afterward.

Although some of the parents expressed reservations about their children's goals, their identification with the American ideology of individualism seemed to restrain them from objecting strongly. Deborah mentioned that when her nineteen-year-old son said, "I might end up Conservative," she said, "You have to do what your heart tells you what to do." Lauren wondered whether she has a right to expect her children to stay *frum*, considering that she did not follow the path her parents chose for her. Brian asserted that he it is up to his children to choose a path that is right for them and hopes they will explore the available options. Yet, he added, "I'll try to be open to whatever they choose, and pray that they make choices that are in alignment with my choices."

Another aspect of the parents' perception of their children is that their children were raised Orthodox, meaning that for those whose parents were already *frum* at the time of their birth, the children were *frum* from birth (FFB). As Sarah, *frum* for twenty-two years, said to her interviewer, her practically FFB children have not had to struggle in the ways she and the *baalat teshuvah* interviewer did:

> And that's how I feel that this whole process is, that it's a challenge for you and I, but for our kids, because this is their lifestyle since they were almost born [*frum*] . . . but they don't have to work as hard as we do in the challenges of having to have been in two different worlds.

In addition, others mentioned that the children of BTs do not experience the excitement of discovering Judaism that their parents experienced.

For the most part, the *baalei teshuvah* in this study conveyed positive feelings about parenting. Several, like Allison and Brian, described parenting as spiritually uplifting. Allison remarked:

> Spiritual moments for me is every morning watching my girls walk out the door. And knowing that this is the last year they're together here, walking out the door. And, I know that it's a simple act, but I just watch them walk out the door together, and for me that's spiritual, and I just look at that and I go, thank God,

to me that's a *nes* [miracle], that I can watch them walk out the door every day. And get on a school bus.

Brian noted:

Raising children is by far the most challenging and joyful combination of experiences that God could ever bestow on people. In my opinion, it's the most humbling and the most inspiring, for me, and sometimes the most overwhelming part of my life. Thank God, we have six kids.

Their role as parents also created a significant link between themselves and their parents and siblings.

Relations with Family of Origin

The families of origin of the *baalei teshuvah* were described previously in chapter 1. As I explained there, most of the families were intact and identified with Jewish institutions or culture while the participants were growing up. At the time of the interviews, some parents were deceased, divorced, or widowed and all their children (BTs and their siblings) had left home for marriage or independent living. A few of the widowed or divorced parents had remarried. Thus, the families of origin were at the stage of "families in later life" where the emotional process had to do with "accepting the shifting of generational roles" (Carter & McGoldrick, 1989, p. 15). This stage is characterized by parents' retirement, becoming grandparents, loss of a spouse and other losses, and, in some cases, declining health and dependence. The parents relinquish old roles and take on different ones. At the time their children became Orthodox, however, some of the parents were at the previous stage of "launching children and moving on," when they faced the challenge of accepting multiple exits and entrances into the family system (Carter & McGoldrick, 1989, p. 15), that is, children leaving the home and the addition of new members, sons- and daughters-in-law and grandchildren. Thus, the time when the BTs became Orthodox was a time in which the BTs and their families of origin were in the process of changing their structures and the way in which they related to each other. Parents and their adult children separate and pursue differentiated lives.

In prior research in which mothers of *baalot teshuvah* and their daughters were interviewed about their reactions to a daughter's becoming *frum* in different national settings, Roer-Strier and I found changes in the mothers' reported initial responses as compared with their responses over time. The results varied, depending on the population we studied, but in most cases mothers became more ambivalent over time. In a study of South African mothers and daughters, the mothers reacted primarily with ambivalent and positive feelings at first and over time became more ambivalent and less positive (Roer-Strier & Sands, 2001). In a similar study of mothers who lived in the United States and BT daughters who had immigrated to Israel, we found that mothers were primarily negative and secondarily positive in the beginning but over time became more positive and ambivalent (Sands & Roer-Strier, 2004). In another study that includes mothers and daughters, both of whom lived in the United States, the results were similar to those of the U.S.-Israel study (Sands & Roer-Strier, n.d.). Argentine mothers started off mostly negative and ambivalent and became mostly ambivalent and positive (Sands & Roer-Strier, n.d.). Clearly, attitudes change after increased exposure.

In the study described in this book, we did not ask participants specifically about their parents' feelings and reactions to their religious change, but almost everyone addressed this when asked about their relationships at various periods in their timelines. The few who did not discuss this had lost their parents before they became Orthodox. The predominant parental initial reaction to the religious change was displeasure. BTs said that their parents "freaked out," were "appalled," or were "shocked." Reportedly, parents used terms such as "nuts" or "crazy," implicating their adult child's mental health. Parents were said to have expressed concern about what their child was getting into, wondering whether it was a cult. One participant said that his parents sent him to a psychologist to see whether he needed to be deprogrammed. Another said that her father thought she had been brainwashed. A few parents conveyed negative attitudes toward Orthodox people (e.g., "dirty") and did not want their child to become "too Jewish." The mildest reported negative reaction was by three sets of parents who initially thought (or hoped) it was a passing phase.

Participants spoke about parents' difficulties understanding the type of Judaism their children had adopted: "They didn't get it" or were "clueless." Furthermore, parents seemed baffled by their children's refusal to eat non-kosher food and allow the grandchildren to eat at homes that were not kosher. As Maya said:

> With my children, my mother could not understand why they had to eat kosher in her house. Because "What do they know?" You know, so she wouldn't get it. It took a long time, she would always

prepare a stew or something in a pot, and then give it, want to give it to the children and I said, "They can't eat it. It's cooked in your pots." And she just didn't understand it.

Several participants told similar stories about parents' difficulties understanding why their *baal teshuvah* children were so inflexible about *kashrut*, and the parents' feeling insulted over their not accepting food. Another aspect of Orthodox life that parents reportedly complained about was Shabbat. Karen spoke about her parents' objecting to her being unavailable by telephone on that day:

My mother couldn't understand [that] even if she calls me on *Shabbos* I'm not going to answer. "But I'm your mother" . . . "Isn't that more important?" "How can God tell you not to answer your mother's phone call?" . . . Trying to manipulate, you know, she knew enough about *kibud av va'em* even though she wouldn't call it *kibud av va'em*, she called it honoring your parents. Well, how can you honor your parents if you're not going to answer the phone?

Parents who spent Shabbat with their BT children had objections that went well beyond being inconvenienced. Joel's mother reportedly stopped staying with them for Shabbat because, unlike his *frum* but more flexible brother, Joel will not tolerate her turning lights on and off. His mother also objects when Joel's child tells her what she should or should not do on Shabbat. Two participants described explosive events during Passover seders, when family members could not tolerate the restrictions and could not wait to leave and eat bread. Shabbat and holidays spent together provide occasions when cultural differences within the family come to the surface.

Several *baalei teshuvah* recalled parents' questioning them. Some parents who considered themselves knowledgeable said that the customs were strange and outdated. For example, when one mother heard about *shidduchs*, she reportedly said, "That's so old fashioned. . . . People still do that?" A father asked his son when he was going to trim his beard. Participants also reported being questioned about the immutability of Jewish laws and having arguments that ended badly. It was difficult for parents with scientific training to understand their children's beliefs, and it was challenging for BTs to give rational explanations to their horrified parents.

Participants offered interpretations of their parents' objections. Batya, who grew up in a Mainstream Reform family, said that her mother views her becoming Orthodox as "a rejection of who she is and her Judaism. She is very, very resentful. And she thinks that I think that I'm 'holier than thou.'" Other interviewees attributed their parents' attitudes to guilt and anger over depriving them of a rich Jewish education. Howard, who grew up in a Minimalist home, said that when his father realized how much Howard's soul craved for Judaism, his father became angry at himself for going along with his wife and restricting their son's exposure to Judaism. After recognizing this late in life, his father apologized and voiced pride in what his son had done.

Several participants said that their parents were supportive and, like Howard's father, proud. Sherry, whose home was Modern Traditionalist, said that her parents had always encouraged her to be creative and to follow the path shaped by her gifts "because that's what God wants you to develop." When her parents saw where their daughter's inclinations were, they encouraged her to explore further. Tamar, *frum* for twenty-four years and also from a Modern Traditionalist home, said that her parents have expressed pride to other people rather than directly to her. She depicted their words as follows:

> Very proud of her, we're proud of her. She's sticking to her convictions, she's strong about her convictions, she's doing what she thinks is right, and she does a lot of *mitzvahs*, and it's great how she helps all these people and gets involved with all these people. And even though we don't understand it all, it's great, and she's happy doing it, and dah, dah, dah.

Other participants reported that despite their parents' initial reservations, when they saw how well their grandchildren were being raised, they understood and appreciated the benefits of Orthodox Judaism more. As Liora, *frum* for six years, said of her mother:

> I know for sure now she's so happy that we've made this choice. And she sees how it's working for us, and how . . . when my family sees my kids, they understand what we're doing, and that they appreciate what we're doing and the way we're raising them in a very solid way. And I actually feel like my actual family has come back in closer.

In our study of Argentine Jewish mothers and daughters, the grandchildren, with whom the mothers of BTs wanted to be connected, served as bridges between the generations (Sands, Roer-Strier, & Strier, 2013).

Although we did not interview parents in this study, from the comments of participants it appears that parents who were initially displeased became more accepting over time. For example, Marcia said that her parents, who at first worried that she had joined a cult, became more relaxed over their daughter's religious change after she met Marcia's friends. Karen's parents, who also found it difficult to accept their daughter's religiousness at first, later became more positive. Karen put it this way:

> So now, like let's face it, how can they look at me and say there's anything wrong with what I'm doing? I have a great husband, a gorgeous child, a beautiful house, a great job, my husband has a great job, we're not, like, you know, crazy strange.

In the three cases just mentioned (Liora, Marcia, and Karen), the BTs had been observant for six to eleven years, long enough for parents to see how Orthodox Judaism was working for their children and grandchildren.

A four-year BT, Ariella said that her parents, who had a difficult time adjusting to their son becoming *frum*, gave Ariella an easier time than they did with her brother:

> They've learned to adapt, and I've learned to be more accommodating . . . as much as I can. And they've seen me become more family-oriented, so they see some value in that. And now they have a grandson! So they're thrilled! (laughs)

Likewise, Simcha told co-participants in Focus Group 1 about how his parents, influenced by the arrival of a grandchild, became more accepting than they were initially:

> It did not take to long for her to not only decide, but also . . . to *kasher* certain parts of her kitchen, and for her to have a special place [for him] to play, and for her to work within our system, would be to her benefit and ours. And then it turned out that every Shabbos they came. Every Friday night they came. And it ended up bringing us much, much closer together, even though it started off with difficulty.

The BTs also spoke about the reactions of their siblings. Ten of the forty-eight interviewees had siblings or stepsiblings that preceded or followed them into Orthodoxy, which was conducive to acceptance and relatively smooth relationships. Negative sibling reactions included being sarcastic, dismissive, or poking fun. In one case, the BT had conflicts with her sister and brother-in-law over theological issues, which led to emotional distancing. In another instance, the siblings told Greg that religion was a crutch that may have helped him but they did not want any part of it. Greg wishes that they would be "on board" with him but said sadly, "I still love my brothers and my sister, you know, [but] they just don't share that aspect, they don't want to share that central aspect of my life with me at this point." Other siblings had married partners who were not Jewish, complicating family relationships. Mordechai, from Focus Group 1, said that he avoids situations that would bring his children in contact with the children of his intermarried brother because they are not Jewish. In this case, the emotional tie to his biological brother was insufficient to overcome the intermarriage barrier, depriving his children and his brother's of this family connection.

Parents, BT children, and siblings used a variety of means to adapt to and cope with their differences. Several parents found ways to address food issues, such as using special dishes, buying special food, becoming kosher, or raising their standards of *kashrut* if they were already kosher. Three parents and, as mentioned, ten siblings identified with their religious family member by becoming *frum* themselves. *Frum* for ten years and from a Modern Traditionalist home, Allison said of her parents:

> Eventually, my parents became *shomer Shabbos*. They became *shomer Shabbos* after we did. I don't know whether to take credit for that, but there were lots of reasons; I can explain that to you if you want how they became observant. My father was raised in a European home, so it wasn't difficult for him. But my mother, you know, and she embraced it. She was a real *baal teshuvah*, my mother! She was a panic! Very proud. Very. She was out there doing *keruv* on her own. It was terrific!

One coping method mentioned in relation to siblings but also used by parents is joking, making light of something that probably bothered them. In addition, several spoke about not talking about their difficulties. Ellen, who was observant three years at the time of her interview, made a comment that is typical of families that avoided conflict:

> I guess I have a lot of conflicting and mixed feelings, to be honest. I don't let on like that, really, ever. I go visit them, and I talk to

them. Mom bought me, in fact, I just picked it up today, some tabbouleh and some hummus with a U in an O². She said, "It has a U on it!" But there's a lot . . . there's a lot that's not really discussed or said or acknowledged. I don't know, I just feel like they can't handle it. And it's so funny because they feel like I can't handle it. So meanwhile, no one really says anything really meaningful to one another.

Clearly, there are underlying issues that are disturbing to parents and children that are not addressed in a direct manner. Arguments, however, are also problematic. Some BTs cope with their alienation by seeking substitutes. As Nina, also observant three years, said:

> I think it's a pretty common thing among the *baal teshuvah* community (that) friends become the substitute to family. But as my father used to say, there's no substitute for family. It becomes a second best. And you become close, and you go through a lot of these events because they have the same issues, your friends. But it makes me sad, because I don't believe that that's the way it's supposed to be.

One can surmise from this that Nina is suffering from the loss of a close relationship with her biological family.

Baalei teshuvah with secular relatives are out of synchrony with members of their religious communities who were raised Orthodox and have multigenerational Orthodox families. Aside from having to deal with suppressed issues and intermarriages in their families, problems crop up from time to time that intrude upon their existence. For example, Susan described receiving an emergency telephone call about her father-in-law during a holiday that fell on the Sabbath when she was not supposed to use electricity:

> This *yom tov* . . . somebody kept calling and calling and calling. His father was in a rehab. I told his father ahead of time we couldn't answer the phone. But his girlfriend kept calling and she didn't know. She's not Jewish. And she didn't know. And I ended up knocking the phone off with my elbow to tell them I can't talk on the phone. And they got all mad at me, why I did that.

Susan responded to the call in this way in order to be what she considered technically in compliance with the rules of Shabbat and the holiday. Her husband and children were the ones who were angry at her for her religious transgression, but, as she later explained, the family subsequently teased her about her "breaking Shabbos." Susan seemed to feel torn between her religious obligations and the needs of her secular family.

Summary

As they live out their lives after making a commitment to Orthodox Judaism, *baalei* and *baalot teshuvah* become further socialized about norms around dating, marriage, and parenting, and try, as Orthodox Jews, to relate to their families of origin. Those who date when already Orthodox learn that dating is pursued for the express purpose of finding an appropriate marriage partner and that physical contact is not permitted. They meet potential partners in Jewish contexts or through friends, intermediaries, or the "*shidduch* system." Some become Orthodox after meeting a potential spouse who is already observant or is moving in that direction. It is considered desirable that courtships be short (Lamm, 1979).

The traditional Orthodox wedding consists of bride and groom meeting guests in separate locations, the signing of the marriage contract (*ketubah*), the veiling ceremony (*bedeken*), the formal wedding ceremony under the wedding canopy (*chuppah*), the departure of the bride and groom to a separate room (*cheder yichud*), and their return to celebrate. *Sheva berakhot* (seven blessings) are recited under the *chuppah*, after the wedding meal, and during celebrations the following week. Men and women sit in separate sections and dance separately. Few participants in this study mentioned having had weddings with all these features, but they did have some of them.

After the committed *baalei teshuvah* were married, they underwent additional life changes. They set up households in communities with large concentrations of Orthodox Jews and settled down (Levinson, 1978). Consistent with Erikson's stage of *intimacy vs. isolation*, they worked out their relationship with each other along religious lines so that they could grow as individuals and as a couple. Those couples who were already married when they became *frum* made adjustments as each of them moved at his or her own pace in taking on mitzvahs. Regardless of when they became Orthodox, couples sought a balance between them in their religious observances.

For *baalei teshuvah*, raising Orthodox children is a major challenge. Lacking parents who could be Orthodox role models, they had to find ways to learn how to raise their children. They read books, attended parenting classes, and sought role models in the community. They did this while still learning the ins and outs of living a *frum* life described in chapter 4. When their children became school age, the parents enrolled them in religious or yeshiva day schools where the children learned about how they are supposed to behave as religious children. In keeping with the generativity pole of Erikson's stage of *generativity vs. stagnation*, some parents learned with their children, creating a bond and enhancing the education of parents and children. As time went on, some parents were disturbed that the schools were socializing their children to be Torah scholars rather than professionals with secular academic educations.

Becoming Orthodox has implications for the BTs' relationships with their families of origin. As explained by participants in this study, a number of parents had negative initial reactions to their child's religious change. They were critical and lacked understanding of what their children had gotten into. Several were upset that their adult children's keeping kosher would interfere with family relationships. Yet some parents were supportive or became supportive and more understanding over time. Some siblings poked fun at their Orthodox brothers and sisters, yet a good proportion of them later became Orthodox themselves. Parents, siblings, and BTs made adaptations to maintain relationships with their Orthodox family members, including grandchildren. In some cases, the community became a substitute for family, but some *baalei teshuvah* felt sad over distant relationships with their families of origin.

Chapter 6

Spiritual and Religious Struggles

While religion and spirituality offer *baalei teshuvah* comfort, meaning, and guidelines for living, they also may be the bases for struggle and strain (Exline & Rose, 2005, 2013). During their movement toward commitment, the BTs grapple with ideas, practices, and religious requirements that conflict with their personal, familial, or secular values. After making a commitment, they may continue to have such conflicts but they also struggle when their experiences do not match the ideas and ideals that drew them to Orthodox Judaism. They may be troubled over adverse events in their lives, question the fairness of suffering, or have regrets over what they are missing in the secular world. They expected a diminution of life problems, but instead they are anguished over new ones. The biblical narrative about Jacob's wrestling with a divine being prior to meeting with his estranged brother is a paradigm for such spiritual struggles.

Exline and Rose (2005) describe four types of religious and spiritual struggles. The first type has to do with the problem of suffering; the second, with living up to the requirements of the religion; the third, with the perception that one is being attacked by supernatural forces; and the fourth, with interpersonal relationships. Whereas the first three types have to do with individuals' relationships with God, the fourth has to do with individuals' relationships with each other and the religious community (Exline & Rose, 2005). Elsewhere, Exline, Pargament, Grubbs, and Yali (2014) modify and expand upon this typology to include *divine struggle* (conflict over beliefs about a deity or a relationship with a deity); *demonic struggle* (worry about the devil or evil spirits); *interpersonal struggle* (negative experiences with religious institutions or religious people); and *intrapersonal struggle* (related to one's inner thoughts or actions). Intrapersonal struggles are over moral issues, doubts, and questions about ultimate meaning.

The spiritual/religious struggles of the *baalei teshuvah* were largely intrapersonal and interpersonal (Exline et al., 2014) but also had to do with suffering (Exline and Rose's first type; also in the authors' 2013 chapter) and the requirements of Orthodox Judaism (Exline and Rose's second type). In this chapter I discuss a variety of challenges the *baalei* and *baalot teshuvah* faced before and after they became Orthodox. I begin with a discussion of their struggles over feminist ideology, struggles that had to do with living up to religious requirements and were intrapersonal and interpersonal. Then I address challenges over infertility, illness, and death, which had to do with suffering and their relationship with God. Next, I discuss challenges to maintaining beliefs, which is followed by intrapersonal and familial issues. I conclude with a discussion of a lingering attachment to the secular world.

Struggles over Feminist Ideology

Before the participants in this study became *frum*, feminist ideas had infused public consciousness. Whether they took women's studies classes in college or learned about feminism from the media or peers, they were aware of the women's movement for equal rights in the political, economic, religious, and domestic spheres and of the constraints imposed by traditional gender roles. Some of the women, like peers, were breaking barriers by becoming doctors or lawyers or attaining high positions in the workplace.

Although there are a variety of feminist frameworks that are described in women's studies courses (e.g., liberal, socialist, and cultural feminisms), most are critical of patriarchy, the dominance of men. In some Christian feminist writings of the last quarter of the twentieth century, the patriarchy in the cultures surrounding the early Hebrews was attributed to the Jews. As Plaskow (1980, p. 11) said in her classic response to this perception, it is a myth "that the ancient Hebrews invented patriarchy" and that the patriarchal aspects of Christianity are rooted in Judaism. Even though the Hebrews did not create patriarchy, it is nonetheless present in Judaism. Within Orthodox Judaism, gender separation is normative in synagogues and children's schools, and is instituted in some celebrations, such as bar or bat mitzvah dinners and wedding parties. Men are privileged in having significant roles in religious services, such as being called to the Torah (*aliyot*) and reading from it and leading services. The quorum (*minyan*) necessary for a religious service that includes the essential components comprises ten men. Not only are women not counted in a *minyan*; in many synagogues they are expected to suppress their voices when singing. Within Orthodox communities, women's domestic role is valorized, even if the woman holds a responsible position outside the home. Women are expected to be primary caretakers of their children, prepare meals, and keep the house clean. On the path to becoming Orthodox and afterward, many women encountered practices that challenged their feminist values, struggled with the decision to commit, and/or grappled with taking on particular practices after they committed.

Most of the women interviewed in this study had difficulty taking on one or more of the religious practices that were normative for women in their Orthodox communities.[1] These included covering their hair with a headscarf (*tichel*), hat, or wig (*sheitel*); modesty in dress (*tzniut* or *tznius*); restrictions on women's singing in mixed company (*kol ishah*); and sitting behind or beside a *mechitzah* (barrier separating men and women during services in Orthodox synagogues and, less often, in other settings). On the other hand, the women took pleasure in some of the *mitzvot*, such as *chesed* (acts of loving-kindness, such as visiting the sick) and lighting Sabbath candles. Some women initially struggled over going to the *mikveh* (ritual bath), whereas others found this experience spiritually exhilarating from the beginning.

For the most part, the women who were struggling over feminist issues did not explicitly discuss the reasons for their discomfort. It is likely that they found these practices diverged from those in Reform, Reconstructionist, and Conservative communities in which they were raised. These religious movements have extended privileges such as reading from the Torah, being counted in a *minyan*, leading services, and having an *aliyah* to women. Women and men sit together in synagogues, where women may sing aloud. Women in these three movements may, if they wish, cover their heads with hats or yarmulkes (*kippot*; skullcaps); they also may wear a *tallit* (prayer shawl), worn only by men in Orthodox environments, while *davening*. Although the latter practices by women are not universally adopted by non-Orthodox women, they are frowned upon in Orthodox environments.

Struggles over modest dress and hair covering may have to do with the emphasis on women's beauty in the larger society, which women internalize. Dressing modestly means *not* wearing pants, sleeveless or short-sleeve tops, scoop-neck dresses or sweaters, and short or tight-fitting skirts. Modestly dressed Orthodox women generally wear medium to long-length skirts, blouses with sleeves covering their elbows, and closed-necks, obscuring the shape of their bodies. The requirement of covering one's hair applies to married women only. In the wider society, it is atypical to cover one's hair except perhaps when one has a "bad hair day." *Tichels* and hats favored by Orthodox women tend to cover all or most of their hair. Wigs (except for falls) cover all of it. Hair contributes to women's attractiveness[2]. The glut of ads for women's shampoo, conditioners, and hair coloring attests to the significance of hair. Women who follow Orthodox norms for dress and hair look less attractive by secular standards and may even stand out as dowdy, different, or strange. Discussing her struggles during Focus Group 2, Rachel said, "The *tznius* thing was so difficult for me, was so painful, because it really touched, you know, tapped into my identity. Who am I now if I can't wear the clothes that I wore before?"

The married women interviewed for this study spoke of struggling over covering their hair. At times, this became a source of conflict for the couple, with one party wanting her to cover her hair and the other objecting. During her interview, Deborah, *frum* for twenty-five years, spoke of consulting her rabbi before she covered her hair to find out how to do it and when. "How do I come out of the closet with all of a sudden I'm wearing a hat?" The rabbi told her "that of all the *mitzvot* this is the one that there seems to be the most regression. Women take this on and some women don't end up keeping up with it." In an article based on a study of Brazilian *baalot teshuvah*, Topel (2002) reported that most of the women she observed who kept kosher, observed Shabbat, and adhered to the laws of family purity did not cover their hair. After numerous attempts to get women to discuss this issue, she learned that they found this *mitzvah* particularly difficult, one that they took on gradually. They described a series of stages they experienced:

> In the beginning, women only accepted covering their heads while celebrating *shabbat* in the synagogue. Soon and progressively they accepted this practice on other occasions. First, this occurred in clearly Orthodox settings such as, for example, Jewish holidays, religious commemorations, and weddings. Afterwards this took place within the bounds of their households—until they finally accepted wearing the *shaitl* in public non-Jewish places. (Topel, 2002, p. 335)

Although I was not able to observe the participants in my study over time, it was clear from the transcriptions of the interviews that the *baalot teshuvah* from the United States also took on this *mitzvah* hesitantly and incrementally. Interestingly, the men we interviewed also struggled over covering their heads in public. They did not want to draw attention to themselves as Jews.

In a report on three ethnographic case studies of the covering/uncovering practices of Orthodox Jewish, Muslim, and fundamentalist Orthodox Christian women, Galman (2013, p. 436) defined "uncovering" as ceasing to hide or play down their religious identities. When women "cover" their bodies through modest dress and hair covering, they "uncover" who they are and reveal their resistance to pressures to conform to the norms of the dominant culture. Women in these three minority religious communities announce through their appearance that they choose "not to 'fit in'" mainstream culture and its assumptions. While their distinctive dress signals membership in a minority religious community and may aid their acceptance in such a community, it may also draw negative attention to themselves in the wider community. Similarly, the *baalot teshuvah* described in this book viewed covering their hair as a sign of membership and a willingness to accept the norms of the new community over those of the secular community.

Some aspects of Orthodox practice appear to oppose the egalitarian values and sense of justice that are fundamental to a democratic society. Sitting in the women's section behind a *mechitzah*, which could block their view, can be construed as tantamount to being separate and unequal. Similarly, the prohibition against women singing in the synagogue or at dinner tables where men are present can be viewed in more fervently Orthodox groups as discrimination if not a deprivation. Not being counted in the *minyan* sends a message that women do not count at all.

Even if they struggled over feminist issues in the past, most of the interviewees did not seem to be struggling at the time of their interviews. Six of the twenty-four women called themselves feminists and described earlier difficulties they had. These women and others who did not self-identify as feminists referred to struggles over particular practices or over their gender role. At the time of their interviews, they had either reinterpreted the troubling practice in feminist terms (cf. Kaufman, 1991), reframed it according to Orthodox precepts, or found a way to work around a restriction.

Several women struggled initially with the requirement that they immerse in a *mikveh* a week after the cessation of menstruation. Allison, *frum* for ten years at the time of her interview, said that she was surprised to learn at a time when she already considered herself Orthodox that the *mikveh* was one of the three mitzvahs required of (married) women:

> I had . . . a lot of bad baggage about *mikveh*. Because in my family
> *mikveh* was a dirty thing. My grandmother, sort of unfortunately,
> who was from Europe, gave this bad image of *mikveh*, sort of

communicated that to my mother; my aunt had a terrible experience about being inspected when she got married, so *mikveh*
was a bad, archaic, backward, dirty thing. I'm reading Telushkin's
book and he's describing the different Judaisms. And finally he
says, Orthodox Judaism, what distinguishes it from all the other
branches [is] *kashrut, Shabbos* and *taharas mishpachah*. So . . . I'm
reading the book lying in bed next to [husband] . . . , [and say,]"You
know, I'm doing two of the three. We're not doing the third. If
we're calling ourselves Orthodox, [it's inconsistent that] we're not
doing the third. . . . I've got to do the third."

Allison's extended family's associations with the *mikveh* have to do with the
normative practice of inspecting oneself prior to immersion, but a mikveh atten-
dant may also do this, an action that could be interpreted as intrusive. At the
mikveh or beforehand, one needs to bathe, wash one's hair, and cut one's nails
prior to immersion. These procedures could suggest that women are physically
unclean because of menstruation and thus need to be cleansed. On the other
hand, Allison's aunt's *mikveh* in Europe may not have been well maintained.
Although the *mikveh* is traditionally considered spiritual cleansing, Allison's
family seemed to view it differently. The statement on the three mitzvahs
most likely came from Rabbi Joseph Telushkin's book *Jewish Literacy* (1991),
where he describes and distinguishes the various Jewish religious movements.

The term *taharat* (or *taharas*) *hamishpachah* (family purity) refers to laws
restricting sexual relations when a woman is *niddah* (ritually impure). Consistent with Leviticus 15:19, women and men are not supposed to have sexual
relations during the time she is menstruating and for a week after she ceases
to discharge blood. For some, this prohibition extends to having any direct
physical contact. The woman is supposed to use a cloth for inspection (called
bedikah) or the equivalent to assess whether she is no longer bleeding, after
which she counts seven days. If there is doubt whether the blood is menstrual,
the woman might show the cloth to a third party—a woman with expertise
in this area or a rabbi. After seven "clean" days, the woman immerses herself
in a *mikveh* and may resume sexual relations with her husband.

Eliza, who was observant nineteen years, said that she found the separation when she was a *niddah* difficult:

Keeping the *mikveh* was very difficult. Exceedingly difficult. It
turned out to be an absolutely terrific thing, but it took a long
time to both get used to the idea of no contact for that period of

time, and, you know, not having sex when you want to have sex, and then the stringencies about what you had to do to prepare to go to the *mikveh*, and that can be very inconvenient if you're out of the house someplace or something.

Yet she, like many of the other women, came to view this experience positively. Liora, who was *frum* for six years, also had difficulty with being sexually separated from her husband. She reported that she and her husband learned how to communicate in a non-physical way and that, overall, it has led to a maturing of their marriage. Other women, like Deborah, found the mikveh spiritually uplifting:

> I look forward to it. I love just being in the water. I feel like there's like this beam of light that goes directly [to me]. And it's my time of, it's kind of like when you light candles, also. I hope other people feel that, too. That you're just surrounded in this aura, and it's like you have all of a sudden a direct line. Instead of being distracted by everything else that goes on in life.

Regardless of whether they objected to a mitzvah in the beginning or took it in their stride, the *baalot teshuvah* came to reframe it as "empowering," a term frequently used by feminists. Much of the change had to do with their increased learning. Erica, for example, who in a women's studies course had been exposed to the idea that the *mikveh* is degrading, came to see herself "as in charge of whether or not my husband is in violation of the laws of *niddah*. He doesn't ask to see the *bedikah* cloths, and he doesn't ask to see a receipt from the *mikveh*." During her seven years of observance, she had learned that it is incumbent on men, through their wives, to adhere to the laws around separation when the woman is considered ritually impure. Some women came to see the *mechitzah* as similarly empowering because it gave them space in which to talk to God.

Besides reframing mitzvahs as positive, the BTs found ways to work around practices that challenged their feminist sensibilities. Several women struggled with restrictions on women's singing in the presence of men (*kol ishah*), observed in more stringent Orthodox settings, where it is held that the singing voices of women arouse men. One work-around available in some more liberal environments is to participate in women's *davening* groups that are led by and include only women. In some of these, women read from the Torah and have *aliyot*, activities from which they are barred in the synagogue and that also obviate the need for a *mechitzah*. When Tamar, *frum* for twenty-four years, invited groups of women to her home for festive meals as a work-around, she came to understand the rationale for *kol ishah*, with which she had struggled:

> I've had women-only meals, where I'm hearing these gorgeous voices and harmony that just radiated through the whole apartment. And I realized, not all the time, but some of the time, there are some men with great voices, too. But in general, when men just kind of get together at a table and sing . . . it's not the same as when women sing. That helped me realize why it could be very distracting for a man to hear a woman sing, because it really can be very beautiful and elevating and enticing, whatever the words are. I would say it was not one of my easiest, but it wasn't overly terribly difficult either.

Considering that Tamar sang publicly before she became *frum*, she may have understated the challenge of *kol ishah*. Nevertheless, she, like other women who had difficulty with various mitzvahs and customs, came to accept the norms of her community.

Aside from the struggles over particular *mitzvot* that have been described, another issue was apparent in the interviews. The women felt overwhelmed with the responsibilities that they experienced in the traditional roles of mothers and homemakers. As noted by Davidman (1991), who described women's role in Orthodox Judaism as "labor intensive" (p. 202), they talked about feeling burdened with preparing the household for Shabbat and holidays and taking care of the children. Lauren, *frum* for twenty-four years, spoke of how difficult it was "to run a *frum* house, and it's hard to wear a *sheitel*, and it's really hard to make Shabbos every week." She had this conversation with her interviewer:

> LAUREN: It was a rude awakening to cook and clean and also pay Jewish school tuition. Big rude awakening. And you have to work on your resentment toward that also and being happy with being *frum* but realizing the physical burdens that go with it.
>
> INTERVIEWER: So how do you make peace with that?
>
> LAUREN: Well, sometimes you don't. Sometimes you just say, "I can't believe how much this chicken cost me. This is ridiculous"

(laughs). But you know that it's for the right thing. And then when you sit down at a Friday night table, and sometimes a kid thanks you. "The soup was so good, Mom." And you say, "Okay, fine. Fine, I'll do it." Or they say a *d'var Torah* from school. So you just wait for those times and you can get through the cooking and the cleaning and the laundry (laughs).

As she suggested, there are intangible benefits she receives from her children that compensate for the cost of the children's schooling and the labor she puts into food preparation.

Another woman, Susan, *frum* for eight years, who felt overwhelmed with food preparation and getting ready for Shabbat and holidays provided details on what she has to do:

The problem is I haven't had time. You would think I would have time; it's not like I have a nine-to-five job. But this whole getting ready for *yom tov* is a whole process. You have to start shopping, and then you have to start cooking. And then you have to start serving. And then you have to clean up. And it's like, okay, by the time that's all over, then you have to get ready for your normal life. And doing everything else that's been piling up. So I find it so hard to have time to enjoy life.

Shopping and cooking must occur in advance because one cannot cook on the Sabbath. When Shabbat precedes or follows a two-day holiday (*yom tov*), and when there are guests, preparation is obviously more extensive. Clearing the table and cleaning up afterward are also taxing. Susan did not have time to catch her breath. At the same time she complained of being burdened, she asserted that her household responsibilities are important. They are her priority. In contrast with her feminist *baalot teshuvah* friends, she does not attempt to do everything her husband does. As she explained:

I told one of my girlfriends recently, I said, "Listen," I said, "Even if you don't go to *shul*, and even if you don't do all these things that [the men do], they're not [as] important [as] what you're doing at home, and you're enabling your family to do. . . . But don't get upset and don't make your husband or your children think that you have to do it." First of all, women aren't obligated to do the same things that men are. A lot of women, a lot of *baal teshuvahs* get hung up on that. . . . But you can't make it so hard on yourself, because being in the house and cooking and cleaning and taking care of your family, that's the hardest of it all.

As Susan explained it, her friends seem to think that women should take on the same mitzvahs as men, a carryover from liberal feminist ideology. But as Kaufman (1991) points out, feminist thinking has moved away from a simplistic focus on equality to a consideration of women's differences. Susan has learned that Orthodox Judaism recognizes these differences, leading her to the conclusion that she can dispense with what she previously considered obligations and by focusing on her home and family, she can lighten her load. Nevertheless, she views her household responsibilities as difficult.

Three women who described themselves as feminists made gradual transitions to Orthodoxy, enabling them to deal with their concerns slowly. All three had the early life experience of attending a brother's bar mitzvah but not having their own bat mitzvah; two had bat mitzvahs as adults. One of the two (Marilyn, *frum* for three years) had an adult *bat mitzvah* at age fifty, when she read from the Torah and recited the *haftarah*. She described wearing a *kippah* and a *tallit* in her Conservative synagogue in the past. As she has become more knowledgeable and comfortable in Orthodox settings, Marilyn explained, she no longer feels the need to demonstrate that she can do the same things as men. She has come to accept the explanation she was given by Orthodox authorities that women have an innate sense of piety that makes it less necessary for them to do what men do. As she said:

> I've done a lot of reading, I've availed myself of some classes. . . . As items would come up: why did we do this, and . . . why doesn't a woman do this, and why does a woman do this, and finding out that there's really nothing that a man does that a woman can't do. But that women have chosen, and it's tradition, that these are the traditions that have been set aside for men, and these are the basic reasons for them. A man wearing *tallis* and *tefillin*, there's no reasons that a woman can't. And I have. But it's now explained where a woman has a much more ingrained sense of good and not good. Mothering. And things that go with that, nurturing. Whereas a man doesn't. A woman doesn't need reminders to say a prayer of thanks. A woman will just automatically, when something good happens, [say] thank you. A man has to be reminded much more

so than a woman does. And some of the sages have said: this is why a man has to wear a *tallis* and see the fringes to be reminded, to keep it in front of his eyes; whereas a woman doesn't need that. She has it much more internally ingrained in her; it's in the genes.

Although the assertion of innate gender differences may be an excuse for male privilege, Marilyn accepts the explanation she was given.

Eliza and her husband became increasingly observant after being exposed to Shabbat by their Conservative congregational rabbi. They gradually took on various *mitzvot*. The couple's paths diverged, however, over feminist issues. Eliza was trying to push her Conservative synagogue to expand women's participation, while her husband was moving toward Orthodoxy. She eventually joined him and became Orthodox, too, but with some difficulty. She reflected on how much more difficult it is for women than men to become *frum*:

> I think it's a lot easier for a man because, if anything, he gets to take on more, not less. And if anything, when a woman leaves the Conservative movement and moves into Orthodoxy, there are things she's giving up. Which I guess, maybe if you've never had [them] it doesn't matter. I couldn't state that [and] probably it's different for everybody. But if you've been used to going up for *aliyos*, and being near the Torah and feeling part of that whole scene, and used to being able to kiss the Torah on Shabbat, it feels like a great loss to be that far away and be more like a spectator.[3]

Eliza laments the loss of active participation she experienced before she became Orthodox and misses the pleasure she previously took in having an *aliyah* and being in close proximity to the Torah. The *mechitzah* separating the women's section from the men's hinders women from feeling part of the action. Eliza has "worked around" this perceived deprivation by attending a synagogue in which the *mechitzah* does not entirely block her view and by participating in women's *minyans*. In contrast, a woman in Kaufman's (1991) study preferred *davening* when men were present in the same synagogue but in a separate area. She said, "It makes two statements simultaneously—that we are separate, different, yet together" (Kaufman, 1991, p. 48). Other women in the current study have found *davening* in a separate area liberating. Erica, for example, explained that *davening* in a separate section enables her to talk to God without being distracted.

Struggles over Infertility, Illness and Death

Several interviewees struggled with experiences that opened them up to the presence of God or challenged the tenacity of their faith. These experiences had to do with infertility and birth complications, illness of a family member or oneself, and the death of a family member or friend.

Infertility and Birth Complications

Four women and one man mentioned infertility or birth complications as trying experiences for them. One of the women, Karen, *frum* for eleven years, spoke of getting married at age thirty-five and not conceiving until she was forty. As she explained:

> They always say that Hashem, sometimes where even Hashem gives us *tzaros* [troubles], [it] is so that we'll need Him. And so, you know that we had difficulty having a child. So a lot of the things that we did to grow spiritually I think were motivated also by, okay if we take on one more *chumra* (stringency), you know, someone told me this, that if you do this, maybe (you will conceive).

Here we see Karen and her husband viewing their difficulties around infertility as a message from God to increase their spiritual-religious growth.

During the first six years of her marriage, Shifra had difficulty becoming pregnant. During this period, she had several surgeries and she and her husband cared for a foster child who had behavioral problems. Then she gave birth to a child, after which they came to the realization that they could not deal with the emotional needs of the foster child while caring for their baby. Her husband in particular was concerned that the foster child would have a negative effect on their biological child. In response, they returned the foster child to the agency, which placed him in a group home. Shifra said that she felt terrible about this and cried for a year. This was a trying spiritual struggle, as she felt blessed with a baby but bereft of another child that she loved.

One of the male interviewees, Jerry, *frum for* three years, spoke of the difficulties he and his wife had in conceiving their fourth child. He attributed their problems to his prostate infections. He spoke of their difficulties with his Chabad rabbi, who said that he should write a letter to the office of the Lubavicher rebbe, Rabbi Menachem Mendel Schneerson, after his wife goes to the *mikveh*. The letter would be brought to the grave of the late rebbe, who the faithful believe continues to have spiritual powers. Shortly after they followed this advice, his wife became pregnant. Jerry believed that this happened because they "were on the path that Hashem wanted us to be on. And [our son] is the product of that."

Sarah, observant for fifteen years and fifty years old at the time of her interview, spoke about having had spiritual encounters around problem pregnancies and childbirths. Her first child, a son, had to be resuscitated three times after he was born. She had problems with her next pregnancy, and in the second trimester she learned that the baby had died in utero. Throughout both pregnancies, Sarah had worried that she might have a girl. Having grown up surrounded by women with whom she had complicated relationships (her mother, grandmother, and sisters), she did not feel ready to handle a baby girl. Even though it was difficult to lose a child during pregnancy, Sarah was relieved that this baby was a girl. As she explained:

> When they woke me up from [the anesthesia], I was only half-awake obviously, to tell me (what) was going on medically, they said that it was a girl, and I said something like, "Thank God. I didn't want a girl anyhow." And, so you can imagine, saying that, maybe it was Hashem's way of saying, I will take care of this. You're not ready to have a girl. You're not ready to parent a girl. It was loaded, let me tell you. Very, very, very loaded spiritually.

Reflecting on this experience during her interview, Sarah said that the ideas she then had about God's role in deciding that the child would be a girl were immature. Yet she said that when she later had a daughter, she felt ready.

Marilyn described having had a problem pregnancy and delivery early in her fifth month. Based on her son's low birth weight and other medical signs, the doctors said that they did not expect him to make it. Yet he did survive and today he is a college professor. This experience strengthened Marilyn's faith and brought her spirituality to the forefront. As she explained:

> As hurdles were gotten over, and he did survive, and all of the horrible things that they said would absolutely be there were not there, you had to have faith. And you've got to find out where is it coming from, and what does it mean for me. . . . I owe thanks to something, someone, something. . . . Becoming a *baal teshuvah* gives me the comfort in a lot of realms, but it also allows me to say thank you.

In all these examples, the individuals endured life events that would have been challenging to anyone, regardless of their religious orientation. Each of them engaged in religious behavior and/or discovered spiritual meaning in the event whether it was becoming pregnant or witnessing the wondrous survival of one's child. In *Expecting Miracles*, Weisberg (2004) describes the experiences with pregnancy and childbirth of *baalot teshuvah* and other religious Israeli Jewish women as deep spiritual encounters. She also shared some of her own experiences, concluding, "These experiences have made me see that pregnancy and birth take place in an altered spiritual reality, in which the dividing curtain between this world and the next is left slightly open" (p. 24).

Illness and Death

Just about everyone who was interviewed referred to the illness and/or death of a relative or friend in the course of describing significant life events. Only some, however, spoke of such losses as crises that challenged their beliefs. Sherry, observant six years, recalled witnessing the illness and subsequent death of a childhood friend, Richard, who died of leukemia a couple of weeks after he had a bone marrow transplant. As she explained it, Richard's parents were atheists:

> And I remember saying to his mother after he died, "He doesn't feel pain anymore. He's in a better place." And she said to me, "I don't believe that. And if you believe in God, then God killed my son. And how does that make you feel?" And I think that was a pivotal moment for me, because I realized that either I was looking at nothingness, or I could look at everything. And I chose . . . to look at it as if it was just the beginning of something for him.

This was also a beginning for Sherry. Subsequently she went to a seminary in Israel to learn more about Judaism, and after she returned to the United States, she continued to learn. Years later, the illness and death of her father became a turning point for her:

> Because he suffered unbelievably for a long time and . . . was in such agony, I started . . . thinking more clearly about my soul and my purpose. And it helped me to focus. I think when a parent dies, hopefully you have a major growth spurt. And I think I did when my father died. . . . I think all suffering, the purpose

of suffering is so that you'll grow. And so I look at suffering in a different way now than I ever did before. Before, I was afraid of it. And now I really see it as a tool that God uses to strengthen you ultimately.

Later in the interview, Sherry said that she has wrestled with suffering throughout her journey:

I think suffering, really, is something I can never really grasp, because if I think about my own evolution, I think about the things that stick out in my mind are people that I loved that died, that really suffered when they died. Somebody who was my age, and then my father, I mean, real intense suffering. Like them, I know what exquisite pain means. And because I'm very empathic, I think that I just felt somewhat motivated to understand why God would do such a thing to just kind, gentle people, to cause such unbearable suffering. And I still don't have an answer to it, but it makes me [think] there has to be, if God made death, then there has to be something good in that, too. And so, if this isn't all there is, then you really have to be careful how you tread in this world. Because it obviously must have an effect on what happens to you after this world.

Sherry's struggle to understand the suffering and deaths of her friend and father led her to examine the purpose of her own life and God's reasons for creating suffering. She concluded that there is meaning in suffering. In contrast to her friend Richard's mother, she determined that there is more to life than physical being; that there is a world after death.

Allison, too, struggled to find meaning in a family member's illness and subsequent death. Her mother was diagnosed with advanced stage cancer while Allison was in the process of becoming Orthodox. She coped with this by promising God that she would keep the Sabbath:

I go and I strike a deal with God. And I go, okay, I'll do the whole nine yards. I won't touch lights, I won't touch the phone, won't rip paper, do anything. By this time, I'm knowledgeable enough to know what to do, right. If You help me out here, okay. Anyway, she goes into remission. So I feel like my observance is holding her, is tethered.

Prior to her mother's diagnosis, Allison was struggling with some of the beliefs held by Orthodox Jews. Ambivalent about becoming Orthodox, she nevertheless took on increased observance, reminiscent of Kubler-Ross's stage of bargaining described in *On Death and Dying* (1969). In the process of keeping up her end of the deal and incorporating Sabbath observance into her life, Allison came to appreciate the value of being observant. She saw positive changes in her children and her family life and in her connection to the religious community. She found that she was no longer performing the *mitzvot* as part of a "deal" but because it made sense to her. Before long, she became convinced that "no human being could have thought this up." Subsequently, her mother and sister became Orthodox, too. Striking a bargain was not a rare event among the BTs. Karen told God that she would become Sabbath-observant if her seriously ill stepfather recovered. This promise gave Karen a push to become *frum*.

During the course of conducting the interviews, we learned that two interviewees had physical health problems. One interviewee said that she is struggling to figure out the lessons Hashem is trying to convey through her illness. Some time ago, she visited the late Lubavitcher rebbe, hoping for a complete healing. Instead, "He blessed me to have the strength and the insight to understand, to accept and understand my illness, and to live with it gracefully." In retrospect, she thought that this was a good blessing, which would apply whether she got well or continued to be sick. The other participant with an illness expressed feelings of dissatisfaction with her life. She missed the excitement she had when she first became Orthodox and wondered if she could recapture that by studying Kabbalah.[4] She reported tiredness, boredom, and depression, which may be symptoms of her illness. Two male participants said that they were worried about ill spouses. No one expressed anger at God for these illnesses, but they did seek to understand what God was trying to teach them.

There is a growing literature on spirituality and health care (e.g., Abu-Raiya, Pargament, & Exline, 2015; Miller & Thoresen, 2003). Health and mental health providers are encouraged to be sensitive to the spiritual needs of patients and family caregivers. As this literature and these examples show, illness is a time in which many people seek meaning and strength outside themselves. According to Kleinman (1988), a psychiatrist and anthropologist, cancer is loaded with symbolic meaning as it is malignant, seems to occur randomly, and makes one feel powerless. As he explained, "Cancer is an unsettling reminder of the obdurate grain of unpredictability and uncertainty and injustice—value questions, all—in the human condition" (p. 20). Formal religions provide a framework and structure in which meaning can be made. For someone who is Jewish and Orthodox, or is on the path of *teshuvah*, taking on and engagement in religious practices can help them connect with God and cope with difficult situations.

Maintaining Belief

It was difficult for interviewees to accept world events and personal experiences that disrupted their assumptive world, which Beder (2004–2005) explains as follows:

> The assumptive world is an organized schema reflecting all that a person assumes to be true about the world and the self on the basis of previous experiences; it refers to the assumptions, or beliefs, that ground, secure, and orient people, that give a sense of reality, meaning, or purpose to life. (p. 258)

Deborah's assumptive world was disrupted by the terrorist attack on the World Trade Center. She said, "You can't understand why things happen. And really you have to just accept them." Although this event was disturbing to non-Orthodox Jews and gentiles as well, it is an example of how some BTs seemed to have expected life to go more smoothly. It was challenging, some said, to place their confidence in God when life is unpredictable or when adverse events occur in the United States or Israel.

Orthodox for thirty-eight years, Paul continues to have difficulty accepting the way God is running the world and, like Sherry, would like to attain a better understanding of why people suffer. In response to being asked where he saw himself moving spiritually, he said that at this point in his life he would like

> to be able to look back and understand why things happened. So that's what I'm rooting for (laughs). And, you know, there's hardly a person in the world without pain of some sort. Some have very great pain, some have very minor pain, but there's hardly a person who does not have in their life some pains. And that's an issue. It's an issue for me when I see really good people who are suffering in some way. I can't come to terms with it. And that bothers me on an individual basis when I see that, more than the Holocaust because that's so far removed from me, it's just six

million people and I can't relate to that in any way. But if you tell me the story of one person from the Holocaust that I can relate to. . . . Maybe there is not a reason for the Holocaust. Maybe there are six million reasons. And that's the way to think of it. So, not understanding. It's like I said once half in jest, "When I was young I wanted to understand everything. Now I would settle for understanding anything."

In addition to his struggle to understand God's purposes, Paul was troubled on the personal level over the values of his son-in-law that were guiding the upbringing of Paul's grandchildren. In contrast with his son-in-law who said that there is no goal for Torah life, that one only has to *daven* and perform mitzvahs, Paul would like to improve the world, "to make it into the ultimate place that the Ribono Shel Olam [Master of the Universe] wants it to be" and to bring holiness into the world. Paul was disturbed that his grandchildren were being educated in a closed community where information is filtered through the religious press and rabbis and mitzvahs are performed without attention to their meaning. He was also concerned that his grandchildren were not allowed to participate in activities such as going to the zoo where they would encounter non-Jewish and non-religious people. It appears that Paul is struggling with his secular value of openness in the face of his son-in-law's adoption of a more restrictive approach to childrearing.

Ezra, *frum* for ten years, felt challenged by threats to the unity of Judaism (*achdut* or *achdus*). He described a recent experience that troubled him:

> I guess I wish that, that there was *achdus*, that there was unity in the Jewish people. I went to a wedding Sunday in a Conservative synagogue, performed by a gay rabbi. And I went there because . . . these people I've known for thirty years, and . . . so they, he asked me to come. He asked me to sign his *ketubah*. I told him I couldn't do it and I explained to him why I couldn't do it. But I was there anyway. And there were parts of what was going on that I realized . . . there were two Jewish people getting married. And I thought to myself . . . they, they really don't know. They're really nice people. You know, they feel they're getting married in an appropriate way, and why isn't there a way to bridge all of that? And [that's] one of the things . . . that I really have some difficulty with in the *frum* community . . . you know, especially in a place, people in my own *shul*, things like that.

Like Paul, Ezra seems to partially embrace ideas from the more liberal Jewish movements, here by advocating inclusiveness. Knowing that his *frum* community disapproves of attending weddings in Conservative synagogues, especially those performed by a gay rabbi, he decides to attend the wedding anyway. His refusal to sign the *ketubah*, however, reflects his conflict over being inclusive.

Achdut is a topic of contemporary concern with the Reform, Conservative, Reconstructionist, and Orthodox branches of Judaism in the United States and diverse movements within Orthodox Judaism. Ferziger (2015) discusses divisions within Orthodox Judaism in *Beyond Sectarianism: The Realignment of American Orthodox Judaism*. He sees some movement toward openness because of the *keruv* movement. Krakowski (2015), who reviewed Ferziger's book, attributes the openness to the American context.

In contrast to Ezra's concern with *achdut*, other *baalei teshuvah* had questions about the truth of the Torah and the sacred writings. Baila, observant twenty-four years, struggles over the actuality of events described in traditional understandings of the Torah:

> It's just incredible to me that Avraham went into a furnace and came out unscalded. The miracles. I know that God can do whatever He wants, but it's just hard to believe that every single blade of grass and every single person in this world. . . . He's out there, He looks upon the world, and He's in control of every single thing. It's just hard to fathom. Not that I don't believe it. It's just hard to fathom. Like, these people were righteous, and they were the greatest *tsaddikim* [righteous men] like the brothers [of Joseph], but they threw their brother into a pit? Just all the things in the Torah that it talks about. [Pause] I just have trouble understanding the Torah. Like Dovid Hamelech [King David] was great, but he sent this woman's husband off to war to die so he could have his wife. Those kinds of things bother me.

Baila appears to have been instructed to believe in the literal truth of the events described in the Torah and in the Midrash, and with rabbinic characterizations of figures who engaged in deceitful actions as admirable. It is curious why she did not take her questions to a rabbi who may have helped her derive other meanings from the text. Other *baalei teshuvah* acknowledged that they could not accept all that they have been told. Karen admitted that she sometimes has doubts about "the whole thing," but what keeps her going is that the lifestyle works for her. She and others found in Orthodox Judaism a structure, community, and framework for raising children that motivated them to remain *frum*.

Several participants accepted struggling as part of their lives as Orthodox Jews. Jacob, *frum* for twenty-two years, said:

> There's always wrestling. A lot of it is with my parents and family that was not supportive. That was a huge wrestling, that continues to [this] date, of how far do you go, and . . . how far do you listen to your rabbi, and how far do you listen to the texts, and as you learn you become cognizant of the fact that there are so many different opinions out there and the diversity of views, and where do you fit in.

In recognizing a diversity of interpretations of texts, Jacob seemss to be more intellectually sophisticated than Baila. Like others, Jacob is aware that struggling is an ongoing experience.

In chapter 1, I noted that some *baalei teshuvah* grew up in homes that were culturally Jewish but not God-centered. They were conscious of being Jewish and attended Hebrew or Sunday school but were unaccustomed to incorporating God into their lives. As they evolved as Orthodox Jews, some had spiritual struggles over experiencing God's presence in their lives. Yossi, observant for twenty-eight years, explained that while his children speak easily about Hashem's presence in their lives, he has struggled:

> When Hashem was coming into my life in the beginning, it was all very in my head, meaning I was trying to understand, because no one had explained it to me growing up, what does it mean to believe in God? . . . So I guess you might even say it was very, like if you fulfill all the *halachas*, then you have God in your life. But that just means you're doing the *mitzvahs*. It doesn't mean you're feeling God's presence. And I've always wanted to . . . feel God's presence but never had a natural [entry?]. So I had to try to develop it on my own. It's something that you can only learn by people modeling it for you. That's my understanding. And then you have to do it yourself. Then a person has to figure it out for themselves, and I have to figure out for myself. So I'm always at that point, in a sense, figuring it out for myself. What does God want me to do, and how Hashem has given me so much, and

how [do] I need to be appreciative? Trying to integrate that very,
I guess you might call it a spiritual experience, because it's not a
physical thing, with the physical life that I lead.

At the time of his interview, Yossi was working on having "God awareness"
and incorporating this awareness into his family and work life.

Struggles over Personal and Familial Issues

Several *baalei teshuvah* spoke about intrapersonal and familial issues that affected
their spiritual growth. The intrapersonal issues were expressed primarily by
individuals who had faced problems such as divorce or addiction or were
abused when they were children. When they experienced adversity as *frum*
men and women, they felt angry or disconnected. They directed their anger
at God or their religious community. The individuals who spoke most directly
about their personal issues were in Focus Group 2. Marla, for example, said
that she felt betrayed by God when, after she had been following the Orthodox "cookbook" by performing mitzvahs and contributing to the community,
she had to deal with her son's addiction. Embarrassed by this, she withdrew
from her religious community to focus on her son, while at the same time she
blamed the community for not caring. Upon reflection, she realized that the
problem had more to do with her than with the community. It appears that
she did not previously recognize that performing mitzvahs does not guaran-
tee a trouble-free life. Other focus group members discussed the impact of
adversity on their spiritual development. Some became stuck in their spiritual
development whereas others grew from the experience.

In chapter 1, I mentioned that seven interviewees were children of
Holocaust survivors. In addition, the two focus groups also included children
of survivors. The parents' Holocaust-related experiences affected the BTs'
decision to become Orthodox, their spiritual lives, and their struggles. One
common characteristic of their families was isolation. For example, Nora, *frum*
for twenty-two years, grew up with a family limited to her nuclear family and
her aunt and uncle. She attributed her decision to become Orthodox to the
absence of her Orthodox grandparents in her life:

It was because my grandparents were Orthodox that I had never
known. And I remembered thinking consciously that I wanted to

recreate the life that my grandmothers lived so that I wouldn't have let Hitler obliterate their lives and their memories. So I remember thinking that, consciously, that I wanted to . . . resuscitate, rejuvenate, revive, the Jewish life that had been in our family, so that Hitler wouldn't have [succeeded].

Nora's desire to revive her family's legacy had a downside, however. As an Orthodox Jew living in a community in which many of those who were brought up Orthodox had large extended families of previous generations, she felt deprived of relatives who might have been in her life. She expressed "grief for what I didn't have . . . that other people had." Nora struggled with loneliness, creating a surrogate family of friends as well as her immediate family, arriving at a point in which she was able to reclaim her heritage:

Before I became observant I saw myself as someone without a past or a history. And since I became observant, I feel connected to my past and I feel a connection to the family that I lost, I feel connected to the community, I feel connected. . . . I feel, especially I think because I didn't have a big family growing up, I feel more connected as a person to a larger family, of the Jewish people, and also it's made me closer to my family now, who are not even observant, but I feel more committed to being . . . connected to them.

A member of Focus Group 2 who was also a child of Holocaust survivor parents has experienced some restoration of family in her children and grandchildren. She said:

And the other thing that's been really significant that was really a high (thank you, God), is when my grandchildren were born. I have two grandsons. And I think, connected to the Holocaust background, we grew up with no family; my parents were the only survivors of huge families, so I remember when my son was *bar mitzvahed*, that was like, I can't even (fathom) . . . that we were a family doing this, and then when my grandchildren, so I have children in the neighborhood, with grandchildren, this, it's like a return to normality within the Jewish world. You know, there's something about that that's rooted in the Holocaust piece that is enormously powerful.

Struggles over Religious Requirements in the
Face of a Lingering Attraction to the Secular World

Having grown up secular, the BTs found it challenging to adhere to religious rules knowing that they were free to do what they wanted before they became observant. Depending on the level of stringency they adopted and the norms of the community with which they affiliated, they gave up pleasures such as reading particular secular novels, going to the movies, eating in non-kosher restaurants, and watching television. Some wondered whether the benefits outweighed the sacrifices. This is how Joshua, *frum* for twenty-five years, described his struggle:

> How much do I want my life to have some kind of meaning, which means commitment to things and doing things that I might not otherwise choose to do? And not doing things that I might otherwise choose to do? And how much, you know, how much of my life is just meant to like live? And, if it feels good, do it? I mean there's a real conflict between those two. There's an irreconcilable conflict between those two and . . . it took me years and years and years. Even since I've been *frum*, I mean that's not something that just goes away.

Participants pointed to a number of facets of being observant that they found difficult. A couple of people spoke about getting restless over Shabbat and two- and three-day holidays. While some expressed concern about missing work, others felt confined. Zvi, *frum* for fifteen years, fit the latter category:

> My struggle was more from being a totally physical person into . . . trying to adapt a more spiritual reality to my life, which I was never really able to do. You know, some guys are just naturally like singing and spiritual and finding meaning in everything. And I was more like, alright, how do you do this, and let's get it over with. So I always struggled with that, [and] I struggle with it today. I mean, three-day *yom tovs* make me want to shoot myself. I mean, by eight o'clock on Shabbos night, right before Shabbos ends . . . I'm ready to kill. It's painful, you know.

Zvi was one of several men who presented themselves as religious but not spiritual. As he explained here, his focus was on performance of the mitzvahs, some of which he found difficult because he could not sit still.

Raised in a Modern Traditionalist home and Orthodox for ten years, Uri also found Shabbat observance to be confining and expressed concern about missing activities involving secular and non-Jewish friends that take place on Shabbat and holidays.

> Sometimes I look out and say, well, you know, we only have two days of the weekend and here we spend a whole day, a whole day is cut out, and we can't get things done. And isn't that kind of weird? Or, that doesn't come up so much as, but there have been times where we've decided not to go to a reunion, you know, we had a ten-year BBYO [B'nai B'rith Youth Organization] reunion and it was all happening on Shabbat and no one was *shomer Shabbat*, so we just passed on that. Or, you know, very good friends getting married on a Saturday that we've missed or, we had a friend, you know, got married on Rosh Hashanah, so that made sense, so we skipped that. . . . To . . . miss some of that stuff because of these . . . regulations that are in there, sometimes creates doubts. And there are other, there are certain *halachot* that just seem kind of crazy. You know, not being able to carry or push a stroller in a place that doesn't have an *eruv*;[5] it's just there are things that just don't seem that logical. So there are definitely some doubts around following some of the things.

Uri seems to have a lingering attachment to secular friends and activities he engaged in before he did *teshuvah*. His ambivalence over standard practices and criticism of some Jewish laws lead one to wonder whether he will remain Orthodox.

Some BTs recalled being happier before they became *frum*. Once they got beyond the "BT high" they experienced during their initial learning and after commitment, they lost much of their earlier passion. Steinsaltz (1982, p. 38) used the term "spiritual fatigue" to depict such a loss of enthusiasm. He attributes this to excessive tension over mastering new spiritual demands and the tendency to take on too much. It may also be caused by recognition of what they have given up. Orthodox for three years, Nina thought her family life was better previously. They had more down time on weekends when they could take bicycle rides or have picnics. Because of the restrictions on working during Shabbat, the children do their homework on Sunday. She longed for more family fun, such as taking a trip to Disneyland, but she recognized that in her religious community this activity was not considered compatible with a life based on Torah. (In more open Orthodox communities, going to Disneyland is considered normal.) A number of BTs used expressions such as "it's hard," "it's not easy," or "it's difficult" when they described their spiritual/ religious struggles. They found it challenging to keep certain mitzvahs and were troubled by the impact of their Orthodoxy on relationships with their families of origin and friends. A few relatively recent BTs commented as follows:

> There are definitely times . . . where you say, wow . . . keeping all these *mitzvos*. It's hard. It's rewarding and fulfilling but it's hard. You know, this isn't the way I grew up. (Dov, *frum* for two years, Minimalist Plus family)

> [Parents are] used to it already that you don't call on Shabbos and that I don't come to them for Rosh Hashanah and that we don't have the *yomin tovim* (holidays) together. Which, by the way, is difficult. I mean. It's hard not to be with your family on *yom tov.* (Karen, *frum* for eleven years, Mainstream family)

> It's not easy to do *minchah* [late afternoon prayers scheduled to be recited during his long trip home]. It's not easy to do *maariv* when you get home, and you're tired, and you got four hours sleep, and you haven't eaten yet, and you just don't want to do it. It's hard to motivate yourself to do it. (Elliot, *frum* for five years, Mainstream family)

Another recent *baal teshuvah* had a different set of problems. *Frum* only three years, Jerry was frightened by the rapid changes he was making in his life. Like other relatively new BTs, he quoted rabbis in his interview. Here he explains his challenges taking on religious practices:

> I felt my heart just going much faster than I could keep up with. . . . I was scared because I saw things changing in my life and . . . growing up I would look at the black hats and thought, boy those are weird. Those people are real weirdos. And here I was becoming one of them! And it was like, okay, there's no turning back. My rabbi said, once you take on something, that's it, you got to keep on going forward. Am I going too fast? But what if I really don't want to do this? What if I really don't want to be *shomer Shabbos*? What if I really don't want to wear my *kippah*

every day, or my *tzitzis* every day. You know, once I do it, that's it. That's my commitment. . . . I'm a reflection of Chabad, of the Rebbe, of Hashem; well, what type of representative am I? Am I an embarrassment? Can I really do all this stuff that they're asking me?

Several of the key informants said that they advise newcomers to take on mitzvahs slowly. It appears that Jerry received advice like that, too, but was also told that he could not reverse himself. He was frightened over making commitments he might not be able to keep.

The struggles of *baalei* and *baalot teshuvah* over a lingering attraction to the secular world and spiritual fatigue over taking on too much too soon had much to do with the context of their lives. As a minority group within the Jewish community and within Orthodox Judaism, they experienced an uncomfortable marginal status. Even if they lived in an Orthodox Jewish enclave, they were constantly bombarded with reminders of the secular world. Many of them worked in mainstream occupations where they encountered individuals from all walks of life. Most of their families were embedded in the secular world. As described in this section, they received invitations from families and friends to attend events that occurred on the Sabbath or holidays, when the BTs could not drive and/or where kosher food was not available. The desire to live in both worlds stayed with them, leaving them with an underlying sadness.

Summary

In the processes of making a commitment and living as Orthodox Jews, the *baalei teshuvah* have experienced spiritual struggles that arouse heart-wrenching pain. They have struggled over ideas, untoward life events, maintaining their beliefs, intrapersonal and familial issues, and a lingering attraction to the secular world. The struggles were in part due to their retention of values from the secular world that clashed with those of their religious communities. For the most part, they viewed their struggles as opportunities to grow or to learn what God had in mind for them, yet they were distressed by seemingly incomprehensible situations.

The study participants grew up aware of feminism and some took women's studies courses when they were in college. Not surprisingly, the women were wary of patriarchal practices within Orthodoxy either at the onset or while they were becoming oriented to Orthodox Jewish communities. In contrast with the Reform and Conservative synagogues in which most of them were raised, women encountered restrictions in their synagogue participation and in their presentation of themselves. Their lives were separate, with emphasis given to the women's traditional roles of wife and mother. Women who initially objected to these and other Orthodox gender norms came to accept them, reinterpreting them as positive, reframing them as empowering (Kaufman, 1991), or working around them. Still, many felt burdened by the household responsibilities that fell on them.

Other struggles were around infertility, illness, and death. A few women and one man had had difficulties with infertility or with problem pregnancies. These painful experiences provided opportunities for some of them to increase the stringency of their observance and others to experience the presence of God in their lives. Participants also struggled over the illnesses and deaths of family members or a friend and their own health issues, finding the suffering difficult to fathom. They coped through seeking meaning in the suffering and bargaining with God (Kubler-Ross, 1969).

Struggles over maintaining belief had to do with attempts to understand disruptive events like the terrorist attack on the World Trade Center. Some expressed disillusionment over how life has turned out for them, for their grandchildren, and for their communities, whereas others were skeptical about the truths they thought they were supposed to accept. While some conveyed discomfort over their divergent thinking, others considered struggle a part of life.

Additional participants had personal or familial issues over which they struggled. These included divorce and a personal or family member's addiction. Such issues were the source of shame or embarrassment. A number of interviewees and focus group participants were children of Holocaust survivors. Their small families of origin led them to suffer from the absence of relatives in pro-family communities and recreate the families they lacked through Orthodox friends and through their own children and grandchildren.

The last section of this chapter dealt with the challenge of a lingering attraction to the secular world. This was the consequence of continued exposure to the larger secular society and to secular relatives, friends, and colleagues at their places of work. An invitation to an event that takes place on the Sabbath or holiday when they cannot drive can provoke a troubling conflict over relinquishing activities they enjoyed in the secular world.

Chapter 7

Psychological and Social Integration

The spiritual transformation of *baalei teshuvah* entails psychological and social integration. Psychological integration refers to the achievement of a sense of wholeness, which occurs through the acceptance of oneself. For BTs, this involves recognizing one's secular past, reworking aspects of one's self to fit one's new religious orientation, and revising one's identity such that one's spiritual/religious identity as an Orthodox Jew is central. These changes should cohere comfortably within the individual. Social integration refers to the process of becoming part of a new group, here an existing Orthodox community. In this chapter, I discuss the perceptions and experiences of those who became Orthodox in relation to their psychological and social integration. I show that their spiritual journeys did not lead to extensive psychological and social integration but the BTs were on a path leading in these directions.

Psychological Integration

When one changes one's religious orientation and the beliefs and values that go along with the new orientation, one changes one's identity. These changes evolve over time along with movement to a new community, changed religious practices, consumption of different types of food, and a revised clock and calendar that encompass daily *davening*, fast days, Shabbat, and religious holidays. The changes are particularly salient to the individual in the early years of his or her adoption of Orthodox Judaism, but the awareness of being different from family, friends, and associates who live secular lives continues. For *baalei teshuvah*, psychological integration is a developmental process that is ongoing,

191

nonlinear, and rarely completed. Based on the research data, it seems to involve several tasks, namely: (1) separation-individuation; (2) blending who one was with who one is; (3) being oneself while conforming to community norms; (4) integrating religion and work; (5) dealing with loss; and (6) consolidation.

Separation-individuation

The child psychoanalyst Margaret Mahler used the term separation-individu-ation to describe a developmental process associated with the first three years of life and beyond (Mahler, 1974; Mahler, Pine & Bergman, 1975). It refers to the child's moving away from a symbiotic relationship with his or her pri-mary caretaker, becoming differentiated, and achieving a stable sense of his or her self and the ability to relate to others. Other scholars have affirmed that separation-individuation continues after early childhood. Blos (1967) described a second individuation stage that occurs during adolescence, when the young person develops independence from his or her parents, and Colarusso (1990, 1997, 2000) wrote about third, fourth and fifth stages associated with early, middle, and older adulthood, respectively. The adult stages are not reiterations of those of childhood because adults engage in activities beyond the ability of children, such as establishing intimate relationships with other adults, pursu-ing intellectual interests, work, and adult forms of play (Colarusso, 2000). Separation-individuation in adulthood involves both the taking on of new challenges such as becoming a baal or baalat teshuvah and the relinquishment of others, resulting in further development as an individual.

For some BTs, becoming frum is a way of separating from their fami-lies of origin and asserting their individuality. They proclaim their Orthodox religious orientation and take on a way of life that is markedly divergent from the one in which they were raised. A few interviewees discussed melodramatic encounters with their parents when they were becoming frum in their early twenties, such as refusing to eat at their parents' home (where adaptations could have been made) or insisting on wearing a yarmulke on the street, which embarrassed the parents. Ariella reported having had a difficult relationship with her parents during her post-college years when she blamed them for her depression:

> It was really strained, because I was rebelling against who I was, because I thought that that was part of why I was depressed. Because I thought that I had had such a repressive, traditional life, that if I could break out and be myself, then I would be this

creative individual that would be self-identified. I was trying to throw away my roots, and find out who I really was. I think I had a really strong, I'm going to call it *yetzer harah* [evil inclination]. Because . . . I was trying so hard to be free-spirited, and liberal, and open-minded (that) I threw out the things that were central to me that I didn't want to have anything to do with at that time.

Frum for four years at the time of her interview, Ariella had individuated to the extent that she found a satisfying profession, was married and had a child, had an improved relationship with her parents, and was no longer depressed. Ironically, her adoption of Orthodox Judaism positioned her as more traditional than her parents.

In the second focus group, a few mental health professionals described "enmeshed" or overly close relationships with their parents from whom they struggled to separate. One woman, Michele, described fears of abandonment, rejection, and discomfort she experienced while separating from a home in which her father abused alcohol. She spoke of her developmental process in relation to Erikson's stage of *autonomy vs. shame and doubt*, which she experienced as doubt-ridden with reversals along the way:

> It took me a long time to, it was kind of like . . . up one, back two, no, up, whatever, up two, back one, kind of process. And a lot has happened over the years and I look back I'm like, "Oh my gosh, how did I get to this place?" But I'm very comfortable with my *yiddishkeit* [Jewishness] now and who I am, and it's interesting because, a lot of it I did at the beginning without really knowing what I was doing, just because my need to, as I used the word before, "unenmesh" from my family and sick system that I came from. . . . Now at this point I've integrated it into kind of my own identity, my own emotional, social, concept of what it means to be a Jew, as well as obviously putting the intellectual thing, and I'm very comfortable with myself and who I am.

Michele's normative developmental process of separation from her parents, ordinarily a task of late adolescence, was complicated by family dysfunction. Most likely, she had an ambivalent attachment to her parents. It appears that in the beginning, Orthodox Judaism helped her separate but she realized that she needed to own Judaism in a positive way rather than embracing it out of a psychological need. Michele and other *baalei teshuvah* who had experienced childhood adversity had a difficult time with separation-individuation. Typically, however, individuals experience some anxiety when they separate but are able to move into adulthood without being weighed down by memories of trauma. As a member of the first focus group remarked, healthy attachment to Orthodox Judaism is because Judaism is inherently attractive, not because it is an escape from pathology.

Blending Who One Was with Who One Is

Teshuvah involves a reassessment of earlier activities and relationships that are detrimental to the spiritual-religious life one takes on (Steinsaltz, 1982). In their narratives about their process of becoming *frum*, participants described pre-commitment activities that would be considered strange or unacceptable in their new communities, such as meditating, celebrating Christmas, or having sexual relations outside of marriage. A minority alluded to abuse of drugs and alcohol. Many of these activities no longer fit into their religious lives, but they are part of their pasts and contribute to who they are today. The psychological task is to accept the past as irreversible, using some aspects of the past in service of one's new life, and feeling comfortable with the blend that has resulted.

Frum for 13 years, Ruth is an example of a BT who integrated her past spiritual practices into her current observance of Orthodox Judaism. She grew up in what she described as a culturally Jewish, politically liberal home in which there was no talk of God and no synagogue affiliation, a Minimalist home. The extended family was close, getting together for secular meals on the Sabbath and holidays, but had conflict in their later years. Ruth described herself as a sensitive child who had unfulfilled spiritual yearnings. During her college years, she explored spirituality by attending a yoga ashram and taking meditation and yoga classes. At that time, she was skeptical of Judaism, believing that it created barriers between people, and embraced diversity in her friendships. After graduating, she went to Israel, inspired by a *baal teshuvah* cousin. While there, she studied in a seminary where she was adversely affected by an instructor who spoke disparagingly about non-Jews. She returned to the United States conflicted over her "liberal secular values" and "the Jewish part" of her and struggled with this over a period of years. When she delved further into and moved closer to Judaism, she had difficulty accepting certain (unspecified) beliefs shared by observant Jews. With some help from others, she came to the realization that "you can't force yourself to believe something" you don't believe. Still, she found other aspects of Orthodox Jewish life attractive.

While living in a large city as a single adult, Ruth experienced a strong sense of community with other Jewish young people. She attended classes and developed friendships with others who were becoming or were already observant and decided to become shomer Shabbat. As she thought about the conflict in her extended family and her aspirations for the future, she came to this conclusion:

> I felt really committed . . . to wanting to create as best I could a healthy family. You know, not that I do that ideally, but I knew that I had to have a good marriage, and I really felt like Judaism [as a] religion was going to be a big part of creating that. So these experiences really affected my choices . . . and I really wanted my kids to have a framework and a structure, and . . . a meaning system, . . . which I felt like I . . . need[ed] it so badly as a child and didn't have.

After meeting the man who became her husband and incorporating more rituals into her life, she has felt "grounded" and less troubled over ideas she could not accept:

> It's more like accepting that there are things that I can't answer, accepting that there's things that I might not ever understand, or might never believe, and that's okay. And then, sort of questioning more, with other things. Like how do I want to teach my kids about this, or how do I want to, how do we want to do Shabbos so that it's more meaningful? . . . How do I want to *daven* in a way that's more meaningful?

In the past, Ruth's struggle was between a liberal, secular upbringing and a belief system about which she was skeptical. She has shifted her focus to the quality of her religious life, which has provided a structure for her family and has offered her a community and friends. She is active in her synagogue, *davens* regularly, and learns. She continues to practice yoga and sometimes picks up her guitar. She feels some discomfort over her children's religious school, which is "more to the right" than she is, but she is working on accepting that. Consistent with her early desire for diversity, she interacts with Jewish and non-Jewish people in her work as a therapist and part-time college teacher.

Two men in their forties spoke about a return of their repressed selves in recent years. According to Jung (1933), around age forty one begins to undergo an inner transformation in which one becomes more reflective and parts of the personality that were previously submerged seek expression. Brian said that in the first 15 years after he made a commitment, he focused on "complying with religious laws and customs." While raising his children, he was concerned with integrating into the Orthodox community. In recent years, he has broadened his interests to encompass how the Jewish people integrate into the world. Brian, as well as Yossi, mentioned participating in a men's group in which they engaged in inner psychological work to integrate their spirituality with their personal lives. This involved getting in touch with their feelings and using their love of God as a pathway to understanding themselves and improving personal relationships. As Yossi explained:

> And when you come into the forties, age forty years old, I can be more objective and more aware, more aware of how I'm behaving and how I'm affecting other people, by my good *midos*, and also by my bad *midos*. And seeing that, you know, so much of it is from my childhood and how I was raised, and how I think, even though there's this layer of being a Torah-observant person on top of all that. That's still down there. And some of it needs to be reexamined in light of new spiritual understanding. I think that's kind of where I am right now.

Yossi is describing a process of examination of his childhood influences, Torah learning, and spirituality, which are steps toward creating a more coherent and integrated spiritual identity.

Cheryl, who became *frum* at age 17 and was interviewed when she was 35, reflected on her integration of her feminist values into Orthodox Judaism:

> I guess I'm not a traditional *baalat teshuvah* if there is such a thing, in the sense that I became *frum*, but it was very important to me to retain certain values that came from the secular world, like the values of women's issues and other things like that. And combining them has been a journey. And I think that I've managed to fuse it with some amount of peace. And the thing that I felt as a child that I wanted to live a *frum* life has never faltered. So the fact that I can integrate that with these other values in my life is maybe not that shocking because in the end, it's about living a religious life. In the end, it's about being connected to Hashem, being connected to an Orthodox community, being connected to

klal Yisrael [the Jewish people]. And if I can find a way to bring these other things in, then it's complete. And I think mostly I've managed to do that.

As Cheryl and others indicated, the process of integrating past values with their present way of life is ongoing. It involves self-awareness, reflection, the experience of comfort, and awareness of expectations of their religious community.

Being Oneself While Conforming to Community Norms

While living in Orthodox communities, *baalei teshuvah* experience social pressure to conform to community norms about religious observance, dress, and social behavior. Those interviewees who were early in their processes seemed to have been particularly sensitive to these expectations. One man recalled a time while he was moving toward commitment when he was afraid of being seen driving on the Sabbath by his *frum* neighbors. Others, who had enrolled their children in religious day schools before they fully embraced Orthodoxy, spoke of not wanting their children to be ashamed of parents who were not Sabbath observers or mothers who wore pants. After committing to being Orthodox, they continued to be conscious of community expectations.

Considering that the *baalei teshuvah* grew up in a culture that valued individualism, and their *teshuvah* was an act of individual assertion, they did not want to renounce their hard-won individuality. On the other hand, they wanted to be accepted by their new community and to fit in. Their deficient knowledge of Judaism and the culture of Orthodox Jews made it difficult for them to feel comfortable in their new environment. Their psychological task was to adapt while retaining their individuality.

In the context of a discussion about internal struggles experienced by *baalei teshuvah*, Leah, a member of the second focus group, articulated this conflict:

> I think one of the struggles for me, both when I started to become *frum* and it continues to be a struggle, is being able to maintain a balance with conforming and maintaining my own personality and individuality. I think initially I felt like I had to fit into something, you know, a mold that was there. And I think I did. Like I fit into it probably for four years where things went pretty smooth. You know, every Shabbos is amazing, every *tefillah* [prayer] was [moving], couldn't wait to get up and *daven* . . . everything was so

unbelievable! And then, when things started to get a little more difficult and I started questioning again, and I had to keep choosing what I had already chosen, I had to keep choosing it. But . . . just to navigate . . . what to keep myself and not to lose myself, I think that, for me, has been the theme throughout. . . . And being okay with, if I don't fit in completely to the mold or to a box, that that's okay.

As Leah explained, when she was a brand-new *baalat teshuvah*, she tried to fit in while having a reaction characterized as a "BT high." After Judaism became more fully incorporated into her life, questions that she probably had earlier in her journey resurfaced. She struggled—and continues to struggle—with being herself at the same time she sees herself conforming to a pattern she sees around her. Along the same lines, Eva, a member of the same focus group who described herself as a former hippie, stated that she has kept certain parts of her alive:

And then it started becoming like part of me and today I still struggle with it, but I feel more integrated, because I've kept certain parts of me alive, and just accepted that and accepted the fact that I'm different and this is great. I like that. I want to be, I don't want to be a mold, I want to be me.

Benor (2012) used the term "deliberate distinctiveness" to describe BTs' efforts to maintain parts of their former selves, such as music preferences and style of dress.

The process of being oneself is more complicated for some people than the scenario Eva portrayed. Being oneself may mean being open about health and mental health problems in one's family, which can jeopardize the marriage prospects of one's children. Furthermore, depending on which Orthodox community one joins, there may be no place for secular interests such as reading secular novels, going to the movies, listening to rock music, and playing tennis. A number of BTs in this study spoke of shame about problems in their families, and interests that they recognized as undesirable, leading them to withhold information about themselves from people whose acceptance they wanted. A BT who studied at a yeshiva in Israel for ten years said that if the teachers at his yeshiva knew how little learning he was doing now, they would probably be very disappointed in him. These BTs were sensitive to others' opinions and aware of aspects of themselves that others were likely to perceive as failings.

One way that some BTs were able to be themselves and have community, too, was to channel previous Jewish ethnic interests into religious activities. For example, Jacob was active in Hillel and other organizations supportive of Jews or Israel when he was a college student. While this involvement supported his Jewish identity, it did not contribute to his knowledge of Judaism as a religion. Today Jacob sees himself as "the same person" who expresses his activism differently:

> Just like I got involved in all my other [activities], that Jewish pride and the Jewish activism that I had in my pre-Orthodox days stays with me, and I just redefine it, and refine it, into the halachic lifestyle. And of course now I have a greater understanding . . . as to how it fits into a larger picture of being a Torah Jew.

At the time of his interview, Jacob reported being active in his synagogue and other Jewish communal activities. Similarly, Eli has redirected his attachment to the Grateful Dead to *davening*.

As mentioned, psychological integration is rarely complete. Nora, who regrets not having known more about Judaism while raising her children, had this to say about the 22 years she has been *frum*:

> I think for the first three quarters of my life as a *baalat teshuvah* . . . so much of me wanted to be like other people and it wasn't until I was happy being myself and with my own Jewish Orthodoxy and my own spirituality that I became comfortable and . . . happier in my *yiddishkeit*, and not feeling like I had to be like other people. And, when I developed the ability to accept myself and be happy with where I was Jewishly, then I was easier on my children and on my spouse and on everybody, and was able to give more and do more.

Nora, along with others, seems to suggest that there is a connection between one's personal psychological growth and one's growth as an Orthodox Jew. At first, one wants to be like those who were raised Orthodox, to fit into a "mold." Once one accepts oneself and one's level of observance and spirituality, one feels more self-confident and is able to engage more effectively with one's family.

Integrating Religion and Work

Another psychological task is to integrate religion/spirituality into other life domains. As a recent BT, Elliot, said, it is difficult to balance "learning goals, Torah learning, family, and work." Integration with marriage and parenting was discussed in chapter 5. Here I look at the way in which the *baalei teshuvah* integrated work with their religious life. (This section applies to the, twenty-three men and seventeen women participants who worked outside the home.)

Baalei *teshuvah* need to make decisions about how they present themselves at work. Jacob, a lawyer, discussed his initial struggles over "yarmulke off–yarmulke on, *kashrut*, (and) the level of *kashrut*." A woman in the second focus group, Naomi, described how, in the course of a social work job she held for twenty-five years, she changed into a *frum* woman. As she explained, she works in a secular mental health agency:

> One aspect that, I guess, I thought maybe we would touch on but that's been an area of concern for me, is that my professional growth and my spiritual growth have moved in two different [directions], have not been exactly parallel. So I work in a secular agency. . . . I've been at my agency twenty-five years, so it's been a very odd kind of thing where people have known me, both professionals and, since we run a day program, I actually have consumers[1] who know me twenty-five years, which [is] before and after, and in-between. And up and down. So, it's interesting, so like, my professional life is totally in the secular world, as my personal life has moved almost ninety percent in[to] the Orthodox world.

It is likely that consumers and co-workers who observed Naomi over the years saw her change from wearing slacks to skirts and other changes in her appearance. Because of the split between her professional and personal life and changes over time, she experienced dissonance, if not a lack of integration.

Those who worked within the Jewish community (nine interviewees) experienced less conflict. The BTs who worked in secular environments or were not self-employed had to request adaptations from employers to accommodate to their observances of Shabbat and holidays. During the winter months, one needs to leave work early on Fridays in order to be home before the Sabbath begins. In the fall, there are several Jewish holidays that necessitate absence from work, and in the spring there are two more. Some are two-day or weeklong holidays. Karen spoke of struggling when she first became observant with being a *frum* working person in the business world:

> Just that kind of pull to be like everybody else and socialize with work people and all that kind of stuff. It's very hard to be out there, especially when it's something new to you . . . or, you know, you work at a certain job for four, five years, and, you know, you work on Friday just like everybody else, and then one day you say, I have to leave at two o'clock on a Friday afternoon. I mean, that's a really hard thing to do.

Now married, a mother, and working in another position, Karen still finds it difficult to integrate her work and Orthodox Judaism. She continues to be too embarrassed to tell her co-workers that she cannot eat with them in non-kosher restaurants. A few women worked part-time, excluding Friday, giving them time to prepare the Sabbath meals. One BT mentioned that his work as a professor enabled him to have time off for Shabbat and holidays.

Some BTs changed their focus from work to religion. Ezra, for example, who was previously a successful lawyer who enjoyed the material comforts and prestige his practice brought, radically changed his priorities in the ten years he has been *frum*. He asserted, "Now work is just something I do in order to . . . support my family. And my real, my real, entire being is being observant and teaching Torah and learning." As he suggests, Ezra has become sufficiently knowledgeable to teach others, which is a great accomplishment for a *baal teshuvah*. Several men spoke about overvaluing material success before they did *teshuvah* and appreciating life more now. For example, Dov, who grew up in a modest, Minimalist Plus home and has been *frum* for two years, used to view the acquisition of material possessions as the route to happiness:

> I would drive through expensive neighborhoods and look at houses and say, gosh, you know, I gotta have a house like that one day. Or have to have this kind of car, have to have this much money in the bank. And, now, I can see, it's nice to have those things, there's certainly nothing innately wrong with that; there's something innately wrong, though, with that being the pursuit of life. And I developed huge sensitivity toward this in a good way, that that's not the route to happiness. If you get those things along the way, great. You know, maybe it makes life a little more comfortable, a little more enjoyable in some ways, but, it's really . . . the pursuit

of something spiritual [that matters]. . . . That spiritual part of myself has emerged in this process, and, you know, the little things are [what] make my every day really happier. You know, I get the first diaper in the morning. I go in and I get [son]. And he's smiling. Every day when I go in and . . . I come home and my wife and I have dinner together.

As Dov explained, since he did *teshuvah*, he has attained an increased appreciation of the joys of daily life and greater spiritual fulfillment as he adjusted his aspirations to better integrate Judaism.

Similar to Ezra and Dov, Jerry said that he used to consider financial success his main goal, but now he attaches greater value to "Hashem, and my family, and my *yiddishkeit*, and how I represent myself to the outside world as a representative of all those things." Jerry commented on personality changes he experienced during this shift. He used to insist on winning every argument, antagonizing other people in the process, whereas now he is more tolerant of others' points of view. Other participants told similar stories of behavioral changes. Gabe, for example, who used to get into political squabbles at work, has learned to avoid such situations.

Religion offers BTs a meaning system that that gives the sacred a central place (Silberman, 2005) and provides them with a framework to interpret the challenges they face at work. A few men who spoke of professional crises reframed these events as blessings in disguise. Greg described his focusing too much on work in the past as *avodah zarah* (idol worship). With help from his rabbi mentors, he came to realize that he was not spending enough time with his children and was not studying Torah. With changed priorities, he now attributes his professional achievements, in which he had prided himself, to Hashem.

Two psychotherapists discussed their efforts to bring spirituality into their work. Ruth said that she tries to use her relationship with God and her spirituality in a way that is healing to people, and Joshua said that he thinks about relevant Torah concepts during his work. Nora, an assistant teacher at an Orthodox day school, said that she applies Jewish values to her work:

I've tried to put spiritual [matters], like the kindness and the patience and the understanding of the children that I work with every day, [first]. I feel like, every day I try to be better with them, and better with my relationships with people and reach out more to people.

Two women who struggled with integrating feminism and Judaism reinvented themselves as teachers. Cheryl relinquished her law career and acquired a new mission in life from giving *shiurim* for women, while Tamar created music and dance classes for women and girls. As Tamar said, "I think it's important to take the gifts Hashem gives you, and do it in a kosher way, versus don't do them at all." Tamar was reflecting on restrictions on women's public performance that could have prevented her from using her ability to teach music and dance.

Dealing with Losses

During adulthood and in some cases earlier, *baalei teshuvah* experience the death of parents, grandparents, and other family members. These are inevitable events, though the timing varies from person to person. Aside from these losses, BTs face losses that are less visible but nonetheless painful. These are what Boss (1999) calls "ambiguous losses," which are vague, indefinite losses that are not marked by death or other overt signs. Of the kinds of losses Boss describes, those relevant to *baalei teshuvah* are ones that are suffered even though the person is alive or the situation continues. These stressful losses are difficult to resolve.

As shown in previous chapters, the decision to become Orthodox entails a radical life change. *Baalei teshuvah* give up many of the previously taken-for-granted features of secular life, such as eating in non-kosher restaurants, using electricity whatever day of the week it is, sexual experiences before marriage, and, for those who identify with more stringent streams of Orthodoxy, television, movies, and the internet. Orthodox communities expect men and women to dress modestly. Even though relinquishing their secular life entered into the decision to become a *baal* or *baalat teshuvah*, the sense of loss lingers. Living in an Orthodox community provides some protection against loss, but feelings resurface when a secular family leaves a phone message on the Sabbath, when BTs are invited by friends from their previous life to events that take place on religious holidays or Shabbat, and other experiences. Weddings of siblings and other family members who are marrying someone of another faith also evoke feelings of loss.

In chapter 5, I discussed the impact of the religious change on the family of origin. For the most part, family relations become complicated, at least initially, with families challenged by the BTs' need for kosher food, proximity to an Orthodox synagogue, and protection of their children from secular influences. Visiting back and forth is not easy. Both parents and adult children experience the loss of the kind of extended family they may have wanted.

Relationships with close friends can also be problematic, another ambiguous loss. A number of BTs reported distancing themselves from friends from the past because they no longer had anything in common with them. Several BTs who were *frum* only a few years attempted to preserve these friendships but ran into difficulties when they could not accept invitations to eat at friends' homes or could not find a restaurant that would satisfy both parties, and when they were invited to bar and bat mitzvahs held in Conservative or Reform synagogues. While transitioning to Orthodoxy they engaged in awkward social behaviors, such as asking friends who kept kosher about the level of *kashrut* they kept,[2] and insisting on eating on paper plates where the level was unacceptable to them. Nina attended a bat mitzvah of close friends' daughter in a Conservative synagogue but her husband, who followed the advice of his rabbi, said that it was not acceptable for him to go to this synagogue. Instead, he went to Shabbat services at an Orthodox synagogue in the same community:

> Now [husband] just couldn't *daven* there, he just couldn't. And that's fine. And, as I said, there are a lot of halachic reasons why I probably shouldn't have either. But I didn't want to hear that. That's why I didn't ask. . . . I find that there's sometimes a conflict between halachah, and kind of being a nice, good person. Nobody would really fault me, I'm sure.

Whatever the halakhic reasons were, Nina did not care. She was more concerned with maintaining her friendship than with the stringency recommended by her husband's rabbi. Nina is a recent *baalat teshuvah* who is still finding her way in Orthodox Judaism. She has not fully accomplished the psychological task of acknowledging losses of lifestyle, family, and friends and engaging in some grieving. Because the persons that are the subject of their grief are, for the most part, still alive, this is an ambiguous loss that is difficult for the BTs to acknowledge and grieve.

Consolidation

Consolidation entails the coming together of and working through all the tasks that have been described, increased comfort with oneself and others, and greater knowledge and competence in living as an Orthodox Jew. This is performed, experienced, and expressed in everyday life. Accordingly, *davening* regularly, eating kosher food, dressing modestly, eschewing gossip, learning, observing the Sabbath and holidays, and other activities feel natural. There is an acute consciousness of God's work as creator and a feeling of divine presence in one's life. *Baalei teshuvah* feel content in having found purpose, meaning, and direction, as well as a sense of community.

Consolidation is more easily described than achieved. As a *baalat teshuvah* interviewee remarked, "I am a work in process." Relatively new BTs experience a great deal of anxiety over what they do not know and what they anticipate having to learn to "catch up." Those who have been *frum* for many years may feel more confident, but they are still likely to face situations for which they are not prepared. As Breina remarked in Focus Group 1, "Once a *baal teshuvah*, always a *baal teshuvah*." David, who had been observant twenty-six years, was the only interview participant to assert the opposite sentiment:

> I don't see myself as a *baal teshuvah* anymore. I see myself as ingrained in the Orthodox mentality and way of life. . . . It's like just a way of life, now it's more, I'm more into the religion and more into what I do on a day-to-day basis. It becomes part of my life as opposed to being a new thing and always learning new things about it.

On the other hand, some of the interviewees seemed to be quoting rabbis and other instructors in a way that reflected unassimilated ideas. For example, Gabe used the idea of predetermination to explain his difficulties obtaining or holding onto a job. Another participant, Susan, spoke of seeking guidance from a book, possibly a "how to" book that explains Jewish laws that apply to everyday life or, with help from someone who can read it, the Shulkhan Arukh, which is a compilation of Jewish laws:

> Now I feel like I'm doing *mitzvos*, and I have a purpose of living, and there is a reason, and there is a Book that tells you how to live life. I mean, even if you don't do everything that's halachically right, there are still certain ways that you try to do your best, the way you treat people and the way you treat your family, and you work toward that. It doesn't mean it's gonna happen right away. But you try to do your best. And that's all you can do.

The BTs in this study spoke about internal and external changes but not in their core personalities. Those who described themselves as always intense became intense about observing religious laws and rituals. Those who had been activists in the secular Jewish world became activists within the Orthodox world. The men and women who described themselves as spiritual seekers during their journeys found new outlets for their spirituality. As Jacob said:

> I'm the same person. I still look at things, as I mentioned to you before, whether it's an *Ashrei* or a Jewish music, you know it brings back the core spiritual personality, I think that is there, and kind of remains the same. And then it's a question of the trappings and the trimmings around it that will change and be modified, and, I guess, the way you look at things. But . . . I still think I'm kind of the same person and I try to express that.

Using their core personalities, they revise and expand upon them. They learn to be less self-centered, less materialistic, and more oriented toward others in their own community and to Jews around the world. Motivated by the obligation to improve their character traits [*midot*], they strive toward personal growth through service to others. This results in increased self-awareness and self-acceptance.

As indicated, the consolidation process is rarely complete. *Frum* for thirty-eight years, Paul spoke of questions that had appeared to have been resolved in the past returning later. Others continue to feel conflicted over certain issues and uncertain about their ability to maintain their individuality. Clearly, consolidation does not mean that one eliminates spiritual struggles, questions, and doubts that are part of the experience of being human. In contrast with the struggles that they had prior to making a commitment, however, later struggles are based on lived experiences as participants in a religious community.

Social Integration

Social integration refers to the process of joining, adapting to, and becoming part of a new community.[3] The term can be applied to a wide range of contexts including but not limited to immigrating to another country, becoming a professional, and moving into a higher social class. In all these examples, one begins as an outsider, learns the rules of the new situation, and gradually enters into the fabric of life in the new milieu. For *baalei teshuvah*, social integration entails joining and becoming part of a preexisting Orthodox community and is the outcome of leaving one's former social group, learning the norms of the new group, conforming to the new community's standards, and achieving acceptance (Danzger, 1989).

When one joins a preexisting community, the norms, values, and standards of that community are already in place. Although some Orthodox Jewish norms such as those pertaining to Sabbath observance are explicit, some are implicit, knowable through socialization. One becomes socialized through observation, asking questions, practicing what one sees others practice, direct instruction, and being corrected for mistakes. Agents of socialization such as rabbis, rebbetzins, and community members assist in this process. An additional aspect of the new community is its own hierarchical structure based on its own values and history. In Orthodox communities, one may have status by virtue of being born into a family that has high status, such as that of a prominent rabbi, a head of a yeshiva, or a well-respected Torah scholar. The Yiddish term *yichus* is sometimes used to denote a prestigious religious lineage. One can also achieve status by being learned in sacred texts and through leading an exemplary religious life. In some Orthodox communities, status is based primarily on religious education, whereas in others it is through a combination of religious and secular education. In either case, those who were raised Orthodox benefit from early learning of the Hebrew language and religious practices at home and at school, as well as from participation in social networks (schools, summer camps, youth groups, and yeshivas) that are socially advantageous. Orthodox insiders (often those who are *frum* from birth) are privileged in having access to authoritative sources of knowledge about how to live a *frum* life from having grown up in a *frum* environment and being educated at religious schools. Accordingly, those who were raised Orthodox have the religious and social capital they need to succeed in Orthodox communities (Iannaccone 1990; Portes, 1998), while those who have adopted Orthodoxy lack these advantages.

Because they do not have the experiences that insiders have, the position of *baalei teshuvah* is marginal. Although they make efforts to learn, for the most part they begin the process of social integration deficient in the education and socialization they need to navigate comfortably in their new communities. They cannot follow the traditions of their families of origin because their families were not Orthodox. Unless they furthered their knowledge of Hebrew in classes in the United States or Israel and interacted closely with Orthodox Jews where they could observe their way of life, they lack important cultural "tools" (Swidler, 1986) they need in their new environment. Furthermore, they may be viewed as tainted by experiences in the secular world, such as dressing immodestly and having sexual relations before marriage. As Ebaugh (1988) explains, it is difficult for "exes" to leave a previous status without being perceived as retaining residuals from their past.

For these reasons, it is challenging for *baalei teshuvah* to become integrated into a preexisting Orthodox community and problematic for some members of that community to accept previously secular members. Recognizing that their lives have been different, *baalei teshuvah* are wary of those who were raised Orthodox, and the reverse is true of some of those who were raised *frum*.[4] Beyond these experiential differences are differences in knowledge, ideas about appropriate behavior, aspirations for their children, and interactional norms. These cultural differences are expressed in language, dress, ideas about sacred time and space, nonverbal behavior,[5] and other aspects. Even with remedial Jewish education in synagogues, yeshivas, and seminaries, large gaps remain. When they become aware of their differences initially, they have mixed feelings.

Initial Reactions: Amazed, in Awe, and Intimidated

The *baalei teshuvah*'s social integration should be seen in the light of their initial reactions, which lasted several years and changed with increased social integration. Early in their journeys, when *baalei teshuvah* are first exposed to Orthodox communities, they find themselves in what seems to be a different universe. As Allison remarked on her first meeting with a woman with a "yeshivish" background:

> I'll never forget the first time I met someone in this neighborhood who is one of fifteen [children in her family]. And I remember being at a dinner table with her and it came out that she was in this family. And she's from a yeshivish-type family. She doesn't live the lifestyle now. And I remember thinking, you know, she could have come from Mars as far as I was concerned.

While Allison was amazed at the cultural differences between this woman and herself, others were in awe of those who were raised *frum*.

Initially, the *baalei teshuvah* were impressed with the personal qualities they found in those who were raised Orthodox, idealizing them. They described them as "sincere," "sweet," and "wonderful," with a sense of gratitude and appreciation "that just shines forth all the time." They contrasted the constancy and centrality of the FFBs' graciousness with the superficial expressions of appreciation they hear in the secular world. They described FFBs in hyperbolic terms. Two people who were impressed with the authenticity and knowledge of FFBs said that they thought that almost all the men were rabbis. Another BT who was awestruck remarked that there are "no better people than *frum* people in the world. . . . They'd give you the shirts off their backs."

As they moved toward becoming Orthodox, the *baalei teshuvah* viewed those who were raised Orthodox as role models, exemplars of how to live as a *frum* person. Although Ezra did not regard all Orthodox people as exemplary, he described some as "people who . . . [are] a combination of everything that you would want to see in a person . . . warmth and acceptance, and scholarship, and . . . learning, ritual, everything." This opinion was widely shared.

When they joined Orthodox synagogues, they also idealized them. Some referred to their "*shul* communities" as their significant communities whereas others pointed to observant neighbors and friends as such. Liora described her *shul* community this way:

> When I look in people's eyes at our *shul*, I see the striving, I see the striving for people trying to connect, and more than just spiritually, religiously, with God, to bring meaning to their lives, to their families' lives, to connect to all Jews.

Sherry said of her nearby community, which encompassed a neighborhood and *shul*:

> In this kind of community, when people suffer in an Orthodox community, everybody's there for you. And everybody, even if it's not with their words, their presence is there. It's commanded of you. You know, it's what's required of you that makes you a good person. Not how you satiate yourself. It's really a counter-cultural existence, being Orthodox. And, that's something that I willingly embrace.

Others were impressed with the readiness of the community to respond to each other's needs and noted that this was not the norm elsewhere. One woman recounted how her community took in a group of Orthodox Jewish strangers who had been detained on the highway so that they would be able to observe Shabbat before it got dark.

Ariella was impressed with how consistent and principled Orthodox people were whereas Dov expressed admiration for the bar mitzvah celebrations in the Orthodox community: "There's not as much fanfare surrounding a bar or bat mitzvah [as in non-Orthodox bar mitzvahs]. It's more about the meaning behind it, not as much about . . . the big party with the entertainer showing up and that kind of stuff." Overall, the BTs' early impressions were with the personal qualities of the FFBs they met and with the consistency, integrity, and meaningfulness of their way of life.

Steinsaltz (1982) states that *baalei teshuvah* are particularly prone to idealizing the Orthodox Jews whom they view as "perfect." This is "based either on living models glimpsed from a distance or archetypes out of the past. Such a person is imagined to be completely at one with himself and his chosen path, knowing no failure in its pursuit" (p. 35). Such ideal types, Steinsaltz asserts, "have never existed except as figments of the imagination and of literary invention" (p. 35).

Another common early reaction of BTs to those who were raised Orthodox was intimidation. The FFBs seemed so far ahead of them in their knowledge of Hebrew, Aramaic, and Jewish law that the BTs did not think they could ever achieve such a level. As Shimon said, "I feel intimidated by people who were *frum* from birth. . . . I feel lacking." Initially, Orthodox synagogues seemed inaccessible because of the BTs' deficiencies in Hebrew, which made it difficult for them to follow the prayer service. They worried, too, about being accepted. Yet Howard recalled being well received when he was looking into an Orthodox *shul* that someone had recommended:

> It was very intimidating because . . . you don't read Hebrew, and I figured there's gonna be all these people and everything's gonna be in Hebrew, and nobody's gonna say a word in English, and I'm not gonna know where they are or how they are. But I went. And I came home and I said, "This was great. The people are so nice. Mind you that in three years, going every single Shabbos and every single *yom tov* to [a Conservative synagogue], [only] two people ever invited us over for Shabbos. And nobody ever befriended us. Nobody ever tried to *mekarev* us [bring us closer to Judaism]. Not even the rabbi.

As Howard explained, the human interaction and warm reception he experienced the first time he attended a service at an Orthodox synagogue was a significant factor that led him to further involvement in Orthodox Judaism.

Over time and with more contact, the BTs felt less intimidated. Sarah expressed this sentiment:

Initially it was intimidating, but with time I've gotten so immersed in being with so many people that are *frum* from birth that I am comfortable being with them, I'm comfortable speaking with them . . . I know, again, there's *gvul* [a boundary] between us, but it's not an intimidating experience for me. As a matter of fact, I had an experience just a few days ago, where I was invited to sheva brachos, and I assumed it was gonna be a very large sheva brachos. And I got there, and it wasn't so large. And most of the people there were very yeshivish and myself and a few others who did not grow up like that. And it made me feel so good . . . that she invited me. Listen, I'll never be a hundred percent part of their world. . . . You can't pretend that your father was a rosh yeshiva [head of a yeshiva] if he's not a rosh yeshiva, but that if you're a good person and you take yourself seriously, and you take your religion seriously, and you're a nice person, then why can't you get invited?

In view of her lack of status markers in the yeshivish community, Sarah was flattered over being invited to sheva brachos by a yeshivish family. Sarah appears to be socially integrated, though acutely conscious of being different.

Preferences for Other Baalei Teshuvah

During the interviews, participants were asked about their relationships with other *baalei teshuvah* compared with those who were raised Orthodox. Twenty-four of the forty-two individuals who responded to this question (57 percent) expressed a preference for relationships with other *baalei teshuvah*. Only five said that they preferred those who were raised Orthodox, while thirteen expressed no preference. The comments of those who said that they felt more connected to other *baalei teshuvah* made it clear that they perceived themselves as a unique and special group that is different from those who were raised Orthodox. They prided themselves in their passion, excitement with learning, and their commitment. With similar backgrounds and comparable journeys, they gravitated toward people who were like them and formed *baal teshuvah* subcommunities. As Joshua said:

I think most of my friends are *baal teshuvahs*. Most of them are people who are very successful in their chosen fields of endeavor but were Jewishly illiterate and decided to become religious. And . . . I just feel more comfortable with *baal teshuvahs*.

Jacob spoke of the special bond among *baalei teshuvah*:

> *Baalei teshuvahs* definitely have a special bond. Probably the way like born-again Christians, you know, have these conventions. I'm sure it's the same way. It's this life-changing event that you, when you meet others who've done it, it . . . confirms that you, not a question of that you doubted that you made the right decision, but you're very proud that there's a club. You're a member of a club.

Another participant, Zvi, described this bond with more fervor:

> *Baal teshuvahs* are . . . my world! Those are my friends. Like we share common experience. . . . You can relate to someone who's been through what you've been through. The story might be different but it's basically the same.

The bond among *baalei teshuvah* is attributable to their having had similar experiences of breaking away from the pattern in their families of origin, having had to learn a great deal, and feeling insecure among those who grew up Orthodox. Jacob spoke further of the camaraderie he feels with those who those who "were on the journey together" who "were all fumbling and mumbling together, which many of us still feel we do today." Another basis for the bond is the *baalei teshuvah*'s secular-world experiences. While those who were raised Orthodox were learning in yeshivas, kollels, and, in some cases, Jewish-affiliated universities, the *baalei teshuvah* were attending secular universities, some in the Ivy League, getting established in professions and partaking of the broader culture of music, art, literature, theater, and dance, as well as politics. Their frames of reference were different.

Some BTs expressed their "clubbiness" by joining synagogues that had a relatively high concentration of *baalei teshuvah*. One of our key informants, the rabbi of one such synagogue, spoke of his work creating an atmosphere of friendship, warmth, and community at his *shul*, and encouraging a feeling of belonging. He and his wife set the tone by inviting people to their home, and members follow suit and invite each other. He also described the *davening* at his *shul* as animated. Interviewees who affiliated with his *shul* spoke of the supportive, family-like atmosphere they experienced there.

Members of another synagogue with a large proportion of BTs supplemented the activities of their *shul* with a "user-friendly" service held monthly in someone's home. Joshua described it as follows:

> I've organized a sort of a Carlebach-style *minyan* at our *shul*. Meets once a month, it's an outreach thing . . . like a *kiruv* thing, for other people. . . . We call it a user-friendly *minyan*. I would like to think that every *minyan* is user-friendly but they're really not if you don't know what's going on. And so, we have this *minyan* that . . . meets once a month in somebody's house, and we . . . sing everything out loud together, slow . . . narrow the service down to the absolute minimum that needs to be done halachically so that we can spend more time doing that. We take a break in the middle after the Torah reading, we go upstairs and make kiddush and have a social time and parshah discussion. Open [for] any question, [that] kind of thing.

Frum for twenty-five years, Joshua seems to be sensitive to the needs of newcomers to understand, keep up with, and ask questions about the service. Just as he and others in the *minyan* were socialized by FFBs and longtime BTs, so do they socialize newcomers to Orthodox Judaism.

Despite the bonding and mutual support valued by some BTs, others were critical of certain peers. Seth remarked:

> I would put *baalei teshuvah* in different categories. There's the people who are sort of, somewhat normal—you know, who just sort of live their Judaism and don't wear it on their sleeve. And then there are people who wear it on their sleeve and [others who] . . . seem to go overboard, you know, almost as a reactionary to where they were. I'm very accepting of all kinds of people. . . . I try not to judge them, but there are some people just get in your face too much, so . . . those are not the people we're best friends with.

Seth, *frum* for fifteen years, complains that some *baalei teshuvah* flaunt their Judaism. Similarly, Sarah, also *frum* for fifteen years, was critical of *baalei teshuvah*:

> I'm not the type to go out and seek *baalei teshuvah*. I'm surely more than happy to speak to somebody in length about it, but

> somebody who is so fervent and so gung ho, so magically in love
> with becoming religious . . . I don't have the patience for that.

The heightened level of enthusiasm of newer *baalei teshuvah* is a source of
annoyance to some BTs, who act as if they are not one of them and never
experienced a "BT high." In her study of language usage by newcomers to
Orthodox Judaism, Benor (2012) described a pattern of "hyperaccommodation"
in which the BTs who are trying to conform do so in an exaggerated way.

Some *baalei teshuvah* were critical of those who were raised Orthodox.
Uri, for example, had this to say:

> The answer is that I tend to gravitate toward people who are *baalei*
> *teshuvah* in the Orthodox community. I think that my experience
> has been that people who are *frum* from birth tend to be a lot
> more parochial and less, a lot less, interesting. And so I tend to
> gravitate toward people who are *baalei teshuvah* that have really
> interesting backgrounds.

Other participants spoke of finding FFBs complacent, flat in their observance,
dogmatic, judgmental, and materialistic. Paul labeled them "FFH"—*frum* from
habit—highlighting their mechanical observance and lack of passion. Eli said
that he would like to move to a community in which there were more *baalei*
teshuvah, whom he found more spiritual.

De-idealization

Having once been in awe of those raised Orthodox, some *baalei teshuvah* later
became disillusioned. In Focus Group 1, the term "de-idealization" was used
to depict a process in which *baalei teshuvah* lose their previously idealistic
views of Orthodox people and their communities, become disillusioned, and
eventually attain a realistic perception. As Shlomo, a focus group member
explained, initially he experienced Orthodox Judaism as "fireworks" and was
amazed at the wonders he learned. Once he became immersed in a religious
community and was exposed to its politics, his perception changed:

> And it was as if I just realized that this similar thing, that when
> you're a kid you realize that your parents are human beings. That
> they are no longer the idealized parents. That they are actually

human beings. And all of a sudden, now, religion was the same way. It wasn't the fantasy of the *baal teshuvah*. . . . It's now, "Gee. Religious people are like human beings."

The analogy with the parent-child relationship is worth considering. It appeared to the researchers, as well as a number of the key informants, that many BTs were seeking parent substitutes. In chapter 2, I noted that some beginning *baalei teshuvah* adopted individuals and families in the community as advisers. Several BTs spoke of seeking, but not finding, a special rabbi or rebbetzin who could perform a similar function, a spiritual guide, discussed in chapter 4. Carey, a member of the same focus group as Shlomo, spoke of relinquishing her fantasy about finding such a rabbi while she was becoming disillusioned over the last few years:

> Because before, I was looking for, hoping there would be a rabbi, a rebbe, a rebbetzin, people from the community, just that the love and warmth would just sweep me along in greater and greater observance. Now I realize it's just really a solitary decision that one embarks upon really with a solitary relationship with God. And that's what I'm doing after a kind of sad period.

Some *baalei teshuvah* became disillusioned with people in the communities they had joined. Eliza was dismayed about the conversation that took place when she was a Shabbat guest of an FFB:

> So I have a hard time if I go to somebody's home and they're *frum* from birth, and the conversation is no different than the conversation would be on a Thursday. And sometimes even, you know, veers off toward *lashon hara* [gossip]. And I'm thinking, this is Shabbos!

Eliza expected the conversation to be more spiritual, in keeping with the holiness of the day, and would certainly not include *lashon hara*, which is considered sinful. Other people had more global complaints about people in the community:

> People get very petty about their level of observance, and they have this need to condescend. (Sherry)

People are just hung up about who's doing what and who has money and who doesn't and who's going here and who's doing that, and that part of it I don't like. That's what I wanted to get away from when I became religious. (Susan)

And then you see that there are *frum* criminals and *frum* people who are abusive and people who fudge on their taxes. And you realize that everybody is human. It makes it easier for you to be a part of it. But it also makes you feel like, "How could this be?" (Lauren)

These examples show that *baalei teshuvah* reflect on how their previously idealistic perceptions contrast with how they later understood the communities. While they are disappointed, they have grown in their perceptions of what it is like to be human. Their previous perceptions were sometimes found to be distortions that they adjust after living in a *frum* community for years.

Changes in Social Integration over Time

While some *baalei teshuvah* eventually developed a less idealistic, more realistic perception of those who were raised Orthodox but remained part of *baal teshuvah* subcommunities, others moved into the mainstream Orthodox community. They relinquished membership in predominantly *baal teshuvah* synagogues that they joined early in their journeys, feeling less of a need for a built-in support system from rabbis of those synagogues who were experienced with supporting BTs and from other *baalei teshuvah*. Furthermore, they did not always think that these synagogues were appropriate for their children, who were being raised Orthodox. For example, Yossi, who used to be active in a *baal teshuvah*–oriented synagogue, attends several other *shuls* now. He explained why he changed:

I felt that [at] Rabbi _____'s *shul*, that there wasn't really anything for me to gain at a certain point. . . . Actually, I was getting a lot from Rabbi _____ over the years, and I was also able to give and learn with other people, and connect with other people. And I think that I got to a point where my family responsibilities, my children growing up and getting married, I had a family. I had my own family, so I wasn't that much in need. I didn't need a *shul* family. And I honestly didn't have time for a *shul* family.

He added that he was looking forward to making other changes in his life, such as teaching.

Another participant, Brian, spoke about becoming less compulsive over his religious observance so that he could deal more effectively with other parts of his life that he thought he was neglecting:

> So in order to, in my own mind, free myself up to address other things that I thought needed to be addressed, I felt justified in relaxing some of my behaviors around ritual that I felt became overly compulsive. And so I loosened up my observance among certain details, so that I would have more time. More time for other people, more time to focus on making a living for my family, more time for myself, to be with myself, and to process what I was going through.

Brian's progressive relaxation of his formerly rigid practice of Orthodox Judaism is similar to a pattern Benor (2012) describes as the "bungee effect," where one hyper-accommodates as a beginning BT and later reaches a plateau. *Frum* for twenty-five years, Brian has come a long way from his Minimalist family background to studying in both university and yeshiva environments, and to taking on different levels of practice. His changes appear to be a natural development as seen in someone who has matured over time.

Longtime BTs expressed feeling more comfortable with and accepted by the FFB community than they did in the past. With increased contact, they felt less intimidated and more relaxed in their company. Nora, who has been living an Orthodox life in an Orthodox community for twenty-two years, spoke of her changed feelings this way:

> And, people who are *frum* from birth . . . I don't feel like as in awe anymore. . . . I see them more as regular people and just people that are my friends and I can relate to but . . . over time, I've been able to just relax and . . . see that we share, you know, we have a lot in common and, but the thing that we don't have in common is family ties that are *frum*.

Passing

In his sociological study *Stigma*, Goffman (1963/1974) discussed how individuals with a discrediting characteristic that is known to some but not to others are able to slip into situations in which they present themselves as "normal." Although, on the surface, one would not consider being a *baal* or *baalat teshuvah* stigmatizing, some FFB communities hold unfavorable views about BTs (see, e.g., Levin, 1986). The criticism of BTs made by some interviewees presented earlier demonstrate a distancing of themselves from others who, like them, became Orthodox. Members of Focus Group 2 vacillated between expressing shame and pride over their status. As Edward said:

> I feel compelled to say . . . that, although on one hand, I feel like, yeah, I'm a *baal teshuvah*, and I'm sort of proud of it, there's also part of me that thinks, uh oh, I hope people don't know that I am.

The shame and embarrassment are attributable to gaps in their knowledge on the one hand and, as Edward later suggested, impressions held in the Orthodox community that there is something wrong with people who become Orthodox, or, as was mentioned earlier, they go overboard or are too gung ho.

A few people boasted about their ability to pass. Men who had been *frum* for some time spoke about their ability to *daven* like someone who grew up Orthodox. For example, Yossi said, "I could fit into a regular like Agudah kind of *shul*[6], and people don't even know that I'm a BT, because I'm a seasoned BT for twenty-eight years." Still, he said that he connected better with other *baalei teshuvah*. Joshua, *frum* for twenty-five years, bragged that he was accepted by "the top *frum* families in town," whereas Maya, *frum* for thirty years, boasted that her child married the child of a rosh yeshiva. Allison, *frum* for only ten years, said, "I can quote unquote 'pass' very easily. . . . I speak Yiddish a little bit[7]; I can pass. I sound like a black person, but, you know, a light-skinned black person." Allison's claim that she can pass was based on her exposure to the language through her Yiddish-speaking European father. By "black person," Allison was metaphorically referring to the "black-hat," haredi population, with her self-description as a "light-skinned black person" reflecting her marginal position in the black-hat community. Nevertheless, despite boasts like those of Yossi, Joshua, Maya, and Allison, most BTs would agree with Sarah, quoted earlier, who said, "I'll never be a hundred percent part of their world."

Besides those who thought that they could pass, there were those who thought that although they appeared *frum*, they were not fully assimilated. Raphael, a mental health professional in Focus Group 1, described looking like a Yiddish speaker but being unable to speak the language:

> I was in a supermarket . . . maybe eight years ago. My Yiddish was very, very, very rough. Barely existent. And a man walked over to me in the supermarket with a heavy European accent. He starts speaking to me in Yiddish. At that time, I was already wearing a black hat. My beard was long. And I said to him basically, "I'm sorry but I don't speak Yiddish." He says [with accent], "Oh. You're American." . . . So even as I move up the ladder and I look more like the real McCoy, people have different expectations of me and I'm worried a lot of the time that I'm going to find myself in an embarrassing situation. Because there is something they all know and take for granted and I don't.

He, like others who looked the part but did not know all the lines, felt like an imposter.

Baila opened her interview by saying "I don't know if you picked the greatest person to interview, because . . . in one respect . . . I present myself as *frum* in the world but I still have issues with Yiddishkeit, so you know." Her issues, described in chapter 6, had to do with doubting the veracity of stories in the Torah or Midrash that seem implausible or those that point to the shortcomings of the patriarchs and other biblical figures. Thus, some BTs saw themselves as able to pass successfully while others who saw themselves as passing thought that they were misrepresenting themselves. A couple of key informants stated that they can identify *baalei teshuvah* by the way they dress and how they *daven*. This raises the question of how socially integrated *baalei teshuvah* are.

How Well Integrated Are They?

Most of the *baalei teshuvah* interviewed for this study have lived in and participated in the religious activities of Orthodox communities. They *daven* in one or more local Orthodox synagogues, dress modestly, take classes, and do volunteer work in the community. Those with school-age children have sent their children to Orthodox religious schools. They serve on boards, engage in fundraising and program development, and perform committee work for their synagogues and Jewish communal organizations. They volunteer at their children's schools, helping with musical programs and assisting in the administrative offices. A few BTs have offered classes to adults. Giving to the community seemed integral to their religious commitment. As Jacob said of his involvement:

> I'm a real firm believer in everybody volunteering and being involved so I got involved right away in the *shul* . . . what[ever] I can, different committees, different activities, because I believe it's an obligation. . . . I don't look at it any other way. . . . I have to do it. In fact, typically I get overloaded. . . . How could I possibly turn my back on . . . my people, my community?

The kind of community service Jacob described did not require knowledge of Hebrew, Yiddish, or Aramaic or familiarity with Jewish texts. It requires the kinds of skills that *baalei teshuvah* can and do offer their communities.

Several men spoke with pride about leading prayers at their *shuls* or in *minyans* in which they participated. Dov, *frum* for two years, said that serving as chazzan "seemed like the natural next step for me" and that his next goal is to read from the Torah or the *haftarah*. (Dov, from a Minimalist Plus family, had a Hebrew School education plus additional learning while becoming *frum*.) *Frum* for twenty-two years, Jacob served as gabbai for many years, a role that helped him gain competency in the service. Uri, *frum* for ten years, said that he was hesitant to take on a leadership role partly because he was relatively new to the community and had not until recently settled into his own home, but also because "I haven't quite figured . . . what the credentials are to be active in . . . an Orthodox synagogue." Nevertheless, Uri set up learning programs in his community. As he explained, "[I] physically went out and said, hey guys, I want to learn about Soloveitchik.[8] Will you teach it, and I'll get together people? So I've done some of that to try to continue to grow."

Whereas several men referred to roles in religious services, some of the women described roles in the wider Jewish community. This included serving as president of a women's service organization, directing a Jewish nursery school, and participation in a *chevra kadisha*, a group responsible for the ritual preparation of the body for burial. The two interviewees who spoke of the latter explained how meaningful this was for them. Annie said:

> I happen to get a great deal of, I don't know if it's spiritual satisfaction, but comfort every time I help to prepare a body for burial. When I see the decedent first come in and her face might still be distorted. She just looks like a dead person. Through the course of the group working with her I always feel extremely moved by the love and devotion that the women from the *chevra kadisha* pay to her. To the point that if you accidentally bump her head you apologize. Just the care and devotion that goes into that. I always

feel that at the end of the process when we place the decedent into the casket, that she looks so much better prepared to meet her maker. And I think to myself, "This is what being a part of the community is all about and I feel good that I was able to give over this comfort and to prepare her and to make her ready."

Preparing a body for burial is an act of loving-kindness, encompassed by the word *chesed*. BTs spoke, too, of *bikur cholim*, visiting people who are ill, hospitalized, or isolated, taking a frail elderly *shul* member to visit his son in a nursing home, visiting nursing home residents, and visiting their own elderly relatives. They also donate blood, help with food distribution drives, and other volunteer activities. A couple of people mentioned that they always were oriented toward helping others before they became Orthodox and did not know that they were doing mitzvahs, but as Greg said, he now ties his helping to his service to Hashem. Karen said that when engages in bikur cholim, she feels spiritually fulfilled. Another way in which the BTs participate in community life is to reach out to people exploring Orthodox Judaism. It is common for BTs to have guests who are exploring Orthodox Judaism for Sabbath and holiday meals. Some, like Maya, saw reaching out to potentially Orthodox Jews as their mission in life:

> I'm very involved right now, my direction is very much in *keruv*, through Aish HaTorah, and I've made some very wonderful close friends through that. . . . I also get a tremendous amount of spiritual satisfaction in being able to help somebody to learn about their yiddishkeit. And somebody, recently, from Aish HaTorah wants to set up a kosher kitchen, so she's, she's asked me if I'd come and help her do that. It's just, like, so exciting! So, that's very exciting. . . . (It's clear to me) that that's the work Hashem wants me to do.

It is apparent that the *baalei teshuvah* are socially integrated into the community through institutions like synagogues and their children's schools. Furthermore, they are actively engaged in community service activities where they could transfer skills developed in secular environments. Nevertheless, their integration appears to be partial. They are most comfortable in *baal teshuvah* subcommunities, engaging in service and outreach activities through them. For the most part, they felt different from the mainstream. Those who felt more integrated were married to people who were raised Orthodox, were *frum* for twenty or more years, or had made concerted efforts to advance their knowledge and skills. Others were left with residual feelings of inadequacy. Those who became Orthodox prior to having children or soon afterward, thus raising their children *frum* from birth, may achieve fuller social integration through their children, who will have the educational credentials their parents lacked, assuming that the children decide to remain Orthodox.

Summary

This chapter described the internal and external processes that *baalei teshuvah* experience when they live out their commitment to Orthodox Judaism. For BTs, psychological integration refers to the achievement of a sense of wholeness through the acceptance of one's secular past, reworking aspects of one's self to fit one's adopted religious orientation, and creating a revised identity in which Orthodox Judaism is focal. Social integration refers to the process of becoming part of an existing Orthodox community. These processes occur in tandem with each other and influence each other.

Psychological integration is a developmental process that is ongoing, nonlinear, and rarely completed. It has six components, which are (1) separation-individuation; (2) blending who one was with who one is; (3) being oneself while conforming to community norms; (4) integrating religion and work; (5) dealing with loss; and (6) consolidation. The process involves separating psychologically (but not interpersonally) from one's family of origin, retaining parts of one's previous identity, becoming oriented toward a new community, dealing with religious restrictions at work, and revising one's spiritual-religious identity.

Social integration is a social process of becoming part of a new community. It is challenging for newcomers, who have deficits in their knowledge of Hebrew, Jewish law, and rituals, which makes them feel insecure. Initially, they are in awe of and feel intimidated by people who were raised Orthodox, whom they idealize. Later, some of them experience de-idealization, when they recognize that FFBs have human flaws. A majority find community with other *baalei teshuvah*, whose journeys, backgrounds, and life experiences are similar to theirs. Yet they engage extensively in community life in the Orthodox communities they join through their synagogues, outreach organizations, and children's schools, and through volunteer activities. Over time, some *baalei teshuvah* move into the mainstream and seem to pass, whereas others, regardless of the length of time they are *frum*, continue to prefer socializing with other BTs.

Chapter 8

Incorporating Spirituality
into Everyday Life

Much has been said in this volume about the journey toward commitment and the subsequent struggles to acquire academic and cultural knowledge, cope with spiritual-religious conflicts, and accomplish psychological and social integration. I return now to the spiritual experiences of *baalei teshuvah* in their everyday lives. In the introduction, I defined spirituality as both a subjective experience of connection to God and living in accordance with teachings of the Torah and the performance of *mitzvot*. In this chapter, I demonstrate how the BTs live out their spiritual-religious commitments in their daily lives. This entails a radical revision of their previous worldviews and a reattribution of life events to God.

According to *Pirkei Avot*[1], the "Ethics of the Fathers," "The world is based on three things; the Torah, serving God, and active loving-kindness," in Hebrew, *Torah, avodah,* and *gemilut chasadim,* respectively (See Hirsch, 1967, 1979, 1989, trans. into German by Hirsch and into English by Hirschler, p. 7). *Torah* refers to "knowledge of the truth and the will of God," *avodah* means "*dutiful obedience,* serving God by fulfilling His will," and *gemilut chasadim* refers to "selfless active loving-kindness" that fosters the welfare of others (Hirsch, 1989, p. 7, n. 2).[2] Goldin (2003) noted that *Torah* refers to the *Five Books of Moses; avodah* to worship in the Temple; and *gemilut chasadim* to deeds of love. These three fundamental ideas and activities can also be viewed as paths to spiritual development—study, prayer, and loving-kindness (Strassfeld, 2002/2006).

223

The participants in this study pursued all three paths, giving each of them distinct interpretations and emphases. In chapter 4, I discussed the learning activities (*Torah*) and *davening* (*avodah*) in which the BTs engaged. I discussed their anxiety over their lack of knowledge, and the efforts, especially on the part of men, to become proficient in Hebrew and to be able to *daven* in the synagogue. I noted that the women, who felt less pressure to perform publicly, expressed more excitement over their Torah learning and less interest in *davening* than the men did. In chapter 7, I gave attention to the BTs' participation in deeds of loving-kindness (*gemilut chasadim*) in the context of social integration. As indicated in the definition of spirituality, these activities enable people to feel close to God. Study participants used the term *avodat Hashem* (service to Hashem) to explain what they think Hashem wants of them.

Engagement in these three paths is predicated on consciousness of God and expressing this awareness in everyday life. In this chapter, I show how the BTs reformulated their experiences so that God, spirituality, and religious practice are central. I discuss *baalei teshuvah*'s thoughts about spirituality and religion, their ideas about God, what they had to say about their relationship with God, their views on divine intervention, their feelings of gratitude, the healing they experienced, and their spiritual aspirations and growth.

Thoughts about Spirituality and Religion

Although the perspective taken in this book is that spirituality and religion are interconnected, the women and men gave divergent emphases to the two ideas. The women spoke readily about spirituality and the presence of God in their lives, with one exception, and this woman recanted her initial objection toward the end of her interview.[3] In contrast, many of the men expressed uneasiness with the term spirituality, giving greater emphasis to their religious obligations and practices or their intellectual involvement. They seemed to associate spirituality with something non-religious and offbeat. As one male focus group member said, "I've kind of put it into the same category as feeling the energy, you know, eating the yogurt." Nonetheless, several men described their wives as spiritual. This split along gender lines was also evident in the talk in one of the focus groups and in conversations with key informants.

The differences in perspective were apparent in women's discussions about the incorporation of spirituality in their everyday lives. Karen, *frum* for eleven years, said little about *davening*, while highlighting awareness:

If we work under the premise that my aspiration is to always increase my *avodas Hashem*, always to increase my feeling of closeness to *Hashem*, then it's about trying to be aware of that as much as I can, even through my daily crazy schedule.

Sarah, *frum* for fifteen years, also commented on awareness of God's expectations. She said that she was conscious of nonverbal behaviors such as shaking one's head in disapproval, which could be construed as gossip and which she strived to control. Other women focused on working on their character traits, their *midot*, such as controlling their anger, among others. As Nina, three years post-commitment, said, "I try to really work on my personal growth in terms of being more patient, in terms of not judging people."

Some women saw engagement in traditional female role behavior as spiritual. Liora, *frum* for six years, expressed joy over making challah, and Baila, *frum* for twenty-four years, spoke of expressing her spirituality by wearing skirts and long sleeves and covering her hair. Erica, *frum* for seven years, said:

The biggest way I see *Hashem* in my life is through my husband and my children. Everything I do in my home. I mean, I can sweep my floor and I am creating a clean space to raise Jewish children and make a Jewish home. And that's where Judaism revolves. It revolves around the home.

Other women gave attention to *davening*, learning, and *chesed* as spiritually meaningful.

The men focused primarily on religious practice—*davening*, the performance of *mitzvot*, and complying with Jewish law (*halakhah*). They wanted to improve their skills in Hebrew so they could more competently participate in synagogue services. Four men rejected the term spirituality, while others little to say on the topic. Seth, *frum* for fifteen years, described himself as "pragmatic" rather than spiritual. Similarly, Mark, five years Orthodox, emphasized the "doing" of Judaism:

When I do things, I don't feel I'm being spiritual. It's just, I do things, this is the way things are. . . . There are things that you do, there are things that you don't do. If you want to call that spiritual, I don't know if you want to call that spiritual. If I talk to God, is that being spiritual, or is that just talking to God?

Like some of the other men who distanced themselves from the term spirituality, Mark had difficulty seeing his relationship with God as spiritual. In this study, feeling close to God is regarded as fundamental to spirituality.

Some men did see the connection between religious practice, their relationship with God, and spirituality. As Arthur, *frum* for twelve years, said:

> It's hard for me to get past 9:00 in the morning without spiritual beliefs. You wash your hands, and you put on *tefillin*, you wear your yarmulke. You're constantly doing these things. Putting on *tefillin* is just so powerful . . . there's just so much there.

The men who appeared to be most comfortable with spirituality affiliated with Hasidim or non-haredi streams they described as modernist and centrist.

In addition to discussing their religious practices, the men (like the women) discussed working on their *midot* and *chesed*. Overall, however, the men focused primarily on *davening* and learning.

Thoughts about God

In chapter 1, I portrayed the participants' earliest memories of thinking about God. They viewed God as Creator, powerful, and caring, and they located this powerful Being above them (in the sky) or in nature. Some recalled that their parents and Hebrew School teachers did not talk about God whereas others spoke of parents who believed in God but did not demonstrate their belief through religious practices. In the course of their development, the *baalei teshuvah* continued to envision God in ways they did in the past and in other ways.

At the time of their interviews, they described God as omnipotent and omniscient, just, loving, giving, and forgiving. (These characteristics are among the thirteen attributes of God listed in Exodus 34:6–7 that are recited in prayer services.) They saw God as an ethical force that brings meaning to life and as a divine presence that is actively involved in their lives. As Jacob, *frum* for twenty-two years, said:

> So, personally, I am of the opinion that God involves Himself in everything, whether we recognize it or not, whether it's direct or indirect, and that if there is any kind of pain, physical, spiritual, emotional pain, that there is some reason for it and that it is typically meant to be *metaken*, to fix, repair, to affect you in a positive way, and I find that's a very uplifting way of looking at things.

God's active role included protection, emotional support, and divine intervention. For example, Liora (*frum* for six years) said that when she is under great stress, "*Hashem* will hold my hand."

Most of the BTs said that they believed that God was present in their lives and that God's gift, the Torah, was true. Joshua, *frum* for twenty-five years, put it this way:

> I guess [I] discovered what you would call spirituality and grew to understand that the stuff really is true. And there really, there really has to be, it's like whatever God, whatever the word God means, there really is something there because it's just, everything fits together in a way that it just couldn't without that. It just makes sense.

Eliza, *frum* for nineteen years, came to a similar conclusion during medical school when she became astounded by the complexity of the human body:

> And then around twenty-three, thereabouts, I went to medical school. And I was very much struck, awestruck, with the intricacies of the body, and the workings, and it became even clearer to me that this couldn't be a world that just created itself. It's just impossible. There was just too much detail, and too much that, one little thing go awry, the whole thing would fall apart. Chemistry, biochemistry, anatomy, physiology, the hand of God was there every time I looked at something.

This impression remained with her.

Relationship with God

Almost everyone talked about his or her relationship with God and expressed a need for a close connection with God. They connected in a variety of ways, most commonly through prayer, study, following Jewish laws, performing *mitzvot*, improving their *midot*, and talking to God. Cheryl, *frum* for eighteen years, portrayed many of these channels as she evolved:

> I wanted to do what Hashem wanted me to do and observe *halakhah* in the way Hashem wanted me to. But also, and I think I got this from my mother, I had a very strong feeling of a personal

connection to Hashem. That Hashem would listen to me if I *davened*. . . . So I had a very warm feeling that Hashem was listening to my *tefillot* [prayers], that I could talk to Hashem, I could *daven* to Hashem, and Hashem was going to hear what I had to say.

When she began to teach other women, she connected with God through textual study:

But the teaching and the immersion in texts, and also helping other people connect to text, has been for me such a connection to Hashem. Like I feel the presence of Hashem in the room, and I have these women sitting around this table grappling with texts that they've never accessed before, and that they couldn't access before.

In chapter 4, where I discussed *davening*, I referred to a discussion by Schachter-Shalomi (2014) on *davening* with *kavanah*. The idea is to pray with one's whole being, with focus and intentionality. Prayer is directed to God who, one hopes, hears and responds. Some individuals enhance their *kavanah* during *davening* by focusing on certain words and on the meaning of the words. Standard prayer services are organized in a way that foster a relationship with God, with sections sequentially praising God, petitioning God, and expressing gratitude (Strassfeld, 2002/2006).

For some *baalei teshuvah*, their relationship with God is furthered through the chanting of prayers. Those participants who grew up loving the Beatles or the Grateful Dead, hearing Yiddish songs sung by their grandparents, and attending Israeli song festivals found the music they enjoyed in the past a gateway to appreciating Jewish religious melodies. For others, Shlomo Carlebach's music and the singing at Chabad and elsewhere drew them into Orthodox Judaism. Six BTs spoke of connecting with God through music, commenting on how moved they were by the *zemirot* (songs) and the *niggunim* (melodies) sung at *shul* or at the Sabbath table.

The participants spoke of numerous ways in which they enhanced their awareness of God in their daily lives. They recited prayers before eating and afterward and on other occasions for which there are prayers. Several women pointed to covering their hair and dressing modestly as ways they demonstrated reverence to God, and men made similar statements about wearing kippahs in public. Joshua commented on how the meaning of wearing a *kippah* has changed over time for him:

I wear a *kippah*, but the fact is I originally started wearing a *kippah* as an ethnic, as an expression of my ethnicity. I made a point of making sure everybody knew that. You know. It didn't have anything to do with religion or spirituality. It was a cultural icon, kind of thing. But I don't play that game anymore.

Besides attending to their external behavior, the BTs worked on improving their sensitivity to others' needs. Elliot, *frum* for five years, tries to be less selfish, more pleasant, and to seek opportunities to help others. By working on their *midot* and helping others, the BTs strengthened their connection to God.

Another way study participants connected to God was through their children. Several spoke of doing so by teaching their children, learning with their children, or learning from their children. Erica, a *baalat teshuvah* for seven years, captured this sentiment in describing how she interacts with her children:

I try really, really, really hard to be the best mother that I can be. I don't always meet that goal, but I try really hard to nurture them spiritually, to encourage them to learn Torah and to make *brachas* and to be conscious that there is a *Hashem* in the world.

Lauren, *frum* for twenty-four years, said that preparing for Shabbat and the holidays was spiritually uplifting even though it was hard work. Besides preparing the food, she recognizes her own role in creating excitement.

The *baalei teshuvah* said that they worked at heightening their connection to God to understand what God wants of them. Some thought God wanted them to observe the mitzvahs. A thirty-year BT, Maya said that God assigned her the mission of *keruv* work. (She did not explain how she knew that God wanted her to do this.) Batya, *frum* for four years, said that she aspired to be sufficiently aware to "know" and "hear" what God wants from her. In order to do this, they talked to God and listened for a response.

Talking to God

Baalei teshuvah told interviewers that they talked to God in contexts besides *davening*. They spoke of these talks as conversations, jokingly giving examples from popular culture:

> If I'll go into a meeting and I've got to give a talk, you know, I'll go
> and ask the *Ribono Shel Olam* [Master of the Universe], "Help me
> say the right thing here." And then if it goes well, I say, "Thanks."
> So I have this . . . closer relationship now with *Hashem* . . . in
> which we have these transactions. As George Burns would say, "I
> talk and you listen." (Paul, *frum* for thirty-eight years)

> The best example I can think of is in the play and movie, *Fiddler
> on the Roof*. You see how Tevye talks to God. To me that seems
> natural. God's there, you talk to Him. (Mark, *frum* for five years)

Paul is referring to the movie *Oh, God*, in which George Burns plays the role
of God, speaking to an ordinary man played by John Denver. He misquoted
Burns/God, who said, "You talk. I'll listen." Similarly, Tevye in *Fiddler on the
Roof* has one-way conversations with God. Paul and Mark's jocular presentation of these examples may indicate that they think the general public believes
that talking to God is strange.

From the way some participants described their talks, it sounded as if
these were internal dialogues or wishes. Ben, *frum* for ten years, recalled saying,
"'God, what are you doing to me? Why are you doing this to me? Give me
the right answer to this. I know somehow this is important for me, but I'm
not seeing it right now.'" Similarly, Shifra, *frum* for twenty-two years, said, "I
talk to myself all the time in my head: 'Please watch over my son, please let
my husband drive home safely from work.'" In these cases, the *baalei teshuvah*
were asking for help with understanding or seeking protection.

Another aspect of talking to God is determining whether God was
answering. Mark said that he thought he heard God responding to him, but
expressed some doubts whether the voice he heard was internal or external.
He said, "Well, I talk to God all the time. And sometimes, I think, He talks
back to me. I can't always tell whether it's His voice or just my own wishful
thinking." In her book on the Vineyard group of Evangelical Christians, the
anthropologist T. M. Luhrmann (2012) discusses how the men and women
she studied learned to "hear" answers to their prayers. The author suggests
that after becoming a part of this church, the Christian participants radically
change their theory of mind so that it differs from the general perception
that there is a boundary between the internal mind and the external world.
As Luhrmann (2012) explains:

> When you attend a church like the Vineyard, you are presented
> with a theory of mind in which the distinction is all of a sudden

no longer straightforward. You are asked to experience some of your thoughts as being more like perceptions. In a church like the Vineyard, God participates in your mind, and you "hear" what he says as if it were external speech. The general model is clear enough, although no one actually presented it to me as a bullet-point list. God wants to be your friend; you develop that relationship through prayer; prayer is hard work and requires effort and training; and when you develop that relationship, God will answer back, through thoughts and mental images he places in your mind, and through sensations he causes in your body. You still experience those thoughts and images and sensations, for the most part, as if they were your own, generated from within your own mind and body. You have to learn to experience those you have identified as God's as different. (41)

The *baalei teshuvah*, too, altered their theory of mind insofar as they talked to God and believed that God actively intervened in their lives. Unlike Luhrmann's participants, however, Mark questioned whether he was hearing his own thoughts or God. Most likely, the *baalei teshuvah* "heard" God by observing the consequences of asking for God's help. When one asks God to help with a particular situation, such as recovery from an illness, the response is tangible—one recovers, recovers in part, or does not recover. Greg, *frum* for twelve years, described an experience he had in which he observed God's response:

I had an operation and I had some minor surgery and I remember that I was in incredible, incredible pain. And so much pain and the painkiller didn't work, and I took another one and that didn't work, and finally I just lay in bed and I said, "Hashem, I accept the pain. I accept it. I accept the pain." And I waited about fifteen seconds, [and] it totally went away. So, what you have to do is, what He wants to do is that you realize that He's in control of your life and acknowledge that, that's how you become a *botei'ach* [one who trusts God]. And sometimes He sends you tests and when you acknowledge that it's a test from Him and it's for a purpose, then it's already served its purpose, He doesn't need to make you suffer anymore.

Here not only did Greg describe receiving an "answer" in that the pain went away, but he also provided an interpretation of the meaning of the pain.

Allison, ten years post-commitment, said that everything she has prayed for has come out the way she wished. Others, however, asserted that they always get a response but not necessarily the one they wanted. *Frum* for twenty-four years, Annie struggles over God's will when bad things happen to good people.

> What kind of God allows this to happen? Don't get me wrong. I don't necessarily have these answers (laughs). I still struggle with what the will is. But by becoming *frum* at least I feel like there is somebody there who is listening. I might not always get the answers. And sometimes the answer is "No." But at least I feel that somebody's there and somebody is listening.

Annie captures the feelings described by others that they were comforted by the presence of God and the possibility that God will respond to their prayers.

The Hand of God

Participants used the terms *hashgachah pratit* (Divine Providence), *beshert* (meant to be), and *yad Hashem* (the hand of God) to describe God's intervention in their lives. They used these expressions when talking about their spiritual journeys toward Orthodoxy and in depicting later life experiences. They gave examples of events they had experienced as miraculous or demonstrating that God offered them protection and direction. They attributed both fortuitous and unfortunate events to God's caring for them and conveyed the feeling that God took a personal interest in the events in their lives and, through these events, conveyed lessons.

In their retrospective accounts, participants saw the hand of God in experiences that led them to Orthodoxy. For example, Eli, who decided to stay in California rather than travel East to his parents' home for Passover, said that "it was really *hashgachah pratit*" when he went instead to seder at the Chabad house near where he was at that time. There he met a man who was recruiting students for a summer yeshiva program in the Catskills. This led him to further involvement with Judaism and with Chabad. When he was interviewed, he had been *frum* for fifteen years. Howard provides another such example. When he was on an airplane on his way to a ski trip with his fiancée, he met a man whom Howard later contacted on a business matter. In the course of their interaction over a period of years, this man gave Howard reading material on Judaism. Some years later, Howard read this literature, starting him on a religious quest. At the time of his interview, he had been *frum* for ten years. A different example is Erica's period of unemployment, which made it possible for her to attend a Shabbaton, a Sabbath program, usually extended over a weekend, that sparked her interest in Orthodox Judaism.

The *baalei teshuvah* attributed significant life events, such as meeting a spouse, to God. After Karen reached a point of being "sick of being single," and did not think she was handling the shidduchs that others arranged for her very well, she prayed, "I just leave it to You. I am in Your hands." At the time of her interview, eleven years post-commitment and married, she described her life in glowing term:

> My life is beautiful now and so I really believe that . . . when Hashem wants us, He gives us a little, so that we ask for it. You know, we ask Him. So sometimes, even now, I feel like my life is so great, this is when I should feel so close to Hashem, but, you know, everyday life takes over and you don't (feel as close as you should). . . .

Karen enjoys a comfortable standard of living from her husband's work and her own and is the joyous mother of a child. She attributes her beautiful life to God and believes that God gives people a taste of goodness to encourage them on their spiritual-religious path.

A few BTs associated positive developments in their work lives to God. Allen, *frum* for twenty-six years, tries to remind himself that God plays a role in his professional success. He incorporates his recognition of God's role into his morning *davening*:

> And so the 20 minutes a day or, with *Avinu Malkeinu*, the 25 minutes a day that I spend *davening*, is sort of my daily way of acknowledging that there is this higher power. That this isn't just [me], and even if I would say to myself, "Oh well, I'm doing well because I'm smart," or "I'm doing well because I'm hard-working," then my brain came from God and my inner drive, I assume, came from God. It's not just something I could produce on my own without help. So the 20 minutes a day is just a way of acknowledging, reminding me every day, "Look, this is not just me and I really have to be thankful for this."

Greg interpreted a crisis at work and in his personal life as a message from God to put less emphasis on his career or, as he put it, "to alter my altars."

Some *baalei teshuvah* saw the hand of God in their entire life courses. Liora, for example, sees her life as miraculous. Although she grew up experiencing abuse, neglect, and poverty, and felt unloved, her life has changed in ways that she never could have imagined. Before she became *frum*, she did not believe that God existed for her. Now she believes that God was with her when she was given a scholarship to an Orthodox Jewish day school, when she met her husband ("my *beshert*"), and when she had children:

> I survived some really rough stuff. You know, it's miraculous. I think it's miraculous how I had that [Orthodox Jewish day school] base, which is just like a foundation of who I am. And when I actually turned and faced and considered Orthodoxy fully, that I had that under my belt. I think that God put that opportunity there, in a way that my mom couldn't say no, preparing me. Finding my *bashert*, having my kids. Just every day. I connect with God through nature, certainly through *shul*, through the *niggunim*, majorly over *Shabbos*; sitting around my *Shabbos* table, majorly, just listening to my son sing. In the ordinary day in, day out stuff, I see that. . . . I'm forty years old, and this is my life, and it feels like a miracle. And there's no way that God doesn't exist in my life, because it wouldn't be like this.

Like others who reexamined their lives after they became Orthodox, Liora believed that, despite pain, God was looking out for her all the time, paving the way for the fulfillment she came to experience as a *frum* woman, wife, and mother.

Frum for fifteen years, Sarah deals with her past pain by asserting, "Everything is for the good." Earlier in her marriage, she was in conflict with her husband over her desire to be more observant than he wanted. After they worked that out, they moved to a new community that was not "*yeshivish*," as she would have liked. Now she realizes that God placed her where she is for her own benefit:

> I keep saying, why did Hashem put us here? Why? But, in retrospect, I always say, 'Everything is for the good.' And I think that Hashem . . . as smart as I think I am . . . He knows better. And I think that this is probably just perfect for us, 'cause what do you

expect? I didn't grow up in a *yeshivish* home. . . . What makes you think you're gonna do so well in a *yeshivish* community? You're better off here where there's other people like you. And you get a better support system.

Sarah went on to discuss her astonishment at how her life has turned out:

> Then in the end . . . [I say] how is it possible that I have a son in ___ Yeshiva? I shake my head. How is that possible? Didn't I just say that my mother comes from a socialist background? I just think Hashem really takes care of us. And that if you want something, not that you're going to get it, but if you believe in something and you want something, it's gonna come in different ways. Maybe it's not the home that I wanted, you know, the community that I wanted. So I get it maybe indirectly . . . through my children.

Like Liora, Sarah sees her life as miraculous. She understands that God takes care of her in ways that fit her needs rather than her aspirations, but she is able to satisfy her aspirations through the next generation.

Like Sarah, several participants attributed their religious communities to God. *Frum* for twenty-four years, Tamar learned to live out her commitment in her community, which she described as "supportive" and "active." In this environment, she acquired knowledge that she did not acquire in the seminary she attended in Israel, such as learning about the prohibition of *lashon harah* (improper speech or gossip). "And it's all *bashert*. Hashem sent me here," she said.

Gratitude

Acutely aware of the gifts of life, good health, family, employment, and community, the BTs expressed thankfulness. Shifra captures the sentiment of the other participants in this way:

> I've been very blessed. I have a beautiful, wonderful son, *baruch Hashem*, who is *shomer Shabbos* and loves Torah more than anything I can see in my life. And I love my husband, and you know marriage is not easy, but you work at it. And I have a job, *Baruch*

> *Hashem,* and I have wonderful friends and I could not ask for more.
> If I was to leave the world tonight, tomorrow, *chas v'chalilah* [God
> forbid], I feel like I did something. I gave something, hopefully,
> that I can be proud of.

After a long period of infertility, Shifra is especially appreciative of her son,
but she is also grateful for her husband, her job, and her friends. Like Batya,
who expressed her gratitude by pointing to the hunger, starvation, and poverty
in the world, Shifra saw her blessings in comparison with those who lacked
such benefits:

> You know, there are people around us who are sick, who don't
> have jobs, whatever. I say, *baruch Hashem* I have a job, and my
> son is healthy. If my husband is healthy then everything is okay,
> and you do your best, you try to do as many *mitzvot* as possible,
> *daven,* and try to be a good person.

Notably, Shifra emphasizes non-material gifts and connects these gifts to
God's beneficence. Observing mitzvahs and *davening* are important elements
in her perception of the obligations that make it possible for her to be blessed.

Several BTs spoke about morning prayers as reminders that they are
recipients of God's favor. They were referring to the prayer *Modeh Ani* (how
grateful I am) said upon rising and the morning *Shacharit davening,* which,
like the other two daily prayers, includes prayers of gratitude. As Marilyn,
observant three years, said:

> It helps me when you get up in the morning, and you open your
> eyes, and the first thing you say is a blessing. That immediately
> brings you back into it. . . . I've said to myself: thank you, *Hashem,*
> for allowing me to wake up today, and start to live my day. And
> that's a very nice way to start out your day. And then it can only
> be uphill from there.

Jacob asserts that the *Modeh Ani* and *Ashrei* prayers help him feel grateful
for meeting his wife, having children, and living the kind of life he is living.
He feels fortunate that he is not like other Jews who are "lost in the sea of
assimilation."

The BTs expressed gratitude to God even for experiences that were
painful. Howard places thankfulness as central to his perspective on life. As

he explained, "If I've learned anything, it's gratitude. . . . I'm thankful for everything I have. And . . . when things that don't necessarily go my way happen, I'm still thankful for what I have." He recalls how painful it was for his family when his father went bankrupt:

> When I was a little boy, my father went bankrupt, and I literally watched the sheriff come into my house when I was five, six years old and take away the car and the refrigerator and the couch and the washing machine and empty, you know, things that my parents had bought that were, I guess they had to either be sold or they bought them on time or credit or whatever and, they took them away. And, while it . . . probably . . . didn't have an instant effect and even not through my . . . growing up, when I finally started to put things in perspective, I realized that you have to, you know, whatever you have, you have to be thankful for because it can be gone tomorrow.

While Howard learned to be grateful through this traumatic experience in his family of origin, as well as subsequent life experiences, others incorporated gratitude into their philosophies of life without describing past trauma. They recognize that life could be worse and their own lives could take a turn for the worse. Ezra, who glossed over his former marriages in his interview, described himself in this way:

> You know, *baruch Hashem*, I'm kind of like a *gam zu le tovah* [this, too, is for the better] type person. Whatever happens to me, no matter what happens to me, and I don't know . . . where it comes from, but no matter what happens to me . . . I'm very grateful to Hashem and I, you know, I don't, I don't have spiritual crises. I tend to grow from pain.

In the context of his statement, he seems to be saying that one can learn from painful experiences. Earlier in the interview, he was critical of his wife for her frequent spiritual crises. Here he seems to be saying that rather than becoming unglued, he grows through pain.

Men and women who were relatively recent BTs talked about gratitude with great fervor. It appears that they were in the process of integrating learning from yeshivas, seminaries, and classes in the community. Batya, who spoke about being mindful of God "minute by minute," is exemplary of new

BTs. She said, "I woke up in the morning and said thanks to God. I went to the bathroom, I said, 'Thank you, God. My body works.' I ate, I said, 'Thank you, God, for planting this, for growing this, for bringing this to me.'" She was grateful for her own physical well-being and the bounty of God's earth.

Gratitude translates into a positive, optimistic outlook on life. Rather than focusing on their hardships, participants spoke about how fortunate they were. Considering that some of them had adverse experiences growing up and challenges at work, in their health, and in their marriages, the *baal teshuvah* experience became one of healing.

Healing

As noted in chapter 6, over the past couple of decades, researchers have become increasingly interested in examining the relationship between spirituality and religion and physical and mental health (Miller & Thoresen, 2003; Seybold & Hill, 2001). For the most part, religion and spirituality seem to be beneficial, although some negative effects have been reported (Weber & Pargament, 2014). With respect to the *baalei teshuvah* in this study, Orthodox Judaism seemed to promote their mental health and sense of well-being. They gained a sense of purpose, resulting in greater self-confidence, more self-awareness, greater focus, and stability. They spoke of improved marital relationships and self-esteem and the reduction or elimination of emotional pain. Although some of these developments may have occurred naturally with maturation, others can be attributed to their religious-spiritual transformation.

Two interviewees spoke about the diminution of their psychological symptoms since they became *frum*. Ariella, who had struggled with depression from the time she was in college until she became observant, was able to go off her medication without a return of her symptoms. Another participant, Adam, previously had seriously disabling back pain for which he had received physical and psychological treatment for many years. Here he explains how his back pain lessened:

> I've had some very bad years of back pain. And it just stopped. Not that I don't have back pain anymore; I do. But that it stopped from interfering with me being able to stand up . . . and I think it's because the more *frum* I became, I think the back pain was just a stop sign. It was telling me to stop, that I'm doing things that are not right for me. . . . The more I became *frum*, the more I became clear on *frumkeit*, then the less I had need for my body

to put out a stop sign, that this is not the way to go through life, to be so angry and depressed, and not connected into God in that way. . . . And so some things in my life had just gotten easier. And I became happier, and being less depressed. . . . And that has to do with the *davening*, and it has to do with the connection to Rabbi _____, and it has to do with the connection with the Lubavitcher rebbeim, and it has to do with being *frum*, and it has to do with those things. My life is more congruent with who I always wanted to be. I'm not fighting myself as much.

Adam depicted his back pain as a psychophysiological expression of alienation from his authentic self. Previously he had back pain when he was engaging in what he later considered transgressive behavior. Living an observant life seemed to give him a structure for meaning that he did not have previously. The rabbis he referred to and his *davening* seemed to serve a function akin to psychotherapy. Both Ariella and Adam felt that their connection to God and Orthodox Judaism, as well as the supports they received (in Ariella's case from her husband), healed them.

In an earlier chapter, I alluded to individuals who had made frequent moves and life changes, searching for a place of comfort and meaning. Zvi, *frum* for fifteen years, is a striking example of a wanderer who, after living in different sections of the United States, traveling around Europe, and studying at an Israeli yeshiva for many years, found a home in Judaism. He explained his changes this way:

Well, now I think I'm focused. You know, in the past, when I was younger, as with most people, you don't know what you're gonna do, you're just sort of flying from one minute to the next, and . . . living in the moment, so to speak. And now I have a life that I'm comfortable with, and things work. . . . which is something I never really thought I would have when I was a kid. I moved a hundred times when I was younger. Big moves. Israel, here, there, I was always going somewhere; never stayed anyplace for more than like a year. . . . So now, you know, we're settled, in a house, with kids, so that's different. I mean there was, I never wanted that. So to actually have that and experience it and . . . enjoy that is something different.

As he explained, Zvi has made a remarkable transformation in his life. He has surprised himself with the way in which his life has changed for the better.

Some participants described personality changes that they attribute to their becoming observant. Elliot said that he has become kinder and more authentic and honest, and he experiences less stress. The framework, described earlier in this chapter, through which life is seen as guided by God, enables the BTs to interpret negative events in a positive way. As Elliot remarked:

> I would say one great marketing tool for someone growing in *Yiddishkeit* would be the stress reduction. To think that the burden isn't on your shoulders, to accomplish things, to think that it just isn't all about you, to think that what happens . . . it seemed like really a bad thing, might turn out to be a good thing. This is a great stress reliever. It really is a great stress reliever. So instead of at work getting a manager that you don't like . . . oh, woe is me, okay, so what's God trying to do here? What's He trying to accomplish here? What's the lemonade in this lemon? We just know that the lemonade is there. It's not a lemon. So it's a great stress reliever. So you asked how I'm different? I don't think I get upset about things that I probably would have got upset about before. They either weren't important, or you see that God's trying to help me. I just don't readily see it. And then there are so many things that are simply out of my control. Why worry about things?

Elliot seems to have changed his outlook on life from one in which he would blame himself or others for his problems to a positive one in which he tries to understand the lesson God is trying to convey to him.

Spiritual Aspirations and Growth

Several *baalei teshuvah* spoke of their spiritual transformation as a growth experience. Sarah spoke of becoming more assertive in her marriage. Another woman, Marilyn, said that she has become clearer in her thinking and more accepting and happy. Whereas in the past she experienced great emotional pain and felt alone in the world, she derives comfort in having a loving husband and supportive religious community. She said that living an Orthodox life has taught her to focus on maintaining spiritual feelings, to be calm, and not to blame herself.

As suggested throughout this volume, the BTs have been on a path toward growth throughout their journeys. Most of them began with little or superficial knowledge of their religious heritage and incrementally corrected misinformation and added new knowledge. Joining communities in which learning was a normative religious obligation, they sought to further their spiritual-religious development. Reflecting on her growth at the time of her interview, Allison said, "I think that now I feel that there's much more depth and substance to my own being. And I have a lot more to go. A lot more."

In focusing on growth, a number of participants spoke about strengthening their relationship with God and becoming closer. For Yossi that meant connecting "to the power that Hashem has given me in a very positive way." He would like to use his strengths "in a loving way" to nurture his children and give to the community. Similarly, Joshua wants to work on

> this idea of wanting to be constantly strengthening my relationship with God and conducting myself closer and closer to what the Torah ideal is. And realizing that I'm still pretty far away from it. But want to keep working on it. . . . I really think it's an ongoing, a lifelong, ongoing process.

For many of the BTs, strengthening their relationship with God had to do with taking on more *mitzvot*. The women mentioned *davening* more regularly and with greater spiritual fervor. As stated in an earlier chapter, *davening* was a challenge for many of the women. Women wanted to engage more in the activities they enjoyed such as service to their synagogues, *chesed*, and outreach to potential and new *baalei teshuvah*. Men spoke about wanting to be more philanthropic and to improve their *midot*. They wished in particular to handle their anger better and avoid gossiping. Both men and women spoke about learning more, which for men meant becoming more proficient in the Talmud, while for women the emphasis was on becoming more knowledgeable about *halakhah* and attending more classes. Men and women articulated plans in the near future to travel to Israel and spoke wistfully of making *aliyah* someday.

In keeping with Erikson's (1959/1980) concept of generativity, giving to the next generation, the *baalei teshuvah* parents appeared to be attentive to their children and proud of raising them Orthodox. A few were already grandparents; most looked forward to having grown children who raise their children Orthodox. According to Erikson's later concept of grand-generativity (Erikson, Erikson, & Kivnick, 1986), grandparenting enables adults to validate their own and their children's generativity. Both generativity and grand-generativity are reflected in the BTs' verbalized their aspirations:

> If I can provide the right foundation for my children and they could teach their children and other people, then I've done my job. (Jerry)

> Moving toward older age and being, looking forward to living with the acquired wisdom . . . that I think has come from this journey, and passing it on to my grandchildren and my children, and also to whoever I meet. (Nora)

> So I guess the answer is that I see myself . . . finding more meaning in it and being able to give that over to my children and creating . . . generations of an identity of Jewishness that's been lost in my family for the last five or six generations. (Zvi)

As these quotations show, the BTs' spiritual aspirations are rooted in their own journeys, the benefits of which they would like to pass on. They are hoping that the efforts they exerted and the meaning they found will be passed onto their children and their children's children.

Summary

Despite objections to the term "spirituality" by some of the men, all the participants were able to describe ways in which they expressed spiritual-religious behavior in their daily lives. The women favored experiences involving service to others and working on their own growth, whereas men preferred the enactment of Jewish practices. Both men and women expressed heightened awareness of God's presence in their lives.

As described in this chapter, the *baalei teshuvah* experienced God as an awe-inspiring presence that actively intervenes in their lives. They portrayed God using some of the categories enumerated in the thirteen attributes of God presented in Exodus 34:6–7. They considered their relationship with God of utmost importance and tried to develop a close connection. They sought to communicate with God through prayer, acts of loving-kindness, talking to God, and performing *mitzvot*. Through these activities and their observations of the consequences, they strove to understand what God wanted of them.

Through their learning and immersion in Orthodox communities, the BTs changed their theory of mind (Luhrmann, 2012) so that they could talk to God and "hear" a response to their prayers. As described, they saw the hand of God in their spiritual journeys, in meeting their spouses, in their children, and in the ways in which their lives have worked out. They marveled at the miracles that they have seen in their lives and felt grateful. In their acknowledgment of their blessings, they focused on the nonmaterial.

For some, *teshuvah* enabled healing. They acquired a framework that helped them see the positive in the negative; appreciate the community that supported their spiritual involvement; and acquire the stability that some of them did not have while growing up. A couple of BTs reported the diminution of physical and emotional symptoms.

Overall, the *baalei teshuvah* were oriented toward growth. As indicated by the number of years observant noted in this chapter, recent and longtime BTs shared this orientation. They grew in their knowledge of Judaism, their relationship with God, their character traits, and in their family relationships. They incorporated their spirituality into their everyday lives, transmitted this to their children, and looked forward to seeing the results of their spiritual journeys in their grandchildren. Spirituality became part of them, indicative of their spiritual identity.

Chapter 9

The Spiritual-Religious Transformation
and Its Consequences

In this volume, I have portrayed the spiritual-religious journeys of Jewish men and women who became Orthodox. I described their starting point in ethnically conscious families that instilled a Jewish identity but gave little emphasis to the practice of Judaism as a religion. For the most part, the families offered their children enough Jewish education for them to perform adequately at a bar or bat mitzvah and socialized them to succeed in the secular world through a university education and a professional occupation. The BTs came to view their families' gestures toward Judaism as superficial and regarded their other expectations as insufficient to developing a meaningful life. Through a gradual process of searching, exploration, and education, they made a commitment to become Orthodox. Rather than the end of the story, this decision ushered in a new process that is open-ended and continuous. Following commitment, the BTs became immersed in Orthodox communities where they continued to learn, experienced resocialization, and moved toward psychological and social integration. Considering that this change affected their lives in a fundamental way, it was a radical departure from their beginnings.

To conclude this book, I begin by summarizing the major changes the *baalei teshuvah* made with respect to their identities, community, family relations, and work. Next, I discuss and assess the costs and benefits, and consider why they made these changes. I revisit the question of gender posed in the first chapter and addressed throughout. Finally, I examine the implications of this case study for the development of theory on the process of spiritual transformation.

The Changes

I used the word "spiritual transformation" to depict internal and external changes that take place as BTs engage in actions that bring them closer to God, which they realize through active participation in Orthodox Jewish life. Internally they change their beliefs, values, views of themselves, and feelings of well-being. Externally, they change the entities with which they affiliate in their communities (e.g., synagogues, educational centers, children's schools) and alter their style of dress, the food they consume, and their everyday activities so that they are in accord with Jewish law and customs. The changes are far-reaching, affecting multiple facets of their lives. Some of these changes are natural developments that occur as one matures while others have to do with beliefs and practices of Orthodox Judaism.

Significantly, they made changes in their identities. The BTs grew up knowing viscerally that they were Jewish but their knowing was largely connected with family, ethnicity, social experiences, and values. They saw their Jewishness in the context of family observances of holidays and other home celebrations in which they ate ethnic but not necessarily kosher food. Although some of their families of origin observed the Sabbath in some way (e.g., lighting Sabbath candles), it was more common for them to celebrate the Jewish holidays of Rosh Hashanah, Chanukah, and Passover. Besides their family observances, the BTs saw their earlier Jewish identities through their experiences at Hebrew or Sunday schools, Jewish camps, youth groups, and/ or their bar and bat mitzvahs. They internalized what they perceived to be Jewish values, such as fighting for social justice, acquiring an advanced secular education, and achievement.

Through study and immersion in Orthodox Jewish communal life, they gradually made changes in their Jewish identities. Their visceral sense of being Jewish gained substance, based on a body of knowledge, skills, and practices that they worked diligently to acquire and incorporate into their daily lives. They came to realize that their Jewishness was based on a religion rooted in the past of the Jewish people and their own family forebears, and that the Jewish religion continues to be relevant to them. They felt connected to their ancestors, going back to the biblical stories of Abraham, Isaac, and Jacob, through the scholars who wrote the Talmud and other post-biblical texts, and to those who lived in shtetls in Europe, many of whom died during the Holocaust. They saw themselves as part of a chain of people who were perpetuating sacred traditions and passing them onto their children. As they moved forward in their development as *baalei teshuvah*, the Jewish religion became central, determining their use of time, influencing their family relationships, restraining some of their desires while opening up other aspirations, and affecting their priorities. In contrast with their earlier Jewish achievement-oriented, ethnic identities, they now focused on God, studying Torah, performing mitzvahs, *davening*, and engaging in acts of loving-kindness.

Their transformed Jewish identities encompassed comportment, behaviors, and activities. They became conscious of their personal conduct and its reflection on themselves and God. As Jerry, a BT of three years learned, he is "a representative of Hashem . . . a representative of a king" and, as such, "you act in a way that honors that king." This includes improving one's character traits, behaving in an upright way, and making the world a better place.[1] They believed that they could bring about changes in themselves and the world through prayer, performance of mitzvahs, and Torah study. For many of the men, this meant going to synagogue or *davening* on their own three times a day; and studying sacred texts on their own, with a study partner, or in classes. Women *davened* less often, mostly at home, and attended classes in their communities. Men and women engaged in community service activities in which they helped other individuals, synagogues, and religious schools, and worked on improving their character traits. They came to see themselves as less materialistic and more altruistic.

At the time of their interviews, their identities as *baalei teshuvah* (more so than as *frum* Jews) were prominent. Those who were relatively recent BTs were sensitive to their position as neophytes, aware of their deficits in knowledge, and anxious about their public performance of prayer and their acceptance as Orthodox Jews. In response, some formed sub-communities of like-minded *baalei teshuvah* with whom they felt comfortable. More experienced BTs were less self-conscious, feeling proud of their accomplishments, while they voiced a preference for friendships with those with similar backgrounds and journeys. Others, however, were critical of their own group, whom they saw as excessively passionate, preferring to socialize with those who were raised Orthodox. Whether they sought refuge with others like themselves or separated from other BTs, in general, they experienced their status as marginal.

Spirituality was integral to the Jewish identities of the BTs. Their "spiritual identities" (Kiesling & Sorell, 2009) were tied to their belief in and relationship with God. They expressed their connection with God by incorporating religious practices into their daily lives, such as eating kosher food, reciting daily prayers, engaging in community service, and preparing for and observing the Sabbath. They communicated with God through prayer and "talks" and interpreted their experiences as lessons from God. As they increased their connection with traditional Judaism, new *baalei teshuvah* and some longtime BTs experienced emotional excitement over their learning and the recovery of a tradition that had previously been absent from their lives. *Frum* for fifteen years, Zvi said that the recovery process was amazing:

> We're five generations in America, (and) totally not observant. . . . So the fact that I was able to rekindle that and become connected to that again, and being able to pass that on, I think that's just, that's an amazing thing. That's the greatness of the whole *baal teshuvah* thing.

Their religious communities became of paramount importance to the BTs. These included other *baalei teshuvah*, with whom they felt most comfortable, and those who were raised Orthodox, whose approval they sought. They had reduced or no contact with the friends they grew up with, embracing their religious community as primary. They established friendships with other Orthodox families in the community, inviting each other to their respective homes for Shabbat and holiday meals. Their contact with these families occurred in a variety of settings besides their homes, particularly their synagogues and their children's schools but also on the street, in Jewish bookstores, at the kosher butcher shop, in classes, and at local communal events. Through association with others who shared their religious orientation, their environment became mainly Orthodox.

The BTs participated enthusiastically in selected activities in their new communities. They chose activities in which they had skills they had acquired in the secular world, and those in which they felt comfortable. This included fund raising, volunteering at their children's schools, outreach toward Jews exploring Orthodox Judaism, and helping with musical programs. Some BTs developed sufficient skills to lead prayer services, while a few others were able to teach. Members of one *baal teshuvah* sub-community set up learning programs on topics or texts that interested a group of people and held "user-friendly" beginners' services for newcomers. Others volunteered to perform community service. Many of them found giving to the community spiritually uplifting.

At the same time they served their Jewish communities, the BTs participated in many of the ongoing activities that were occurring in their communities. They attended classes offered by rabbis, rebbetzins, and other scholars, classes that helped fill gaps in their religious educations. The more recent *baalei teshuvah* described excitement over the array of activities and friends that were available in *frum* communities. Others were pleased to find mentors and supportive friends who contributed to their growth and feelings of acceptance.

The BTs' changes affected their relationships with their nuclear and extended families. The life of the nuclear family became infused with Judaism. Shabbat became a day when families could focus on being together at synagogue and at special meals. Although it was difficult initially for parents who did not grow up in observant homes to transmit Orthodox Judaism to their children, they attempted to remedy this deficiency by attending parenting classes, reading books, observing FFB parents, and consulting with others. Parenting was particularly challenging for those who became *frum* in the middle of their offspring's childhoods. When the parents changed course, the children resisted (see chapter 5). Attendance at religious day schools where there were children their age who kept the *mitzvot* helped smooth out these transitions.

Relationships with families of origin were trying initially as well. Parents worried whether their children had joined a cult or had lost their senses. Siblings made jokes about their BT brothers and sisters. Yet some parents came to admire their religious children, and three sets of parents and ten siblings subsequently became observant themselves. Some extended family members had difficulty understanding and appreciating the *baalei teshuvah* in the family. It does appear that the BTs' religious change disturbed the equilibrium in the family system, in some cases bringing family members closer and in other cases creating distance.

Considering that most of the participants did not have Orthodox relatives, and in some cases had complicated relationships with their parents, it was not surprising that they created families through their friends. Some belonged to synagogues in which there was a large proportion of *baalei teshuvah*, which they experienced as familial. On the other hand, Danzger (1989) noted that members of some synagogues with large concentrations of *baalei teshuvah* saw themselves primarily as *baalei teshuvah* rather than on a pathway toward integration into the existing Orthodox community. Although the participants in this study attended both mainstream and predominantly *baal teshuvah* synagogues, as stated earlier, their primary identity was as *baalei teshuvah*. Even those who boasted about "passing" indicated that they felt most comfortable with their BT friends.

Besides the changes that have been discussed, the BTs reported changes in their work lives (Sands, Spero, & Danzig, 2007). Those who worked in secular environments adjusted their work schedules to enable them to take time off for Jewish holidays and to leave early or not work at all on Fridays so that they could prepare for Shabbat. Those who worked for Jewish organizations had schedules compatible with living a *frum* life, where they did not have to explain their need to adjust their work time. Some who were employed in the secular world came to give less prominence to their careers and more attention to their families and religion. Efforts to remedy gaps in their Jewish educations through attending classes and studying with a study partner took time away from their careers. The women, who, like the men, were well educated in secular studies and had professions, changed their focus to family, community, and learning. Preparing food for Shabbat and holidays took time away from women's careers. Both men and women tried to incorporate their Jewish learning into their work and family lives. For both, career and material success became less central than it was in the past.

Challenges and Costs

The spiritual-religious changes of the BTs presented challenges and costs that they did not anticipate when they embarked on this journey. As alluded to earlier and discussed in chapter 4, they had large deficits in their religious education, comparing unfavorably with members of the Orthodox communities who were raised in Orthodox homes and were educated in yeshiva day schools. With a few exceptions, they entered preexisting Orthodox communities with little religious capital, that is, "familiarity with a religion's doctrines, rituals, traditions, and members" (Iannaccone 1990, p. 299). They lacked sufficient command of Hebrew to understand and engage in communal prayer; were unfamiliar with *halakhah* and the Talmud; and were unacquainted with informal, tacit knowledge they needed to pursue an Orthodox Jewish life. As Ben said, "The average six-year-old knows more than me."[2]

Considering that the ability to participate competently in religious services and knowledge of Jewish sacred texts contribute to status in Orthodox communities, the BTs entered these communities lacking the abilities that would bring them status. Furthermore, they did not have *yichus*, a family history of Jewish scholars, which also elevates one's status. Many of the *baalei teshuvah* had achieved high status in secular communities through relatively high levels of secular education and high status professions. The discrepancy in the ways in which they were perceived in the Orthodox and secular worlds produced stress.

Remarkably, the BTs took on the challenge of trying to remedy deficiencies and become reeducated. Although it was unrealistic for them to catch up with those who were immersed in religious life from the time they were children, the BTs did pursue avenues that were available to them. More than a third attended yeshivas or seminaries in Israel or the United States for varying lengths of time, mostly early in their processes of becoming serious about Judaism. This provided them with basic knowledge and some of the tools that they needed. When they joined Orthodox communities, they took advantage of the classes offered there and studied on their own or with a study partner. They assimilated informal knowledge through social connections and by observing others.

Still, the BTs felt self-conscious over public exposure of their incompetence during prayer or other occasions. Oriented toward achievement, they were troubled over their deficiencies. Some pursued a frenzied pace of taking classes and studying on their own. (One man reported attending nine classes per week!) Others had mentors who provided one-to-one tutoring and explained the intricacies of Jewish laws and practices. Many of the women avoided going to synagogue, partly because they could not keep up with the prayer service, but this option was not open to men. Ensconcing themselves in *baal teshuvah* communities and synagogues was another way some BTs coped with their anxiety. Although this warded off self-consciousness and felt comfortable, they ran the risk of acquiring misinformation from peers, unless these peers were further along than they were. Furthermore, association primarily with other BTs does not help them become socially integrated into the larger Orthodox community (Danzger, 1989).

Some viewed their education as a process, taking pride in their accomplishments along the way. Seth, raised in a Minimalist Plus family and *frum* for 15 years, reflected on his learning in this way:

> I still go to this other *shiur* . . . and there's been other *shiurim* that I've attended and they're good . . . and, definitely, just through almost osmosis of just doing it, my skills and those things have come. I'm still not at the point where I sort of would like to be, because . . . it's like I'm an amateur bike rider, I'm not a professional bike rider. Maybe you have to make choices in life that you never become that professional bike rider, you know, but it's just a question of feeling competent.

Seth recognized his increased skills at the same time he acknowledged his limitations. The choices he alluded to are linked to time. It takes time to take classes and study—time that competes with other priorities such as work and spending time with family. Seth's learning through classes and osmosis has brought him to a level where he can *daven* in public space and avoid being considered an "ignoramus," a term two BTs used.

Aside from the costs in terms of time, becoming Orthodox also entails economic costs. Kosher meat and other food items are more expensive than non-kosher food. The cost rises as the family size increases and when the family has guests for Shabbat and holiday meals, which many do regularly. Tuition at yeshiva day schools, especially for large families, can also strain the family's budget. Because of the need to live within walking distance of an Orthodox synagogue and near other Orthodox Jews, residential options may be limited to expensive houses or apartments (Elbein, 2014). Synagogue membership can also be expensive. Furthermore, religious observance prevents BTs from working for employers that require work on Saturdays and holidays, thus precluding some opportunities for employment and advancement. National Jewish population studies have found that overall, the incomes of Orthodox Jews are lower than those who are Conservative and Reform (Lazerwitz, Winter, Dashefsky, & Tabory, 1998; Waxman, 2005).

In addition to bearing economic costs, the *baalei teshuvah* experienced emotional costs. In many cases, relationships with parents and siblings became strained, particularly in the beginning, before the families gained a better understanding of their child's religious-spiritual change. The *mitzvot* that the BTs took on, such as keeping the Sabbath and eating kosher food, imposed barriers to contact with family members. As mentioned, some parents and siblings followed them into Orthodoxy, reducing the strain. Several BTs reported losing friends after their lifestyles diverged. These losses in relationships with families and friends engendered sadness and discomfort as did vague feelings of loss of their previous ways of living.

Considering the costs and challenges, one wonders what enables them to persist. The transformation process is arduous, entailing struggles with one's core beliefs, an extensive learning and resocialization process, spiritual struggles, and challenges to relationships. *Baalei teshuvah* seem to possess qualities that enable them to maintain their beliefs despite the costs. Those who have become Orthodox seem to be "spiritually resilient" (Blieszner & Ramsey, 2002; Manning, 2014), that is, they have the ability to retain their faith, remain committed, and increase their awareness of themselves and God when they encounter obstacles. The BTs are to be admired for their fortitude, openness to exploring the unknown, and persistence in their journeys toward spiritual fulfillment. They were willing to depart from the orientation in which they were raised, make strenuous efforts to advance their religious education, and sustain losses in order to pursue a dream of a more fulfilling spiritual life.

Benefits

Despite the costs, the *baalei teshuvah* benefited from improvements in their lives. The BTs gained an explanatory framework and structure within which to conduct their own and family lives. This framework gave them a channel through which to understand life events, appreciate positive developments, and see the positive in the negative. Their family lives acquired a focus, which influenced the structure of their days and weeks, the composition of their meals, the children's schooling, and their community affiliations. They had a moral system, based on Jewish law, which guided them in their everyday activities. Crucially, they had the security of knowing that God was present, cared about them, and was accessible to them. They saw God as omnipotent, empowering those who recognized this power. The BTs could pray to God and petition for divine intervention in their lives. If God's response negated their wishes, they saw this as God's way of conveying a lesson.

Although this study did not use instruments to measure happiness and well-being, it did use an inventory that assessed their developmental levels, the Modified Erikson Psychosocial Stage Inventory (MEPSI; Darling-Fisher & Kline Leidy, 1988). As shown in chapter 3, their scores were predominantly in the positive direction. Subjectively, most of the participants reported improvements in their lives. They spoke of having better marital and family lives, and satisfaction in their friendships, community life, and life structure. They formed friendships with other Orthodox adults, especially other *baalei teshuvah*, who were part of their "*shul* communities" or were parents who sent their children to the same yeshiva day schools. They invited friends to their homes for Sabbath and festival meals, and regarded each other as family. They derived satisfaction from being part of a religious community by praying together and/or participating in community service (*chesed*) activities. Those who were spiritual seekers or wanderers when they were younger found answers and stability in becoming *frum*. A few spoke of physical or mental healing through belief in God and living an observant life. Most reported personal growth.

Besides their experiences of growth and life enhancement, the BTs contributed to the Orthodox communities they joined. The newly Orthodox add to the proportion of Orthodox Jews, who were declining in the last quarter of the twentieth century (Sands, Marcus, & Danzig, 2006). More significant, they contribute "spiritual capital" to the Orthodox community. Spiritual capital refers to "resources that are created or people have access to when people invest in religion as religion" such as their relationship with God (Woodberry, 2003, p. 1). The *baalei teshuvah* invigorate their communities with their passion, enthusiasm, and thirst for knowledge (Sands, 2009). Furthermore, they have skills developed in the secular world, such as fund raising and musical ability, and vitality that they offer the Orthodox communities they join.

Why Do They Become *Frum?*

Authors of previous books about *baalei* and *baalot teshuvah* have noted that participants in their studies were searching for meaning (Aviad, 1983; Danzger, 1989; Kaufman, 1991) or, as Davidman (1991) found among women at Lincoln Square Synagogue, "a more meaningful context in which to understand their lives" (p. 91). As Aviad (1983) remarked, such a quest is not restricted to *baalei teshuvah*; Frankl (1946, 1959, 1984) saw it as universal. In this study, participants found meaning in the structure of Orthodox Judaism and in the side benefits of a focused family life and a warm religious community. As Marris (1982) stated, it is essential that we have a "structure of meaning" in order "to make sense of our and direct our lives" (p. 191). Orthodox Judaism offers BTs a meaning system that offers them purpose, direction, and emotional fulfillment. Through religious observance they realize an orderly life characterized by Torah study, adherence to *mitzvot*, and the creation of a family life and everyday routines in which the sacred is central (Silberman, 2005). With the Torah knowledge they continue to acquire, they are able to interpret the spiritual struggles and challenges they face in a restorative way. And yet, the question remains: why did the participants in this study become Orthodox?

In the varied retrospective accounts of their spiritual-religious change, participants did not directly explain why they decided to become Orthodox, but they seemed to concur that something fundamental had been missing in their former lives and that they were able to recover that component after their spiritual-religious transformation. Most of them indicated that they did not have much knowledge about Judaism prior to their searches. The Judaism to which they were exposed as children lacked substance. Yet being Jewish was important to their parents and to themselves. To get another perspective, we asked the key informants (KIs) this question, and found that almost everyone said that *baalei teshuvah* seek meaning and purpose in their lives and that prior to making the life change they experienced a void, something like the existential vacuum described in chapter 2. Aside from this explanation, other interpretations were offered.

Four KIs said that people are looking for spirituality in their lives as Jews. They want to move beyond the ordinary "humdrum" life, exposure to immorality, or the "rat race" at work into something deeper, more elevated, and more purposeful. Spirituality offers them a connection with God that they did not have previously or a more intense connection if they had some connection previously. As shown in many of the quotations included in this book, spirituality was important to many of the interviewees. The KIs also said that some *baalei teshuvah* seek community (cf. Aviad, 1983; Kaufman, 1991) and a feeling of belonging, and they experience this when they get to know and feel embraced by observant families. This is especially true, they said, of those whose families of origin are not warm and accepting.

Two KIs referred to two drives that determine the pathways *baalei teshuvah* take—an emotional and an intellectual one. Some BTs have strong emotional needs. They may be unhappy or dissatisfied or they want to live more fully and to be accepted by others. In an article on emotions and identity transformation, Oatley and Djikic (2002) discuss how central emotions are to religious conversion as described in William James's classic work, *The Varieties of Religious Experience* (1902/1982). James discusses conversion as an experience of rebirth in which there is "a shift from one emotional center to another" (Oatley & Djikic, 2002, p. 101). After the conversion, a new set of goals, aspirations, and actions displaces the previous one. Oatley and Djikic (2002) see the shift in emotions that James described as an identity transformation that anticipates formulations of identity development described by Erikson (1959) and Levinson (1986).

The other drive, the intellectual one, is the desire to learn. Some BTs are attracted to academic knowledge and enjoy learning. Most of them were engaged in secular learning during college and graduate school prior to encountering ideas about Judaism that they had not previously known. They found the new knowledge stimulating. Twelve interviewees discussed the books they read and the classes they took that influenced their paths and spurred them on. Several engaged in serious study of sacred texts in Israel. As one of the KIs said, one may begin on an intellectual path and move into the other or vice versa, or find that the two pathways converge. For example, some *baalei teshuvah* discover "truth" during their studies and become emotionally excited about their learning. The expression "BT high" depicts their excitement, especially in the early stages of their learning.

The word "connection" pervaded the interviews with the KIs as well as participant interviews. The KIs talked about connections with rabbis, the *shul*, families, and the community. Participants talked about connections with rabbis and teachers who led to their becoming Orthodox, friends with whom they spent Shabbat, Orthodox families who were role models, and an emotional connection to Israel, their ancestry, and Jewish music. When, during their searches, they met Orthodox people like them (i.e., "cool" people they could "connect" with), they found a way to integrate past and present as well as the intellectual and the emotional aspects of their Jewish identities.

Related to the desire for community and connections, the KIs suggested a social motivation. Seventeen BTs described a web of relationships that led them to *teshuvah*, such as friends who became observant, people they met at work or in Israel, and a group of friends at college or elsewhere who were on a similar path. Another seven interviewees were either searching for a spouse or became *frum* together with a prospective spouse during their journeys. It is notable that relational ties played prominent roles in each of the states described in chapter 2. This is in keeping with social science research on conversion, which has repeatedly found that relationships with insiders are critical to the process (Gooren, 2007; Greil & Ruby, 1984; Lofland & Stark, 1965).

A few KIs asserted that *baalei teshuvah* seek structure in their lives. One said that some BTs have a need to be "grounded" and a context for Jewish family life. Another thought the structure was helpful for a small number of people who need order. This was also true of a focus group member who reported being frightened by the "disorder" she found in the hippie movement and attracted to the order in Orthodox Judaism. Fifteen of the forty-eight interviewees described themselves as people who like the structure of Orthodox Judaism and thought it provided a good structure for raising children. Interestingly, two BTs intimated that they did not fully accept the precepts of Orthodox Judaism (e.g., that God gave the Torah to Moses at Mount Sinai), but they nonetheless liked the *frum* lifestyle.

Consideration of the interviews and key informant reports points to myriad reasons why people become *frum*. Most prominent are the desires for a structured life, a framework for making meaning, a need for community, and spiritual fulfillment. This does not discount the desire to assert one's individuality in opposition to the dominant secular culture or one's parents. Those who may have begun their journeys to resist the dominant culture, however, discovered that the path they chose was demanding.

Gender

Although this study did not focus specifically on gender, gender differences were clearly identifiable.[3] Women and men experienced pressures associated with their respective roles. The women were in charge of the children and homes while also working. At times, they felt overwhelmed with the responsibility of preparing in advance the meals for their families and friends for the Sabbath and holidays. They enjoyed attending classes, which were a welcome break from household tasks. Men oversaw their families' religious lives while both men and women economically supported their families. The men who were relatively recent BTs were overwhelmed with the pressure to increase their proficiency in understanding sacred texts and to perform adequately when they *davened* in public at religious services. The women did not seem to feel pressured to learn; they sought it out as a way to enhance their lives.

The men and women interviewed for this study were exposed to feminist ideas through college courses and from the wider culture. The women participants were as well educated and accomplished professionally as the men. Thus, it was not surprising that some of the women struggled over patriarchal norms in the Orthodox community. They spoke about initial discomfort with sitting in a separate section in the synagogue; restrictions over singing in the presence of men; not being counted in the *minyan*; covering their hair; and going to the mikveh. As explained in chapter 6, over time they accommodated to these constraints by reframing them as empowering or by working around them. They became resocialized as traditional homemakers and mothers. Although most of the women worked, they departed from the feminist ethic by considering their careers secondary. Similar to a generation of women in the larger society described by Belkin (2003), they "opted-out" of focusing on careers.

Women in this study said that they found certain aspects of Orthodox Judaism particularly meaningful. They relished candle lighting time as an opportunity to make special prayers on behalf of family and friends. They gained satisfaction from performing individual acts of *chesed* such as visiting the sick, and they enjoyed engaging in community service. In line with previous research on *baalot teshuvah* (Davidman, 1991; Kaufman, 1991), they found friendship with other women and a shared sense of community gratifying. The men, too, felt gratified with the friendships they formed and being part of a community. While men and women acknowledged challenges they faced along the way, they expressed pride in their personal as well as academic growth.

Toward a Theory on the Process of Spiritual Transformation

This book presented a case study on the spiritual transformation of Jews who took on a stringent approach to Judaism. It is an example of spiritual transformation within a religion or religious system. As explained in the introduction, a "telling case" such as this can make visible the theoretical relationships of a phenomenon (Mitchell, 1984). Theoretical findings are applicable to the social scientific study of spiritual-religious transformation within a religious system that requires a great deal of academic and social learning (e.g., Judaism and Islam), and, to some extent, conversion from one religious system to another where one changes in fundamental ways. In keeping with the constructivist grounded theory (Charmaz, 2014) approach to qualitative research, I now offer theoretical implications of the study on the process of spiritual transformation.

For one, spiritual transformation is an open-ended, lifelong process that entails ongoing learning and resocialization. It is "a process rather than an outcome" (Pargament, 2006, p. 22) that does not end with a commitment. In the case of Orthodox Judaism, the academic learning can be extensive, demanding time, dedication, and perseverance. It can be particularly arduous and anxiety provoking for those with minimal or no prior education in this religion or religious orientation. Anxiety is pronounced in the early years of joining a religious community when the newcomers' knowledge seems to pale in comparison with those who grew up with this religious orientation. Resocialization is also a process whereby one learns how to function in ways that are consistent with community norms in familiar and new situations. This requires observational learning and guidance from others.

Second, one is most receptive to examining and moving into another spiritual-religious orientation during late adolescence and early adulthood, when one is exploring one's identity, and during times of transition, such as new parenthood, marriage, divorce, and the death of a significant other.

Third, the transformation affects one's life fundamentally. It influences one's core beliefs about the presence of God in one's life and in the world, which, in turn, affect the ways in which one interprets experience and the attributions one makes in the face of adverse life events. The transformation can affect the process and content of eating, the structuring of time, one's choice of a life partner, one's intimate marital life, the ways in which one raises children, career decisions, and one's relationships with family and friends. In all, it affects who one is, how and where one lives, the basis for evaluating experience, and what one accepts as true.

Fourth, spiritual struggles can occur before and after one makes a commitment. Some struggles arise when the practices of the religion conflict with strongly held values such as feminism. Others have to do with illness, death, and other adverse life events. Because one previously had different beliefs and occupied a different social world, one also may struggle over maintaining one's new beliefs and continued attachment to one's previous religion or religious orientation. One may also develop "spiritual fatigue" (Steinsaltz, 1982) from trying too hard to master the demands of the new religious orientation. Spiritual struggles offer the opportunity for new adherents to gain a more mature outlook on what the religion can and cannot do.

Fifth, a supportive community is essential to the continuance and growth of new adherents. Institutional resources and individual members serve as reeducation and resocialization agents. Communities that provide educational resources, such as classes on language, religious law, and sacred texts, help those with inadequate backgrounds expand their knowledge. Likewise, religious communities in which local individuals "adopt" the newcomers provide informal contexts in which the newcomers become socialized to community norms. Most of the participants in this research benefited from mentors, role models, and friends they found in the communities they joined. Through these social connections, they gain acceptance.

Sixth, a peer group of newcomers can also provide a sense of community. The new members feel more comfortable with others who have similar backgrounds and journeys than with those who grew up within a strict tradition. They can discuss their anxieties and inadequacies with peers and learn from others who are further along in the process. On the other hand, if these are the newcomers' only friends, immersion into such a peer group can impede social integration (Danzger, 1989).

Seventh, spiritual transformation involves the processes of psychological and social integration, which are achieved to varying degrees. It is challenging to feel psychologically whole when one is an outsider to a new way of life and community. It takes time to absorb new knowledge and social norms that are different from those connected with early socialization, which feel natural. One has to rework one's identity without denying who one is and one's prior history. Social integration is another process that develops over time. It requires immersion in an adopted community, social support, and participation in the life of the community. New entrants participate to the extent that their skills allow, which can involve using skills attained prior to joining the religious community.

Finally, much has been said in the social science literature about people who claim to be "spiritual but not religious" (Fuller, 2001; Marler & Hadaway, 2002). Several men in the study of those who became Orthodox rejected the term spirituality, viewing themselves as religious but not spiritual. Close examination of their interviews reveals that, in contrast with the way in which spirituality was interpreted in this study, these men did not view their relationship with God as an expression of spirituality. In the light of the definition used in this study, I continue to assert that in the case of the spiritual transformation of *baalei teshuvah*, spirituality and religiousness are intertwined. It is likely that this is also the case in transformations within and between other religious systems.

In Conclusion

The men and women who became Orthodox adopted more than a position within Judaism. They adopted a community of people who shared a belief system and a way of life. They were able to learn *from* some members of this community and learn *with* others, including their children. The community had a regular rhythm that made life stable and predictable, and comprised individuals with whom they established close, familial-like relationships. They also assimilated an explanatory framework that could help them cope with the untoward life events. They changed their perceptions of themselves, experiencing personal growth and in some cases psychological healing. They felt appreciative of and grateful for the lives they led, the families they formed, and all they had learned. Although they continued to have spiritual struggles and did not achieve complete psychological and social integration, they experienced their new lives as a blessing.

Appendix A

Individual Interview Questions

Introductory Questions: Earliest Remembrances

1. What is your earliest remembrance of thinking about God? How did you view God at that time?

2. What is your earliest remembrance of thinking about spirituality? How did you view spirituality at that time?

3. What is your earliest remembrance of thinking about religion? How did you view religion at that time?

Development of Spiritual Timeline

Using this piece of paper, would you divide your life into time periods in your spiritual or religious life? You might think about these periods as chapters of your life. Think about them in terms of age, life stage, what you were doing, where you were, etc. Using these markers, would you mark off each period and give it a title or name that describes your spiritual or psychological state (something like a chapter title). If you would like, you may also want to draw symbols of pictures above each period to help us understand what your life was like at that time.

Questions Based on Spiritual Timeline

For each of these stages or chapters, would you share what your life was like at that time? Would you focus on your relationship with your parents and other

261

important relationships; your religious life; and your community involvement? If the interviewee did NOT address the following topics/questions, ask the following questions:

RELATIONSHIPS

1. How did your relationships with your parents change during the course of your journey?

2. What kinds of changes did you experience over time in relationships with other people who were significant to you earlier in your life?

3. (If married): Is your spouse a *baal(at) teshuvah*? If YES, how did his/her journey affected yours? If NO, how has his/her situation of being Orthodox affected your journey?

4. What new relationships became important to you in the course of your journey?

RELIGIOUS LIFE

1. What kind of Jewish learning, if any, did you engage in during the stages of your journey?

2. What was your synagogue participation like during the stages of your journey?

3. What kinds of religious rituals, if any, did you engage in during each stage?

COMMUNITY INVOLVEMENT

1. What kinds of community activities did you engage in during the course of your journey? How did the importance of these activities change?

2. Describe the religious community that was part of your life during these stages (wherever applicable). What kinds of religious community activities did you engage in during these stages?

LIFE EVENTS

1. Can you recall any personal or family events that affected you during any of these stages? If so, explain what these were. How did they affect you spiritually/religiously?

2. Did you experience any losses, crises, or suffering during any of these stages? If so, please elaborate. (May be redundant with 4a.)

SPIRITUALITY AND MEANING

1. What were you wrestling with during your journey?

2. Were there people who helped you in your journey? How did they help you?

IDENTITY

1. How did you see yourself before you became observant?

2. In what ways does how you see yourself now differ from the way you saw yourself in the past?

Current Associations (Social Integration)

1. How do you connect with people who are *baalei teshuvah* in your life today?

2. How do you connect with people who have always been Orthodox?

3. Has there been a change in your connections with these groups over time? If so, would you explain how this occurred?

Current Spiritual Orientation

1. How does your pain or your sense of vulnerability affect you spiritually?

2. How do you express your spiritual/religious aspirations and beliefs in your daily life?

Concluding Questions

1. Where do you see yourself moving spiritually?

2. Is there anything else pertaining to your spiritual life that you would like to add that we did not address? If so, explain.

Appendix B

Focus Group Questions

Initially, participants were asked to read and sign an informed consent form, complete a socio-demographic form, and construct a timeline on their spiritual-religious development. They were told that their comments are confidential and that the questions pertain to themselves and their clients. Then the facilitators asked the following questions.

Questions for Focus Group #1

1. What are some of the struggles that you and others you know have had when they were in the process of becoming a *baal teshuvah*?

2. What triggered you to keep Torah and *mitzvos*? What were the first steps in the process?

3. How does your process fit with Erikson's developmental stages or other stages you might have experienced?

4. Based on your own and others' experiences, what makes it possible for people to move toward greater observance of *mitzvos*? What allows you to do more? What facilitates it? What may interfere with the process of moving toward Torah and *mitzvos*?

5. Aside from the external processes ("I'm doing my *mitzvos*"), what about the internal processes of examining who you are as an Orthodox Jew? Is that something that goes in stages? Do you get stuck? Also, at what point is a *baal teshuvah* no longer a *baal teshuvah* and part of the mainstream?

6. I'm wondering whether you or the *baalei teshuvah* you're working with seem to be working toward a higher plane in their
   processes or instead reach a plateau and level off? What have
   you observed in that respect?

7. How did your becoming a *baal teshuvah* affect your relationships with those who did not become *baalei teshuvah*, who
   stayed unobservant? Relationships with those who are *frum*
   from birth, and how did those relationships continue? And
   perhaps you have a special, unique relationship or affiliation
   among *baalei teshuvah*?

8. Is there anything you would like to say about relationships or
   your timeline?

Questions for Focus Group #2

1. What are some of the internal struggles that you and others
   you know have had when they were in the process of becoming (a *baal teshuvah*, *frum*, Orthodox, observant)?

2. What prompts people to take the leap and become a *baal* or
   baalat teshuvah?

3. How would you describe your process of becoming *shomer*
   or *shomeret mitzvot*? For example, were there ups and downs?
   Was it an uphill process? Were there reversals?

4. Using an Eriksonian developmental model, which stages do
   you think correlate with the maturational processes of *baalei
   teshuvah* (e.g., identity vs. role confusion, intimacy vs. isolation,
   generativity vs. stagnation, etc.)?

5. We are interested in your thoughts about how spirituality
   changes over time.

   a. Based on your own and others' experiences, what makes it
      possible for people move toward greater spiritual develop-
      ment?

   b. What do you think interferes with spiritual development
      as it evolves over time?

c. We are interested in your thoughts about where people get stuck or regress and why either of these developments may happen.

6. We were wondering whether *baalei teshuvah* seem to be moving to a higher plane in their processes or, instead, they reach a plateau and level off or drop down. What have you observed? What is your experience?

7. Do you have any last comments about your being a *baal teshuvah*—or even any comments about this group experience, anything you want to say about that?

Appendix C

Key Informant Questions

1. Would you share with us the nature of your work with *baalei teshuvah*? (*keruv*, teaching, advising, counseling, etc.)

2. How long have you been working with *baalei teshuvah*?

3. What do you think attracts people to Orthodox Judaism?

4. When people start the process, do they tend to start as individuals, as part of a group, or part of a couple? (Explore especially the social component of process)

5. What kinds of advice, guidance, or knowledge do *baalei teshuvah* seek from you when they first start exploring Judaism? What kinds of questions do they ask?

6. What kinds of issues do people struggle with initially?

7. What kinds of issues do people struggle with as they get more into the process?

8. What keeps people in the process?

9. What "pushes" people out of the process?

10. Have you noticed any differences in the issues that men and women struggle with? What are they?

11. We were wondering whether *baalei teshuvah* seem to be moving to a higher plane in their processes or, instead, they reach a plateau and level off. What have you observed in this respect?

12. What is your sense of the relationship between *baalei/baalot teshuvah* and the rest of the Orthodox community?

    a. How well accepted are they? Are different parts of the community more/less accepting?

    b. (If not well accepted): What contributes to their not being accepted?

    c. (If some are accepted): What contributes to their being accepted?

    d. What can you tell us about the attitudes *baalei/baalot teshuvah* have toward those who have always been observant?

13. (For counselors/therapists): How do *baalei teshuvah* integrate their past lives with present levels of observance (e.g., occupation, family relationships, etc.)?

14. Is there anything else about *baalei teshuvah* that we have not covered that you would like to add?

Notes

Introduction

1. The Hebrew form of the first term is also represented in English as *ba'al* (*masc. sg.*) and *ba'alat* (*fem. sg.*). For the most part, I describe men and women using the masculine plural form (*baalei teshuvah*), but at times I use the plural feminine form together with the plural masculine (*baalot* and *baalei teshuvah*) to remind the reader that I am referring to both men and women. Where I use the feminine forms alone, I refer to women alone.

2. Here and there, I cite authors who are not Orthodox but write extensively about spirituality. Rabbi Michael Strassfeld is one such author. Strassfeld grew up in an Orthodox home and attended an Orthodox day school but later moved in a direction he described as both traditional (but not Orthodox) and spiritual (Strassfeld, 2002/2006).

3. *Baalei* and *baalot teshuvah* would not describe themselves as "masters" (*baalei*) or "mistresses" (*baalot*) of "return" (*teshuvah*), a literal, colloquial Hebrew translation that does not suggest expertise. A better rendering is "those who turn around or repent." The word "return" is problematic because most never were observant. The term "*frum* from birth" or "FFB" is also problematic because one is not born *frum* but is socialized in this way. I used the term "raised Orthodox" in Sands (2009).

4. In Chapter 3, I show that the interview participants became Orthodox when they were predominantly in Erikson's stages associated with young adulthood (identity vs. role confusion; intimacy vs. isolation) and were at the stage associated with middle adulthood (generativity vs. stagnation) at the time of their interviews.

5. Interview participants were recruited through contacts of the core research team and interviewers. Because some *baalei teshuvah* are not open about their BT status, the individuals who suggested potential interviewees were asked to obtain permission in advance for the project coordinator to contact them.

6. The division of years lived as Orthodox (thirteen years) was based on the midpoint in prior studies I had conducted on *baalot teshuvah*.

7. This was a variation of the approach of McAdams (1993), who asked participants in his studies to divide their lives into chapters and to label them.

8. In later chapters, I use the term "participants" to refer to the forty-eight interviewees. When referring to focus group members, I refer to them as "focus group participants" or "members" and refer to key informant participants as key informants (KIs).

9. I have occasionally smoothed out the transcribed interview texts to reduce the distraction of excessive use of "you know" and "like," and to facilitate clarity.

10. The transcriptions in interviews match the pronunciation of participants, which tended to reflect Ashkenazic Hebrew or an amalgam of Yiddish and Hebrew, yeshiva-style (e.g., *aliyos*). In the text, I use the Modern Hebrew word or an Anglicized version of the same word (*aliyot* or *aliyahs*).

Chapter 1

1. Of the eight, the parents of five divorced when the participant was a young child, one when he was fifteen, one at sixteen, and another during college.

2. *Tikkun olam* or *tikkun ha-olam* means "repairing the world." Over time the term has undergone numerous changes, lending itself to many different interpretations and applications (Rosenthal, 2005; Wolf, 2001). It has led to differences in perspective between the more liberal religious movements (Reform, Reconstructionist, and Conservative) and Orthodoxy. Generally, the former movements emphasize social justice and social action, whereas the Orthodox streams stress perfecting human beings through performing *mitzvot*, improving one's character traits, and following *halakhah*.

3. Lobster and other shellfish are not kosher.

4. The participant was describing Carlebach's leading the prayer services on Yom Kippur. Yom Kippur opens with the recitation of Kol Nidre in the evening and concludes with the Neilah service at the end of the next day.

Chapter 2

1. This chapter is an expansion of ideas originally presented in R. A. Danzig and R. G. Sands (2007), "A model of spiritual transformation of *baalei teshuvah*," *Journal of Religion and Spirituality in Social Work*, 26(2), 23–48.

2. Under Jewish law (Orthodox Union, 2018), one generally waits about six hours after eating meat before having a dairy meal or consuming a dairy product. It is permissible to eat meat after consuming a dairy product so long as one cleanses or washes one's mouth and washes one's hands after eating dairy. If the meat is poultry rather than beef, however, the cleansing is not necessary. Nevertheless, one is not supposed to have meat and milk on the same plate and, as Allen indicated, the chicken was not kosher.

3. *Shalosh seudos* (*seudah shlishit*, in Hebrew) refers to the third Sabbath meal. It is usually a light meal served toward the end of the day.

4. Driving is considered to entail the creation of a fire, an activity that is forbidden on the Sabbath.

5. "Off the derech" (OTD) is a commonly used term in Orthodox communities. Usually it is used to describe disaffiliation by Orthodox individuals. For an analysis from the perspective of someone from the Orthodox community, see Margolese (2005).

Chapter 4

1. Classes in *ulpans*, universities, and other settings tend to be in Modern Hebrew. Textual learning uses Biblical and Mishnaic Hebrew. The language is essentially the same but with differences in grammatical structure and vocabulary.

2. For an in-depth discussion of Mesorah Publications, the publisher of the ArtScroll series, and its impact, see Stolow (2010).

3. Benor (2012) discusses the practical importance and symbolic value of prominently displaying holy books in chapter 3 of her book.

4. Fader (2013) describes efforts of Hasidic women to strengthen their faith by listening to audiocassette recordings of lectures.

5. As explained by Heilman (1983), *lernen* (Yiddish for an extensive review and ritualized study of Jewish sacred texts) was a vocation for some European Jewish men before emancipation. In contemporary times in the United States, it is normative for Orthodox men to "learn" *Gemara* in their free time in study circles or groups (Heilman).

6. *Taharat hamishpachah* refers to the laws according to which a married couple abstains from sexual intimacy during and several days after the woman's menstruation. This is followed by the woman's immersion in a *mikveh*.

7. In recent years, some Conservative synagogues have been offering Hebrew literacy classes to adults.

Chapter 5

1. Those introduced through this system are encouraged to consider someone who shares their outlook and goals, but there should still be some personal attraction (B. Moskoff, personal communication).

2. This is a reference to the Orthodox Union's certification of food as kosher, signified by a "U" with a circle around it.

Chapter 6

1. Some members of Modern Orthodox communities and synagogues are more flexible on these practices. For example, some Modern Orthodox women wear short-sleeve blouses and slacks and do not cover their heads on a regular basis.

2. Some *sheitels* are also attractive, but they are easily identifiable as artificial, even if they are made from human hair.

3. Early in her interview, Eliza was skeptical about the notion of spirituality, which she considered a New Age concept. Later in the interview, she acknowledged her own spirituality. Her comment on missing being close to the Torah demonstrates her spirituality.

4. Kabbalah is a general term referring to the mystical movement known in Judaism since the time of the Talmud and continuing to the present (Scholem, 1946/1954/1974). It is associated with thinkers such as Moses de Leon, author of the seminal text, the Zohar, and with Rabbi Isaac Luria and Hasidism. Today it has become popular among Jews and non-Jews as a New Age mysticism.

5. An *eruv* is an enclosure within a community that enables observant Jews who are inside the area to carry objects or wheel baby carriages on the Sabbath; otherwise, one is not allowed to carry. It is usually demarcated by a combination of existing objects (e.g., telephone poles and wires) and additional markers that are put in place exclusively for the *eruv*.

Chapter 7

1. In mental health settings, the word "consumer" is used instead of "client" or "patient" in recognition of client choice and empowerment.

2. There are variations in the degree of stringency observed in the slaughtering of kosher animals, in what qualifies as kosher milk, and in the maintenance of a kosher home.

3. This section is an expansion of "The social integration of *baalei teshuvah*," *Journal for the Scientific Study of Religion*, 48(1), pp. 86–102 (2009).

4. Levin (1986) describes the cool reception he received as a *baal teshuvah* from members of the U.S. Orthodox communities he joined. The attitude was particularly salient when he attempted to date FFB women.

5. For example, in many Orthodox communities, men and women do not shake hands.

6. Yossi seems to be referring to a traditional Orthodox synagogue where the *davening* is in Ashkenazic Hebrew. The term "Agudah" is associated with Agudah Israel, an umbrella organization serving Orthodox communities in the United States (see http://agudathisrael.org/about).

7. With the exception of some Yiddish-speaking Hasidic communities, Yiddish is not the everyday language of Ultra-Orthodox American Jews. None of the BTs interviewed for this study, including those who identified with the Hasidic movement, lived in Yiddish-speaking communities. Nevertheless, they do incorporate Yiddish words in their speech and, for some, in their Torah studies.

8. Uri was referring to the late Rabbi Joseph Soloveitchik, former head of the Rabbi Isaac Elchanan Theological Seminary at Yeshiva University, who was a prominent scholar and author known for combining secular and religious knowledge.

Chapter 8

1. *Pirkei Avot*, a tractate in the Mishnah, is an influential work on Jewish wisdom. It is also known as Ethics of the Fathers, Ethics of Our Ancestors, and Chapters of the Fathers. *Pirkei Avot* traces the Torah as the word of God given to Moses at Mount Sinai and then transmitted in succession to Joshua, the Elders, the Prophets, and the Men of the Great Assembly.

2. The three "things" have been interpreted in various ways by scholars of different religious persuasions. Goldin was a biblical scholar. Strassfeld (2002/2006), who was raised in an Orthodox home and educated in an Orthodox day school, was later ordained as a Reconstructionist rabbi. In his book, Strassfeld describes spirituality in practice.

3. See chapter 6n2.

Chapter 9

1. The BTs seemed to be referring to *tikkun olam* (see Chapter 1n2).

2. Benor (2012, p. 26) described the perception that FFB children know more than they as "infantilization."

3. See Sands, Spero, & Danzig (2007) for an analysis of gender differences in the study population.

References

Abu-Raiya, H., Pargament, K. I., & Exline, J. J. (2015). Understanding and addressing religious and spiritual struggles in health care. *Health and Social Work, 40*(4), 126–134.

Antoun, R. T., & Hegland, M. E. (Eds.). (1987). *Religious resurgence: Contemporary cases in Islam, Christianity, and Judaism.* Syracuse, NY: Syracuse University Press.

Arnett, J. J. (2000). Emerging adulthood: A theory of development from the late teens through the twenties. *American Psychologist, 55*(5), 469–480.

Arnett, J. J. (2001). Conceptions of the transition to adulthood: Perspectives from adolescence through midlife. *Journal of Adult Development, 8*(2), 133–143.

Arnett, J. J. (2004). *Emerging adulthood: The winding road from the late teens through the twenties.* New York: Oxford University Press.

Arnett, J. J., & Jensen, L. A. (2002). A congregation of one: Individualized religious beliefs among emerging adults. *Journal of Adolescent Research, 17*(5), 451–467.

Aslan, L. (2017). Features of Islam in France. In M. Peucker and R. Ceylan (Eds.), *Muslim community organizations in the West: History, developments and future perspectives* (pp. 219–244). Wiesbaden, Germany: Springer VS.

Aviad, J. O. (1983). *Return to Judaism: Religious renewal in Israel.* Chicago: University of Chicago Press.

Bandura, A. (1977). *Social learning theory.* Englewood Cliffs, NJ: Prentice-Hall.

Bandura, A. (1996). Social cognitive theory of human development. In T. Husen and T. N. Postlewaite (Eds.), *International encyclopedia of education* (2nd ed., pp. 5513–5518). Oxford: Pergamon Press.

Batson, C. D., Schoenrade, P., & Ventis, L. (1993). *Religion and the individual.* Oxford, England: Oxford University Press.

Becker, H. S. (1960). Notes on the concept of commitment. *American Journal of Sociology, 66*(1), 32–40.

Beckford, J. A. (1978). Accounting for conversion. *British Journal of Sociology, 29*(2), 249–262.

Beder, J. (2004–2005). Loss of the assumptive world—How we deal with death and loss. *Omega, 50*(4), 255–265.

Belkin, L. (2003, October 26). The opt-out revolution. *New York Times Magazine,* 42–47, 58, 85.

Benor, S. B. (2012). *Becoming frum: How newcomers learn the language and culture of Orthodox Judaism.* New Brunswick, NJ: Rutgers University Press.

Berman, S. J. (1973). The status of women in Halakhic Judaism. *Tradition: A Journal of Orthodox Thought, 14*(2), 5–28.

Berman, S. J. (2002). Holiness, meaning and spirituality. *The Edah Journal, 2*(1), 2–7.

Berry, J. W. (2007). Acculturation (pp. 543–558). In J. E. Grusec and P. D. Hastings (Eds.), *Handbook of socialization: Theory and Research.* New York: Guilford Press.

Blieszner, R., & Ramsey, J. L. (2002). Uncovering spiritual resiliency through feminist qualitative methods. *Journal of Religious Gerontology, 14*(1), 31–49.

Blos, P. (1967). The second individuation process in adolescence. *Psychoanalytic Study of the Child, 22,* 162–187.

Biale, R. (1984). *Women and Jewish law: An exploration of women's issues in halakhic sources.* New York: Schocken Books.

Bockian, M. J., Glenwick, D. S., & Bernstein, D. P. (2005). The applicability of the stages of change model to Jewish conversion. *The International Journal for the Psychology of Religion, 15*(1), 35–50.

Bornstein, M. H. (2013). Parenting and child mental health: a cross-cultural perspective. *World Psychiatry, 12*(3), 258–265.

Boss, P. (1999). *Ambiguous loss.* Cambridge, MA: Harvard University Press.

Brodkin, K. (1998). *How Jews became white folks and what that says about race in America.* New Brunswick, NJ: Rutgers University Press.

Bromley, D. G., & Shupe, A. (1995). Anti-cultism in the United States: Origins, ideology and organizational development. *Social Compass, 42*(2), 221–236.

Burstein, P. (2007). Jewish educational and economic success in the United States: A search for explanations. *Sociological Perspectives, 50*(2), 209–228.

Carter, B., & McGoldrick, M. (1989). Overview: The changing family life cycle—A framework for family therapy. In E. Carter and M. McGoldrick (Eds.), *The changing family life cycle: A framework for family therapy,* 2nd ed. (pp. 3–28). Boston, MA: Allyn and Bacon.

Central Conference of American Rabbis. (1999, May). A statement of principles for Reform Judaism. Adopted at the 1999 Pittsburgh convention. Retrieved December 25, 2012, from http://www.ccarnet.org/rabbis-speak/platforms/statement-principles-reform-judaism/.

Champagne, D. (1983). Social structure, revitalization movements and state building: Social change in four Native American societies. *American Sociological Review, 48*(6), 754–763.

Chapters of the Fathers. Trans. and commentary by S. R. Hirsch (1989). Second, corrected edition. G. Hirschler, trans. from German. Jerusalem: Feldheim Publishers.

Charmaz, K. (2006). *Constructing grounded theory: A practical guide through qualitative analysis.* Thousand Oaks, CA: Sage Publications.

Charmaz, K. (2014). *Constructing grounded theory,* 2nd ed. Thousand Oaks, CA: Sage Publications.

Charmaz, K. (2009). Shifting the grounds: Constructivist grounded theory. In J. M. Morse et al., *Developing grounded theory: The second generation* (pp. 127–154). Walnut Creek, CA: Left Coast Press.

Cohen, S. M. (2017, February). *The alumni of Ramah camps: A long-term portrait of Jewish engagement.* PowerPoint presentation.

Colarusso, C. A. (1990). The third individuation: The effect of biological parenthood on separation-individuation processes in adulthood. *The psychoanalytic study of the child,* vol. 45 (pp. 179–194). New Haven, CT: Yale University Press.

Colarusso, C. A. (1997). Separation-individuation processes in middle adulthood: The fourth individuation. In S. Akhtar and S. Kramer (Eds.), *The seasons of life: Separation-individuation perspectives* (pp. 73–94). Northvale, NJ: Aronson.

Colarusso, C. A. (2000). Separation-individuation phenomena in adulthood: General concepts and the fifth individuation. *Journal of the American Psychoanalytic Association, 48*(4), 1467–1489.

Côté, J. E., & Levine, C. (1987). A formulation of Erikson's theory of ego identity formation. *Developmental Review, 7,* 273–325.

Cowan, P. (1996). *An orphan in history: Retrieving a Jewish legacy.* New York: Quill William Morrow.

Daniel, K. (2010). An assessment of the Catholic charismatic renewal towards peaceful co-existence in the Roman Catholic Church. *International Journal of Sociology and Anthropology, 2*(8), 171–177.

Danzger, M. H. (1989). *Returning to tradition: The contemporary revival of Orthodox Judaism.* New Haven, CT: Yale University Press.

Danzig, R. A., & Sands, R. G. (2007). A model of spiritual transformation of *baalei teshuvah. Journal of Religion & Spirituality in Social Work, 26*(2), 23–48.

Darling-Fisher, C. S., & Kline Leidy, N. (1988). Measuring Eriksonian development in the adult: The Modified Erikson Psychosocial Stage Inventory. *Psychological Reports, 62,* 747–754.

Darling-Fisher, C. S., & Kline Leidy, N. (n.d.). The Modified Erikson Psychosocial Stage Inventory (MEPSI). Instructional material obtained from authors.

Davidman, L. (1991). *Tradition in rootless world: Women turn to Orthodox Judaism.* Berkeley, CA: University of California Press.

Davidman, L. (2000). *Motherloss.* Berkeley, CA: University of California Press.

Davidman, L. (2015). *Becoming un-orthodox: Stories of ex-Hasidic Jews.* Oxford, UK and New York: Oxford University Press.

Davidman, L., & Greil, A. L. (2007). Characters in search of a script: The exit narratives of formerly ultra-orthodox Jews. *Journal for the Scientific Study of Religion, 16*(2), 201–216.

DeGloma, T. (2010). Awakenings: Autobiography, memory, and the social logic of personal discovery. *Sociological Forum, 25*(3), 519–540.

Demerath III, N. J., & Yang, Y. 1998. Switching in American religion: Denominations, markets, and paradigms? In M. Cousineau (Ed.), *Religion in a changing world: Comparative studies in sociology* (pp. 3–10). Westport, CT: Praeger.

Denzin, N. (1989). *The research act.* Hillsdale, NJ: Prentice Hall.

Dresner, S. H., & Siegel, S. (1959/1966). *The Jewish dietary laws.* New York: The Burning Book Press.

Ebaugh, H. R. Fuchs. (1988). *Becoming an ex: The process of role exit.* Chicago: University of Chicago Press.

Edwards, A. C., & Lowis, M. J. (2001). The Batson-Schoenrade-Ventis model of religious experience: Critique and reformulation. *The International Journal for the Psychology of Religion, 11*(4), 215–234.

Ellwood, R. (1986). The several meanings of cult. *Thought, LXI* (241), 212–224.

Elbein, A. (2014, July 11). Grappling with the rising cost of being Orthodox. *Tablet.* Retrieved February 19, 2017, from http://www.tabletmag.com/jewish-life-and-religion/177127/rising-cost-of-being-orthodox.

Englander, L. A. (1985). Rav Kook's doctrine of *teshuvah. Judaism, 34,* 211–220.

Erikson, E. H. (1950). *Childhood and society.* New York: W. W. Norton.

Erikson, E. H. (1959/1980). *Identity and the life cycle.* New York: W. W. Norton.

Erikson, E. H. (1968). *Identity: Youth and crisis.* New York: W. W. Norton.

Erikson, E. H., Erikson, J. M., & Kivnick, H. Q. (1986). *Vital involvement in old age: The experience of old age in our time.* New York: W. W. Norton.

Exline, J. J., & Rose, E. (2006). Chapter 17: Religious and spiritual struggles. In R. F. Paloutzian and C. L. Park (Eds.), *Handbook of the psychology of religion and spirituality* (pp. 315–330). New York: The Guilford Press.

Exline, J. J., & Rose, E. (2013). Chapter 19: Religious and spiritual struggles. In R. F. Paloutzian and C. L. Park (Eds.), *Handbook of the psychology of religion and spirituality,* 2nd ed. (pp. 380–398). New York: The Guilford Press.

Exline, J. J., Pargament, K. I., Grubbs, J. B., & Yali, A. M. (2014). The religious and spiritual struggles scale: Development and initial validation. *Psychology of Religion and Spirituality, 6*(3), 208–222.

Fader, A. (2009). *Mitzvah girls: Bringing up the next generation of Hasidic Jews in Brooklyn.* Princeton, NJ: Princeton University Press.

Fader, A. (2013). Nonliberal Jewish women's audiocassette lectures in Brooklyn: A crisis of faith and the morality of media. *American Anthropologist, 115*(1), 72–84.

Ferziger, A. (2015). *Beyond sectarianism: The realignment of American Orthodox Judaism.* Detroit, MI: Wayne State University Press.

Frankl, V. E. (1984). *Man's search for meaning,* revised and updated. New York: Washington Square Press.

Fuller, R. C. (2001). *Spiritual but not religious: Understanding unchurched America.* New York: Oxford University Press.

Galman, S. C. (2013). Un/covering: Female religious converts learning the problems and pragmatics of physical observance in the secular world. *Anthropology & Education Quarterly, 44*(4), 423–441.

Glaser, B. G., & Strauss, A. L. (1967). *The discovery of grounded theory: Strategies for qualitative research.* Chicago: Aldine de Gruyter.

Goffman, E. (1963/1974). *Stigma: Notes on the management of spoiled identity.* New York: Jason Aronson.

Goldin, J. (2003). Commentary on Pirkei Avot (pp. 257–280). In R. Hammer, *Or Hadash: A Commentary on Siddur Sim Shalom.* New York City: The Rabbinical Assembly.

Gooren, H. (2005). Towards a new model of conversion careers: The impact of personality and contingency factors. *Exchange, 34*(2), 149–166.

Gooren, H. (2007). Reassessing conventional approaches to conversion: Toward a new synthesis. *Journal for the Scientific Study of Religion, 46*(3), 337–353.

Green, A. (1986). Introduction. In A. Green (Ed.), *Jewish spirituality: From the Bible through the middle ages,* vol. 1 (pp. xiii–xxv). New York: Crossroad.

Greil, A. L., & Rudy, D. R. (1984). What have we learned from process models of conversion? An examination of ten case studies. *Sociological Focus, 17*(4), 305–323.

Greil, A., & Rudy, D. R. (1983). Conversion to the world view of Alcoholics Anonymous: A refinement of conversion theory. *Qualitative Sociology, 6,* 5–28.

Grusec, J. E., & Hastings, P. D. (2007). Introduction (pp. 1–9). In J. E. Grusec and P. D. Hastings (Eds.), *Handbook of socialization: Theory and Research.* New York: Guilford Press.

Hay, D. (2001). The cultural context of stage models of religious experience. *The International Journal for the Psychology of Religion, 11*(4), 241–246.

Heilman, S. C. (1983). *The people of the book: Drama, fellowship, and religion.* Chicago: University of Chicago Press.

Heilman, S. C. (2005). How did fundamentalism manage to infiltrate contemporary Orthodoxy? *Contemporary Jewry, 25,* 258–272.

Heilman, S. C. (2006). *Sliding to the right: The contest for the future of American Jewish Orthodoxy.* Berkeley, CA: University of California Press.

Heilman, S. C., & Friedman, M. (1991). Chapter 4: Religious fundamentalism and religious Jews: The case of the haredim (pp. 197–264). In M. E. Marty and R. S. Appleby (Eds.), *Fundamentalism observed,* vol. 1. Chicago: University of Chicago Press.

Heschel, S. (Ed.) (1995). *On being a Jewish feminist.* New York: Schocken Books.

Hill, P. C., Pargament, K. I., Hood, R. W., Jr., McCullough, M. E., Swyers, J. P., Larson, D. B., & Zinnbauer, B. J. (2000). Conceptualizing religion and spirituality: Points of commonality, points of departure. *Journal for the Theory of Social Behavior, 30,* 51–77.

Hoare, C. (2009). Identity and spiritual development in the papers of Erik Erikson. *Identity: An International Journal of Theory and Research, 9,* 183–200.

Hoge, D. R., Johnson, B., & Luidens, D. A. (1995). Types of denominational switching among Protestant young adults. *Journal for the Scientific Study of Religion, 34*(2), 253–258.

Hout, M., & Fischer, C. S. (2002). Why more Americans have no religious preference: Politics and generations. *American Sociological Review, 67,* 165–190.

Iannaccone, L. R. (1990). Religious practice: A human capital approach. *Journal for the Scientific Study of Religion, 29*(3), 297–314.

Iannaccone, L. R. (1994). Why strict churches are strong. *The American Journal of Sociology, 99*(5), 1180–1211.

Immersion of vessels. (n.d.). Retrieved February 25, 2018, from https://www.chabad.org/library/article_cdo/aid/82673/jewish/Immersion-of-Vessels.htm.

James, W. (1902/1958). *The varieties of religious experience.* New York: Mentor/New American Library.

Jones, R. P., & Cox, D. (2012). *Chosen for what? Jewish values in 2012: Findings from the 2012 Jewish Values Survey.* Public Religion Research Institute. Retrieved May 20, 2016, from http://publicreligion.org/research/2012/04/jewish-values-in-2012/#.V0C8dOSSBp0.

Johnston, E. F. (2013). "I was always this way...": Rhetorics of continuity in narratives of conversion. *Sociological Forum, 28*(3), 549–573.

Jung, C. G. (1933). *Modern man in search of a soul.* New York: Harcourt, Brace.

Kaufman D. R. (1991). *Rachel's daughters: Newly Orthodox Jewish women.* New Brunswick, NJ: Rutgers University Press.

Kiesling, C., & Sorell, G. (2009). Joining Erikson and identity specialists in the quest to characterize adult spiritual identity. *Identity: An International Journal of Theory and Research, 9,* 252–271.

Kiesling, C., Sorell, G. T., Montgomery, M. J., & Colwell, R. K. (2008). Identity and spirituality: A psychosocial exploration of the sense of spiritual self. *Psychology of Religion and Spirituality, 5*(1), 50–62.

Klausner, S. (1997). How to think about mass religious conversion: Toward an explanation of the conversion of American Jews to Christianity. *Contemporary Jewry, 18,* 76–129.

Kleinman, A. (1988). *The illness narratives: Suffering, healing and the human condition.* New York: Basic Books.

Kohler, K., & Broydé, I. (n.d.). Transmigration of souls (termed also metempsychosis). Retrieved October 31, 2016, from http://www.jewishencyclopedia.com/articles/14479-transmigration-of-souls.

Kox, W., Meeus, W., & 'tHart, H. (1991). Religious conversion of adolescents: Testing the Lofland and Stark model of religious conversion. *Sociological Analysis, 52*(3), 227–240.

Krakowski, M. (2015). Review of Adam Ferziger's *Beyond sectarianism: The realignment of American Orthodox Judaism. Contemporary Judaism, 35,* 327–329.

Kübler-Ross, E. (1969). *On death and dying.* New York: Macmillan.

Kuhn, T. S. (1970). *The structure of scientific revolutions*, 2nd ed., enlarged. Chicago: University of Chicago Press.

Lamm, M. (1979). *The Jewish way in love and marriage*. San Francisco, CA: Harper & Row.

Lane, R., Jr. (1978). The Catholic charismatic renewal movement in the United States: A reconsideration. *Social Compass, 25*, 23–35.

Laue, J. H. (1964). A contemporary revitalization movement in American race relations: The 'Black Muslims.' *Social Forces, 42*(3), 315–323.

Lawton, L. E., & Bures, R. (2001). Parental divorce and the "switching" of religious identity. *Journal for the Scientific Study of Religion, 40*(1), 99–111.

Lazerwitz, B. J., Winter, A., Dashefsky, A., & Tabory, E. (1998). *Jewish choices: American Jewish denominationalism*. Albany: State University of New York Press.

Lebovits, Y., Rabbi. (1987). *Shidduchim and zivugim*. Southfield, MI: Targum Press.

Levi, M. (1998). *More effective Jewish parenting*. Brooklyn, NY: Mesorah Publications.

Levin, M. G. (1986). *Journey to tradition: The odyssey of a born-again Jew*. Hoboken, NJ: Ktav Publishing House.

Levinson, D. J., with Darrow, C. N., Klein, E. B., Levinson, M. H., & McKee, B. (1978). *The seasons of a man's life*. New York: Ballantine Books.

Levinson, D. J., with Levinson, J. D. (1996). *The seasons of a woman's life*. New York: Alfred A. Knopf.

Lofland, J., & Stark, R. (1965). Becoming a world-saver: A theory of conversion to a deviant perspective. *American Sociological Review, 30*(6), 862–875.

Luhrmann, T. M. (2012). *When God talks back: Understanding the American evangelical relationship with God*. New York: Alfred A. Knopf.

Manning, L. K. (2014). Enduring as lived experience: Exploring the essence of spiritual resilience for women in late life. *Journal of Religion and Health, 53*, 352–562.

Margolese, F. (2005). *Off the derech*. Jerusalem: Devora Publishing Co.

Mahler, M. S. (1974). On the first of three subphases of the separation-individuation process. In *Psychoanalysis and Science*, vol. 3. (pp. 295–306). New York: International Universities Press.

Mahler, M. S., Pine, F., & Bergman, A. (1975). *The psychological birth of the human infant*. New York: Basic Books.

Marcia, J. E. (1966). Development and validation of ego-identity status. *Journal of Personality and Social Psychology, 3*(5), 551–558.

Marler, P. L., & Hadaway, C. K. (2002). "Being religious" or "being spiritual" in America: A zero-sum proposition? *Journal for the Scientific Study of Religion, 41*(2), 289–300.

Marris, P. (1982). Attachment and society (pp. 185–201). In C. M. Parkes and J. Stevenson-Hinde (Eds.), *The place of attachment in human behavior*. New York: Basic Books.

Marty, M. E., & Appleby, R. S. (1991). Introduction (pp. 1–7). In M. E. Marty and R. S. Appleby (Eds.), *The fundamentalist project*, vol. 1. Chicago: University of Chicago Press.

Marty, M. E., & Appleby, R. S. (Eds.). (1991–1995). *The fundamentalist project*, 5 volumes. Chicago: University of Chicago Press.

McAdams, D. P. (1993). *The stories we live by: Personal myths and the making of the self*. New York: The Guilford Press.

McKean, E. (2005). *The new Oxford American dictionary*, 2nd ed. New York: Oxford University Press.

Merriam, S. B., Johnson-Bailey, J., Lee, M-Y, Kee, Y., Ntseane, G., and Muhamad, M. (2001). Power and positionality: Negotiating insider/outsider status within and across cultures. *International Journal of Lifelong Education*, 20, 405–416.

Mezirow, J. (1978). Perspective transformation. *Adult Education*, 28, 100–110.

Mezirow, J. (1997). Transformative learning: Theory to practice. *New Directions for Adult and Continuing Education*, No. 74, 5–12.

Miller, W. R., & C'de Baca, J. (1994). Quantum change: Toward a psychology of transformation. In T. F. Heatherton and G. J. L. Weinberger (Eds.), *Can personality change?* (pp. 253–280). Washington, DC: American Psychological Association.

Miller, W. R., & Thoresen, C. E. (2003). Spirituality, religion, and health: An emerging field. *American Psychologist*, 58(1), 24–35).

Mitchell, J. C. (1984). Case studies. In R. F. Ellen (Ed.), *Ethnographic research: A guide to general conduct* (pp. 237–241). London: Academic Press.

Mock-Degan, M. E. (2009). *The dynamics of becoming Orthodox: Dutch Jewish women and how their mothers felt about it*. Amsterdam: Amphora Books.

Morgan, D. L. (1997). *Focus groups as qualitative research*, 2nd ed. Thousand Oaks, CA: Sage.

Morris, B. J. (1998). *Lubavitcher women in America: Identity and activism in the postwar era*. Albany, NY: State University of New York Press.

Moss Kanter, R. (1968). Commitment and social organization: A study of commitment mechanisms in Utopian communities. *American Sociological Review*, 33(4), 499–517.

Moss Kanter, R. (1972). *Commitment and community: Communes and utopias in sociological perspective*. Cambridge, MA: Harvard University Press.

Musick, M., & Wilson, J. (1995). Religious switching for marriage. *Sociology of Religion*, 56(3), 257–270.

National Jewish Population Survey (NJPS), 2000–01 [Electronic data file]. (2003). New York: NY: United Jewish Communities [Producer]. Storrs, CT: North American Jewish Data Bank [Distributor].

Ner le-elef. NLE Morasha Syllabus. The Jewish View of Marriage. Retrieved May 21, 2015, from http://nleresources.com/nle-morasha-syllabus-index-of-classes/.

Newport, F. (1979). The religious switcher in the United States. *American Sociological Review*, 44, 528–552.

Oatley, K., & Djikic, M. (2002). Emotions and transformation: Varieties of experience of identity. *Journal of Consciousness Studies, 9*(9–10), 97–2002.

Oman, D., & Thoresen, C. E. (2003). Spiritual modeling: A key to spiritual and religious growth? *The International Journal for the Psychology of Religion, 13*(3), 149–165.

Orthodox Union. (2018). The *halachot* of waiting between meals. Retrieved February 11, 2018, from https://oukosher.org/blog/consumer-kosher/the-halachot-of-waiting-between-meals.

Paloutzian, R. F., Richardson, J. T., & Rambo, L. R. (1999). Religious conversion and personality change. *Journal of Personality, 67*, 1047–1079.

Pargament, K. I. (2006).The meaning of spiritual transformation (pp. 10–24). In J. D. Koss-Chioino and P. Hefner (Eds.), *Spiritual Transformation and Healing: Anthropological, Theological, Neuroscientific, and Clinical Perspectives*. Lanham, MD: AltaMira Press.

Pargament, K. I. (1999). The psychology of religion and spirituality? Yes and no. *The International Journal for the Psychology of Religion, 9*(1): 3–16.

Pew Research Center (January 15, 2015). This year Millennials will overtake Baby Boomers. Retrieved April 24, 2016, from http://www.pewresearch.org/fact-tank/2015/01/16/this-year-millennials-will-overtake-baby-boomers.

Pew Research Center. (2013, October 1). *A Portrait of Jewish Americans: Findings from a Pew Research Center Survey of U.S. Jews*. Retrieved October 14, 2013, from http://www.pewforum.org/2013/10/01/jewish-american-beliefs-attitudes-culture-survey/.

Plaskow, J. (1990). *Standing again at Sinai: Judaism from a feminist perspective*. San Francisco: Harper & Row.

Plaskow, J. (1980). Blaming Jews for inventing patriarchy. *Lilith, 7*, 11–12.

Popp-Baier, U. (2001). Narrating embodied aims. Self-transformation in conversion narratives—A psychological analysis. *FQS Forum: Qualitative Research, 2*(3), art. 16.

Porterfield, A. (1987). Feminist theology as a revitalization movement. *Sociological Analysis, 48*(3), 234–244.

Portes, A. (1998). Social capital: Its origins and applications in modern sociology. *Annual Review of Sociology, 24*, 1–24.

Prochaska, J. O., & DiClimente, C. C. Transtheoretical therapy: Toward a more integrative model of change. *Psychotherapy: Theory, research, and practice, 19*, 276–288.

Putnam, R. D., Campbell, D. E. (2010). *American grace: How religion divides and unites us*. New York: Simon and Schuster.

Rambo, L. R. (1993). *Understanding religious conversion*. New Haven, CT: Yale University Press.

Rambo, L. R. (2010). Conversion studies, pastoral counseling, and cultural studies: Engaging and embracing a new paradigm. *Pastoral Psychology, 59*, 433–445.

Rambo, L. R., & Bauman, S. C. (2012). Psychology of conversion and spiritual transformation. *Pastoral Psychology, 61*, 879–894.

Raphael, M. L. (1984). *Profiles in American Judaism: The Reform, Conservative, Orthodox, and Reconstructionist traditions in historical perspective.* San Francisco: Harper & Row.

Richardson, J. T. (1993). Definitions of cult: From sociological-technical to popular-negative. *Review of Religious Research, 34*(4), 348–356.

Richardson, L. (1988). The collective story: Postmodernism and the writing of sociology. *Sociological Focus, 21*(3), 199–208.

Roer-Strier, D., & Sands, R. G. (2001). The impact of religious intensification on family relations: A South African example. *Journal of Marriage and Family, 63,* 868–880.

Roer-Strier, D., & Sands, R. G. (2004). Families challenged by religious change: A cross cultural comparison of mothers' images of their daughters. *Families in Society, 85*(4), 485–594.

Roof, W. C. (1999). *Spiritual marketplace: Baby boomers and the remaking of American religion.* Princeton, NJ: Princeton University Press.

Roof, W. C. (1993). *A generation of seekers: The spiritual journeys of the baby boom generation.* San Francisco, CA: Harper.

Roof, W. C., & Hadaway, C. K. (1977). Shifts in religious preference—the mid-seventies. *Journal for the Scientific Study of Religion, 16,* 409–412.

Roof, W. C., & Hadaway, C. K. (1979). Denominational switching in the seventies: Going beyond Stark and Glock. *Journal for the Scientific Study of Religion, 18*(4), 363–379.

Rosenthal, D., Gutney, R., & Moore, S. (1981). From trust to intimacy: A new inventory for examining Erikson's stages of psychosocial development. *Journal of Youth and Adolescence, 10,* 525–537.

Rosenthal, G. S. (2005). Tikkun ha-olam: The metamorphosis of a concept. *The Journal of Religion, 85*(2), 214–240.

Sands, R. G. (2009). The social integration of *baalei teshuvah. Journal for the Scientific Study of Religion, 48*(1), 86–102.

Sands, R. G., Marcus, S., & Danzig, R. (2006). The direction of denominational switching in Judaism. *Journal for the Scientific Study of Religion, 45*(3), 437–447.

Sands, R. G., Marcus, S., & Danzig, R.A. (2008). Spirituality and religiousness among American Jews. *International Journal of the Psychology of Religion, 18*(3), 238–255.

Sands, R. G., & Roer-Strier, D. (2004). Divided families: Impact of religious difference and geographic distance on intergenerational family continuity. *Family Relations, 53,* 102–110.

Sands, R. G., Roer-Strier, D., & Strier, S. (2013). From family research to practice: Argentine families coping with the challenges of religious intensification. *Families in Society, 94*(1), 53–60.

Sands, R. G., Spero, R. R., & Danzig, R. A. (2007). Gender differences in the construction of spirituality, work, learning, and community by *baalei teshuvah. Sex Roles, 57,* 527–541.

Sarna, J. (2004). *American Judaism: A history*. New Haven, CT: Yale University Press.

Schachter-Shalomi, Z. with Segal, J. (2012). *Davening: A guide to meaningful prayer*. Woodstock, VT: Jewish Lights Publishing.

Scholem, G. (1946/1954/1975). *Major trends in Jewish mysticism*. New York: Schocken Books.

Schwartz, L. L., & Isser, N. (1987). Proselytizers of Jewish youth. *Journal of Psychology and Judaism, 11*(3), 181–195.

Scott, S. M. (1997). The grieving soul in the transformation process. *New Directions for Adult and Continuing Education*, No. 74. San Francisco: Jossey-Bass.

Seybold, K. S., & Hill, P. C. (2001). The role of religion and spirituality in mental and physical health. *Current Directions in Psychological Science, 21*–24.

Shah, S. (2004). The researcher/interviewer in intercultural context: A social intruder! *British Educational Research Journal, 30*, 549–575.

Shapiro, M. B. (2005). How did fundamentalism manage to infiltrate contemporary Orthodoxy: A response to Samuel C. Heilman. *Contemporary Jewry, 25*, 273–278.

Silberman, I. (2005). Religion as a meaning system: Implications for the new millennium. *Journal of Social Issues, 61*(4), 641–663.

Smith, A. C. T., & Stewart, B. (2011). Becoming believers: Studying the conversion process from within. *Zygon, 46*(4), 806–834.

Snow, D. A., & Machalek, R. (1984). The sociology of conversion. *Annual Review of Sociology, 10*, 167–90.

Snow, D. A., & Phillips, C. L. (1980). The Lofland-Stark conversion model: A critical reassessment. *Social Problems, 27*(4), 430–447.

Soloveitchik, H. (1994). Rupture and reconstruction: The transformation of contemporary Orthodoxy. *Tradition, 28*(4), 64–130.

Sroufe. L.A., & Fleeson, J. (1986). Attachment and the construction of relationships. In W. W. Hartup and Z. Rubin (Eds.), *Relationships and development* (pp. 51–72). Hillsdale, NJ: Erlbaum.

Staetsky, L. D., & Boyd, J. (2015). *Strictly Orthodox rising: What the demography of British Jews tells us about the future of the community*. JPR Report: Institute for Jewish Policy.

Stamp, G. H. (2003). Transition to parenthood. *Encyclopedia of Marriage and Family*. Retrieved June 25, 2015, from http://www.encyclopedia.com.

Stark, R., & Glock, C. (1968). *American piety: The nature of religious commitment*. Berkeley, CA: University of California Press.

Steinsaltz, A. (1987). *Teshuvah*. New York: The Free Press.

Stolow, J. (2010). *Orthodox by design: Judaism, print politics, and the ArtScroll revolution*. Berkeley, CA: University of California Press.

Strassfeld, M. (2002/2006). *A book of life: Embracing Judaism as a spiritual practice*. Woodstock, VT: Jewish Lights Publishing.

Swidler, A. (1986). Culture in action: Symbols and strategies. *American Sociological Review, 51*(2), 273–286.

Tapper, A. J. (2002). The 'cult' of Aish Hatorah: Ba'alei teshuva and the new religious movement phenomenon. *The Jewish Journal of Sociology, 44*(1 and 2), 5–29.

Taylor, K. (2013, July 12). Sex on campus: She can play that game, too. *New York Times Magazine.* Retrieved May 21, 2015, from http://www.nytimes.com/2013/07/14/fashion/sex-on-campus-she-can-play-that-game-too.html?pagewanted =all&_r=0.

Taylor, S. T., & Bogdan, R. (1998). *Introduction to qualitative research methods: A guidebook and resource,* 3rd ed. New York: John Wiley & Sons.

Telushkin, J. (1991). *Jewish literacy.* New York: W. Morrow.

Topel, M. F. (2002). Brazilian *ba'alot teshuvah* and the paradoxes of their religious conversion. *Judaism, 51*(3), 329–345.

Ullman, C. (1989). *The transformed self: The psychology of religious conversion.* New York: Plenum Press.

Wallace, A. F. C. (1956). Revitalization movements. *American Anthropologist, 58*(2), 264–281.

Waxman, C. I. (2005). Winners and losers in denominational memberships in the United States. Jerusalem Center for Public Affairs. Retrieved February 19, 2017, from http://jcpa.org/article/winners-and-losers-in-denominational-memberships-in-the-united-states/.

Weber, S. R., & Pargament, K. I. (2014). The role of religion and spirituality in mental health. *Current Opinion in Psychiatry, 27*(5), 358–363.

Weisberg, C. (2004). *Expecting miracles: Finding meaning and spirituality in pregnancy through Judaism.* Jerusalem and New York: Urim Publications.

Woodberry, Robert D. 2003. Researching spiritual capital: Promises and pitfalls. Working paper of the spiritual capital research program, Metanexus. Retrieved July 28, 2008, from http://www.metanexus.net/spiritual_capital/pdf/Woodberry.pdf (accessed July 28, 2008).

Wolf, A. J. (2001). Repairing tikkun olam. *Judaism, 50*(4), 478–482.

Wurzburger, W. S. (1997). Orthodoxy. *Encyclopaedia Judaica,* CD-ROM Edition. Judaica Mulimedia (Israel) Ltd.

Wuthnow, R. J. (2011). Taking talk seriously: Religious discourse as social practice. *Journal for the Scientific Study of Religion, 50*(1), 1–21.

Yokes, R. (2007). Rethinking the anthropology of religious change: New perspectives on revitalization and conversion movements. *Reviews in Anthropology, 36,* 311–333.

Zeidan, D. (2003). *The resurgence of religion: A comparative study of selected themes in Christian and Islamic fundamentalist discourses.* Boston: Brill.

Zinnbauer, B. J., Pargament, K. I., Cole, B., Rye, M. S., Butter, E. M., Belavich, T. G., Hipp, K. M., Scott, A. B., & Kadar, J. L. (1997). Religion and spirituality: Unfuzzying the fuzzy. *Journal for the Scientific Study of Religion, 36,* 549–564.

Index